# Beyond the Veil

## A Journey Through Life After Death

## PART ONE

**What lies beyond is not the end, but a profound continuation.**

**SHREE SHAMBAV**

Beyond the Veil

A Journey Through Life After Death

Shree Shambav

Published by Shree Shambav, Tamil Nadu, India



First Edition, 2025



Email:shreeshambav@gmail.com

Web:www.shambav.org

# DEDICATION

"Isavasyam idam sarvam yat kim ca jagatyam jagat, tena tyaktena bhunjitha, ma gridhah kasyasvid dhanam"

**To the Almighty,**

**the Divine Masters,**

**the family who listens,**

**and my parents who see –**

**your presence shapes the pages of my life's journey.**

"Isavasyam idam sarvam yat kim ca jagatyam jagat"

*Meaning: "God encompasses everything you perceive, see, or touch with your sense organs."*

# DISCLAIMER

*Beyond the Veil: A Journey Through Life After Death* explores humanity's timeless curiosity about what happens after death through philosophical, spiritual, and scientific perspectives. This book invites readers to delve into the profound nature of consciousness and its transformative potential. While the journey may evoke moments of deep insight and reflection, it may also challenge deeply held beliefs or stir strong emotional responses. These reactions are part of the natural process of self-discovery and growth.

If you experience emotional distress, confusion, or discomfort while engaging with the material, we encourage you to seek guidance from a licensed therapist, counsellor, or other qualified professional. Prioritising your emotional well-being is essential as you navigate this exploration.

The practices and exercises included in this book are suggestions to enhance spiritual and personal development. As every individual's experiences and needs are unique, readers are encouraged to adapt these practices to suit their personal journeys, proceeding at a pace that feels comfortable. Personal growth is a deeply individual process, and outcomes will vary based on your engagement, readiness, and circumstances.

The author and publisher disclaim any liability for direct or indirect outcomes resulting from the application of the concepts, practices, or insights shared in this book. By engaging with this material, you acknowledge and accept personal responsibility for your own transformation, mindfulness, and discernment.

This book does not promise specific results but serves as an invitation to explore the infinite potential within yourself. Take what resonates with your journey, leave what does not, and trust your innate capacity for healing, growth, and wisdom.

We are honoured to accompany you on this journey of awakening to the infinite. May the insights offered here inspire you to live with greater clarity, purpose, and connection. May this book act as a catalyst for profound transformation and a deeper understanding of yourself, your soul, and the mysteries of existence.

*Note - If any part of the book, in any sequence, hurts the reader's sentiments, it would be just out of a sheer accident, not intentional*

# EPIGRAM

Beyond the Veil

The pure light of awareness does not merely illuminate the moment of death; it is a constant, guiding presence that shines through every moment of life. It is the essence that reveals the profound truth hidden within the ordinary, inviting us to awaken to the eternal now. Whether in the stillness of reflection or the chaos of daily existence, this light reminds us that life and death are not opposites but intertwined expressions of the same infinite consciousness.

– Shree Shambav

# Beyond the Veil

## A Journey Through Life After Death

## Shree Shambav

**Shree Shambav is a 24x best-selling author renowned for his transformative works in personal development and spiritual growth.**

# Dear Cherished Readers

Dear Cherished Readers,

As I embark on this new literary voyage, my heart swells with profound gratitude and an overwhelming sense of connection. With deep emotion, I extend my heartfelt appreciation to each of you who has joined me on this journey.

With sincere warmth, I invite you to revisit the steps we have taken together through the pages of my earlier works. Our odyssey began with "Journey of Soul - Karma," a book that marked my first foray into the world of words and a testament to the raw passion that ignited my writing adventure.

The subsequent chapters of our shared narrative unfolded through the enchanting tapestry of the "Twenty + One" series, both Series I and Series II. Each page turned was a brushstroke on the canvas of our imaginations, painting vivid stories that I hoped would resonate deeply within your hearts.

And how can I forget the transformative journey we embarked on with the "Life Changing Journey—Inspirational Quotes Series?" Day by day, quote by quote, we delved into reflections that uplifted and inspired us and sought to bring a glimpse of light to our souls.

The release of "Death - Light of Life and the Shadow of Death" promises to shed new light on the timeless mystery of death. Similarly, "Unleashing the Incredible Potential of Programming with Python - Optimum - PYTHON: Ultimate Guide for Beginners Series I" is poised to empower readers with newfound knowledge.

In addition, my technical book, OPTIMUM Python Series II - Exploring Data Structures and Algorithms, delves into advanced concepts in Python programming, offering a comprehensive guide for those seeking to deepen their understanding.

Shree Shambav expands his artistic repertoire with "*Whispers of Eternity: 150 Plus - A Symphony of Soulful Verses*," a heartfelt exploration of the human experience. Alongside this, his "*Whispers of the Soul: A Journey Through Haiku*" distils profound insights into poignant verses. Together, these works showcase his versatility and mastery of soulful expression, inviting readers on a journey of self-discovery. Through his poetry, he weaves a rich tapestry of emotion that resonates deeply with the heart.

Shree Shambav's latest works—*Learn to Love Yourself: A Journey of Discovering Inner Beauty and Strength Through*

*10 Transformative Rules, The Power of Letting Go: Embrace Freedom and Happiness, A Journey of Lasting Peace—are true treasures of self-discovery, The Entitlement Trap: Get Over It, Get On, Whispers of a Dying Soul: Unspoken Regrets and Unlived Dreams, Whispers of Silence - Unlocking Inner Power through Stillness, The Power of Words: Transforming Speech, Transforming Lives, and Awakening the Infinite: The Power of Consciousness in Transforming Life.* Each book offers profound insights into personal growth and well-being, guiding readers on a transformative journey toward inner peace and fulfilment.

In addition to these works, Shree Shambav has recently ventured into astrology with the release of Astrology Unveiled – Foundations of Ancient Wisdom Series I to VI, expanding into the realm of metaphysics. These books explore the foundational principles of Vedic astrology, offering readers a rich and practical understanding of this ancient wisdom.

Your unwavering support, enthusiasm to immerse yourself in my writings, and readiness to embark on these journeys with me have been my greatest sources of inspiration. Your input has been a beacon guiding me through the creation process, moulding these stories into containers of passion, emotion, knowledge, and resonance.

As I unveil this new narrative before you, know that your presence, insights, and shared moments have been my companions. The path we have walked together is etched in the annals of my creative evolution, and it's an honour beyond words to have you by my side once more.

Here's to the readers who have illuminated my path with their presence, who have embraced my stories with open hearts, and who have woven themselves into the very fabric of my literary world. Our journey has been a symbiotic dance of writer and reader, a harmony of souls brought together by the magic of storytelling.

With a heart brimming with appreciation and eyes glistening with anticipation, I extend my deepest gratitude for your unwavering support. Thank you for the memories, the shared emotions, and the countless hours spent in the worlds we've crafted together. As we step into this new adventure, let's continue to explore, feel, and discover the boundless horizons that words can unveil.

Warmly,

Shree Shambav

# Suggested Reads

FROM BEST-SELLING AUTHOR

# Endorsements

"Beyond the Veil is a breathtaking exploration of the eternal questions that have shaped human existence. Thoughtfully blending spirituality, philosophy, and modern science, this book takes readers on an illuminating journey through the mysteries of death, consciousness, and the afterlife. With deep wisdom and compassionate insight, it challenges conventional notions of mortality and offers a transformative perspective on what lies beyond. Whether you are a seeker, a sceptic, or simply curious, this book will expand your understanding and leave you with a profound sense of wonder about the infinite journey of the soul."

— Ganesan, Entrepreunuer

# About the Author

Shree Shambav is a visionary luminary—an internationally acclaimed best-selling author, inspirational speaker, artist, philanthropist, life coach, and entrepreneur. A world record holder, his deep passion for music led him to create soul-stirring albums, drawing inspiration from his celebrated poetry collection, Whispers of Eternity. With wisdom and grace, he has transformed countless lives through his counselling, teachings, and writings, guiding individuals toward profound personal growth and self-discovery.

A 24-time best-selling author, Shree Shambav is renowned for his insightful contributions to personal development and spiritual awakening. His work continues to uplift and inspire, offering timeless wisdom that empowers individuals to embrace their true potential.

Shree Shambav's literary journey took flight with the celebrated Journey of Soul - Karma, where he delved into the depths of human experience to unveil profound insights. Garnering recognition through multiple literature awards, his repertoire includes esteemed works, such as the Twenty + One Series – I, Twenty + One Series – II, and the enlightening Life Changing Journey – Inspirational Quotes series.

As a distinguished alumnus of the Indian Institute of Management and the National Institute of Technology, Shree Shambav brings a wealth of corporate acumen from his tenure in multinational corporations. His most recent publications, including Unveiling the Enigma, Death - Light of Life and the Shadow of Death and Optimum - Python Series I and Series II, demonstrate his mastery of both the literary and technical spheres.

Shree Shambav expands his artistic repertoire with "*Whispers of Eternity: 150 Plus - A Symphony of Soulful Verses,*" a heartfelt exploration of the human experience. Alongside this, his "*Whispers of the Soul: A*

*Journey Through Haiku*" distils profound insights into poignant verses. Together, these works showcase his versatility and mastery of soulful expression, inviting readers on a journey of self-discovery. Through his poetry, he weaves a rich tapestry of emotion that resonates deeply with the heart.

Shree Shambav's latest works—*Learn to Love Yourself: A Journey of Discovering Inner Beauty and Strength Through 10 Transformative Rules, The Power of Letting Go: Embrace Freedom and Happiness, A Journey of Lasting Peace—are true treasures of self-discovery, The Entitlement Trap: Get Over It, Get On, Whispers of a Dying Soul: Unspoken Regrets and Unlived Dreams, Whispers of Silence - Unlocking Inner Power through Stillness and The Power of Words: Transforming Speech, Transforming Lives.* Each book offers profound insights into personal growth and well-being, guiding readers on a transformative journey toward inner peace and fulfilment.

In addition to these works, Shree Shambav has recently ventured into astrology with the release of Astrology Unveiled – Foundations of Ancient Wisdom Series I to VI, expanding into the realm of metaphysics. These books explore the foundational principles of Vedic astrology, offering readers a rich and practical understanding of this ancient wisdom.

Shree Shambav established the Ayur Rakshita Foundation, which is dedicated to promoting boundless growth, universal fraternity, and environmental protection. The charity helps diverse communities while working for societal progress.

To learn more about Shree Shambav and his works, visit his website at www.shambav.org. For information about the Ayur Rakshita Foundation and its initiatives, visit www.shambav-ayurrakshita.org.

Let's Follow him on Social Media: **@shreeshambav**

# PREFACE

From the moment we are born, we begin an inevitable journey toward the unknown. The question of what lies beyond the threshold of death has lingered in the human heart for as long as we have existed. It is a question whispered in moments of silence, pondered in the solitude of night, and shared across cultures, faiths, and generations. Death is our one certainty, yet it remains cloaked in mystery. What happens when we die? Is it the end or merely the beginning of something greater?

This book, *Beyond the Veil: A Journey Through Life After Death,* invites you to join an exploration of one of humanity's most profound questions. It is not a journey of conclusions but of inquiry—an effort to bridge the seen and unseen, the material and the spiritual, the scientific and the mystical. Together, we will delve into perspectives that span centuries and civilisations, seeking not definitive answers but a richer understanding of what it means to live, to die, and to exist beyond.

Death is often approached with fear, but within its mystery lies profound wisdom. It is a teacher, reminding us of life's impermanence and urging us to live with greater purpose and authenticity. Through its lens, we begin to see what truly matters—love, connection, growth, and the evolution of the soul. To reflect on death is not to dwell in despair, but to awaken to the beauty and fragility of the present moment.

This book is structured into two parts, encompassing six sections, each offering a profound exploration of life, death, and the mysteries beyond. Due to its depth and scope, Part One covers the first three sections, while Part Two delves into the remaining three.

The journey begins with an exploration of death and consciousness. What is death, truly? Is it an end or a transition? How have different cultures and spiritual traditions understood it across time? We will question whether consciousness is bound to the body or if it transcends the physical realm, leading us into scientific investigations of near-death experiences, reincarnation, and the soul's journey beyond earthly existence.

The middle sections serve as a bridge between science and spirituality, unravelling the intricate connections between karma, consciousness, and the afterlife. Through personal accounts, ancient wisdom, and modern research, we will explore what may unfold immediately after death—the realms of the interlife and the soul's continuing evolution.

In the final sections, the focus shifts inward, inviting deep reflection on how an awareness of mortality can transform the way we live. How does embracing impermanence influence our choices, relationships, and spiritual growth? What practices can help us prepare for a peaceful transition when the time comes? And how can the mysteries that remain beyond our grasp inspire a life filled with faith, wonder, and gratitude?

Beyond being an inquiry into what happens after we die, this book is a guide to living with deeper meaning, purpose, and a greater connection to the eternal.

This book is not a doctrine, nor is it a promise of what lies beyond. Instead, it is a collection of insights, reflections, and questions meant to inspire your own exploration. It invites you to step into the unknown with curiosity and courage, to embrace the mystery of existence, and to find meaning in the eternal dance of life and death.

As you turn these pages, you may find ideas that challenge your beliefs, affirm your experiences, or awaken something new within you. Allow yourself the grace to sit with these questions, for they are not meant to be solved but lived. The journey through life, death, and the afterlife is deeply personal, and the path you walk is uniquely your own.

May this book serve as a companion and guide, offering clarity where there is doubt, peace where there is fear, and hope where there is uncertainty. Beyond the veil lies a vast and infinite mystery, but within it, we may find the essence of who we are.

Welcome to the exploration. May it deepen your connection to yourself, to others, and to the eternal thread that binds us all.

With gratitude and encouragement,

Shree Shambav

# INTRODUCTION

## The Eternal Question

Since the dawn of humanity, we have looked to the heavens, the earth, and one another in search of answers to the question that shadows every human life: *What happens after death?*

This question is neither new nor obscure. It is perhaps the most universal and timeless of all inquiries—one that has shaped civilisations, inspired spiritual traditions, and stirred the hearts of seekers across generations. It is a question that lingers in quiet moments, that whispers through grief and loss, and that ultimately leads us to the very edge of what we can comprehend. Death is the great equaliser, the inevitable passage that unites all beings, yet its true nature remains shrouded in mystery.

Is death an end or a transformation? A threshold to another existence or a return to the infinite? Are we merely biological beings, or is there something eternal within us—a consciousness, a soul, a spark that transcends the physical world? The veil that separates the known from the unknown is thin, yet beyond it lies a vast and unfathomable expanse.

In *Beyond the Veil: A Journey Through Life After Death*, we embark on a profound exploration of these mysteries. This is not a journey to provide absolute answers—for the afterlife, by its very nature, defies certainty. Rather, this book is an invitation: to wonder, to question, and to embrace the unknown with open hearts and minds. We will weave together philosophy, spiritual wisdom, scientific inquiry, and personal accounts to illuminate what may lie beyond our final breath.

This journey begins with an exploration of death itself—its biological, philosophical, and spiritual dimensions. Across cultures and traditions, perspectives on death range from the finality of the material body to the immortality of the soul. Science, too, has ventured into this enigmatic realm, studying near-death experiences, consciousness, and the possibility of an existence beyond physicality. Though science and spirituality have often been seen as opposing forces, we will seek to bridge them, revealing the ways in which they converge to offer profound insights into the nature of existence.

As we delve deeper, we will explore the soul's journey as described by ancient traditions, the role of consciousness in shaping reality, and the experiences of those who claim to have glimpsed the other side.

Near-death experiences, deathbed visions, and past-life memories challenge our conventional understanding of mortality, while teachings on karma, reincarnation, and enlightenment invite us to consider the possibility of a soul evolving across lifetimes.

Yet, this journey is not solely about what happens after death. It is, perhaps more importantly, about the lessons that death teaches us about life. When we embrace our impermanence, we begin to understand the urgency of living with authenticity, purpose, and love. Death, rather than being an adversary to be feared, becomes a teacher—one that reminds us to cherish each fleeting moment, to nurture meaningful connections, and to align our lives with what truly matters.

As you turn these pages, you may find yourself challenged, comforted, or inspired. You may encounter ideas that resonate deeply or others that provoke new questions. This is the nature of exploring the unknown—it is a deeply personal and transformative process. The goal of this journey is not to impose certainty but to expand awareness, to ignite curiosity, and to deepen our connection to the infinite.

Perhaps, in the end, it is not the answer to the eternal question that matters most. Perhaps, instead, it is the courage to ask, the willingness to seek, and the openness to embrace the great mystery itself.

Let us begin.

With warmth and sincerity,

Shree Shambav

# PROLOGUE

There is a moment in every life—a fleeting whisper of awareness—when the certainty of mortality becomes undeniable. Perhaps it comes in the stillness of the night, as shadows stretch long against the wall. Or perhaps it emerges in the depths of grief as we bid farewell to a loved one and realise that they have ventured into a realm we cannot yet follow. In these moments, we are confronted with the ultimate unknown: death.

What lies beyond this life we hold so dear? Is death a final curtain call, an ending etched in stone? Or is it a gateway, a transition into something vast, luminous, and eternal? For as long as humanity has existed, we have sought to peer beyond the veil, yearning for answers to questions that are both profoundly personal and universally shared.

The stories of those who claim to have glimpsed the other side—through near-death experiences, past-life memories, or mystical visions—offer tantalising hints of continuity. Ancient spiritual traditions have passed down teachings of rebirth, heavenly realms, and ultimate liberation. At the same time, science has begun its own exploration of consciousness and the mysteries of the mind, daring to ask whether death is truly the end or merely a transformation.

This prologue is a bridge between two worlds: the tangible and the transcendent. It is an invitation to journey with open minds and open hearts, knowing that the path ahead will be one of exploration, not certainty; of wonder, not answers.

Death is not a subject we easily embrace. It stirs fear, discomfort, and resistance, even as it beckons us with the promise of understanding. Yet it is in facing death that we begin to truly grasp the beauty and fragility of life. Every culture, every belief system, and every individual has approached this enigma with their own lens, weaving together a tapestry of perspectives that is as diverse as humanity itself.

In Parts One and Two of this book series, we embark on a profound exploration of death—not as an end, but as a gateway to deeper understanding. We will delve into the biological realities of dying, the spiritual traditions that illuminate the soul's journey, and the scientific inquiries that challenge the very limits of human knowledge. Along the way, we will listen to the voices of those who have ventured to the threshold of life and returned with stories that defy explanation—accounts that blur the line between the physical and the transcendent.

This journey is not about seeking simple answers but about embracing the vastness of the unknown. We will ask questions that have no definitive resolution and sit within the mystery, allowing its paradoxes and profundities to unfold. Through this, we may come to see death not as a final curtain but as a transformation—one that calls us to live with greater awareness, meaning, and reverence for the unseen threads that weave through existence.

But this journey is not merely an academic or philosophical pursuit. It is deeply personal. To understand death is to understand life—to see its preciousness, its impermanence, and its interconnectedness with the infinite. To explore what lies beyond is to reflect on our own purpose, our relationships, and the legacy we leave behind.

The veil that separates life from death is thin, yet it is often impenetrable. In its presence, we are reminded of our limitations but also of our boundless capacity for wonder. What lies beyond may remain a mystery, but the act of seeking it enriches our lives in ways that are both profound and transformative.

As you embark on this journey *Beyond the Veil*, I invite you to bring your curiosity, your doubts, and your hopes. Together, let us walk the path toward understanding—not to find definitive answers but to deepen our connection to the eternal questions that unite us all.

Let us dare to look beyond, for in doing so, we may discover not only what lies after death but what it truly means to live.

Welcome to the Beyond the Veil: A Journey Through Life After Death.

# CONTENTS

# At Kanchipuram

## Natures Embrace

*"In death, nature whispers the ultimate truth: nothing truly vanishes; everything evolves, returning to the infinite cycle of creation and renewal."*

*- Shree Shambav*

The dawn embraced the ashram with its quiet majesty, and the sky cloaked in twilight hues as the cool morning breeze caressed the earth. Leaves danced to a rhythm only nature could compose, their soft rustle blending seamlessly with the silence that reigned. Beneath the sprawling canopy of an ancient banyan tree, Akshaya, Vasudeva, and Vidyarthi sat in profound meditation, their forms still as statues, their breaths merging with the pulse of the universe.

Elsewhere in the ashram, figures moved like whispers in the pre-dawn light. Some journeyed toward the Zen Meditation Centre, their footsteps purposeful yet serene. Others were already lost in the flow of yoga, their bodies bending and stretching in perfect harmony with the awakening earth.

As the minutes passed, the silence of the ashram gave way to a deep resonance—the chanting of "OM" filled the air, reverberating like a heartbeat. Soon, the melodic hum of bhajans intertwined with the rhythm, accompanied by the rich timbre of tabla, dholak, cymbals, harmonium, mridangam, and other sacred instruments. The atmosphere transformed, alive with devotion and energy, as if the divine itself had descended to join in the symphony.

After their morning meditation, Akshaya and the others rose slowly, their movements mindful and deliberate. Together, they walked toward the Shambav Bhajan Hall, where the voices of Apeksha and Akshatha soared, deeply immersed in their morning devotion. Passing through the garden paths, they saw Roopa, Abhilasha, Abhirami, Alice, and Sofia gracefully flowing through their yoga postures, their focus unbroken even as the music filled the air.

As the sun ascended higher, painting the sky in strokes of orange and gold, the group gathered beneath another sacred tree in the heart of Brindavan Garden. The tree stood like a sentinel, its branches spreading wide, offering shade and shelter as if blessing the assembly. There, they welcomed Martina, Sujitha, Espen, Astyn, and Kieron—new arrivals at the ashram, their faces reflecting a mix of awe and serenity.

The fog lingered gently, shrouding the surroundings in a mystical veil. Even the trees seemed to sway in rhythm with the dholak's beat, their leaves vibrating as though attuned to the divine energy permeating the space. Devotees passed by, their voices harmonising in songs of devotion, their spirits soaring with every chant.

Kieron, captivated by the scene, remarked with wonder, "This is truly breathtaking. The power of music and chanting is beyond words—it lifts the spirit in ways nothing else can."

Vasudeva, his voice tinged with reverence, nodded deeply. "Chanting is a sacred bridge connecting the human soul to the divine. These devotees are not just singing—they are offering their hearts, letting the music carry their devotion to the heavens."

Kiran gently interrupted the moment. "Let's prepare for breakfast. The day ahead is full, and Guruji's session awaits."

Akshaya smiled and nodded, leading the group toward the Annapoorneswari facility, where the aroma of freshly prepared food filled the air. The hall was abuzz with quiet joy as devotees gathered, their faces glowing with gratitude.

Martina inhaled deeply, her eyes alight with pleasure. "The aroma is heavenly."

Sujitha, watching the volunteers serve with selfless devotion, smiled with admiration. "This is what devotion looks like in action—feeding others with love and humility. Truly, serving those in need is serving the divine."

Kiran agreed, his tone earnest. "Yes, service is an integral part of spiritual practice. It's said that when we serve others, we honour the presence of the Divine within them."

"Come, let's eat," Akshaya suggested warmly. "We'll need our strength for the wisdom Guruji will share today."

The group settled down to share their meal, a sense of peace and purpose enveloping them. Every bite seemed infused with gratitude; every word spoken was laced with joy. They were not merely individuals gathered at an ashram—they were seekers on a shared journey, each step bringing them closer to the eternal truths they yearned to uncover.

# The Eternal Question

*"To the body, death is an ending; to the soul, it is but a moment of passage, like stepping through a doorway into a broader, infinite existence." – Shree Shambav.*

The soft rustling of robes and the faint echo of footsteps marked Guruji's arrival into the serene embrace of the Buddha Hall. The room, bathed in the golden hues of the morning sun filtering through stained-glass windows, seemed to hold its breath in reverence. Each devotee instinctively bowed their heads, hands folded in Atma Namaste, their hearts brimming with devotion and anticipation.

Guruji's presence was gentle yet commanding, illuminating yet comforting. His serene smile radiated a quiet wisdom, a beacon for those seeking answers to the profound mysteries of life. Slowly, Guruji approached the centre of the hall and took his asana, his movements unhurried, each gesture imbued with purpose. Closing his eyes for a few moments, he became utterly still, as though connecting with a deeper realm of understanding, drawing from the wellspring of universal truth.

The devotees waited for the silence in the room, profound and alive, a shared heartbeat of expectancy. When Guruji finally opened his eyes, his gaze swept across the room, tender yet penetrating, reaching the very core of those present.

With a voice as soothing as a flowing river, Guruji began, "Akshaya... The Eternal Question."

He paused, letting the words linger in the air, their depth sinking into the hearts of his listeners. "Humanity has always been captivated by this question—a timeless curiosity about what happens after death. It is a question that transcends cultures, religions, and epochs. Like the waves that tirelessly kiss the shore, the human spirit has ceaselessly sought to understand the mysteries of existence beyond the veil."

"Death," Guruji continued, his tone both solemn and gentle, "is not an ending. It is a threshold—a passage. Imagine life as a great river, flowing with vigour and purpose, winding its way through valleys, forests, and plains. Death is not the end of this river, but it is merging with the boundless ocean. The river does not cease to exist; it becomes something greater, vaster, infinite. And yet, the essence of the river—the journey it has undertaken, the paths it has carved—remains forever imprinted in the fabric of the cosmos."

The devotees sat spellbound, their minds painting images of the river's journey, their hearts resonating with the metaphor.

"Akshaya," Guruji continued, turning to the concept itself, "means that which is eternal, imperishable. The Eternal Question is not merely about what lies beyond the veil of death. It is about the very nature of existence—who we are, why we are here, and what we are destined to become. It is about life, death, and what bridges the two. And so, we must explore this question not just through the lens of one perspective, but through the union of philosophy, spirituality, and science."

He paused again, allowing his words to ripple through the stillness like a pebble dropped into a tranquil pond.

"Philosophy," Guruji said, his voice taking on a reflective tone, "asks us to ponder the meaning of death, to confront our fears and uncertainties. It holds up a mirror to life itself, for to understand death, we must first understand life. Philosophy tells us that death is not the enemy but the ultimate teacher, revealing the impermanence of all things and urging us to live fully in the present moment."

"Spirituality," he continued, "invites us to go beyond the mind, to connect with the eternal within. It teaches us that we are not merely bodies with a soul but souls experiencing a human journey. Death, in the spiritual sense, is a homecoming—a return to the divine, a reunion with the infinite source from which we all emerge."

"And then," Guruji said, his eyes glinting with curiosity, "there is science. Modern science, with all its advancements, seeks to unravel the mysteries of consciousness and the afterlife. It explores near-death experiences, reincarnation, and the persistence of awareness beyond physical death. Science, in its quest for understanding, becomes a bridge—a link between the tangible and the intangible, the known and the unknown."

He leaned forward slightly, his gaze sweeping across the room. "Together, these perspectives form a mosaic—a holistic view of the Eternal Question. They remind us that no single path holds all the answers, but each offers a piece of the puzzle. And in embracing this mystery, we come closer to the essence of who we truly are."

A gentle breeze stirred the air, carrying the faint scent of sandalwood from the incense burning at the altar. The devotees sat in contemplative silence, their minds and hearts alight with newfound understanding. Guruji's words were not just teachings; they were seeds planted in the fertile soil of their souls, destined to grow into deeper awareness and wisdom.

"Let us explore this journey together," Guruji concluded, his voice a tender invitation. "Not to seek definitive answers, but to awaken to the wonder of existence, to embrace the mystery, and to find peace in knowing that life and death are but two sides of the same eternal truth."

*Roopa asked, "Guruji, why has the question of what happens after death fascinated humanity across cultures and eras?"*

Guruji's gaze softened as he turned toward Roopa, her question hanging in the air like a thread connecting everyone in the room to the timeless wonder of existence. He smiled, a gesture both gentle and knowing, and began to speak.

"Ah, Roopa," he said, his voice carrying the weight of centuries of contemplation, "the question of what happens after death is humanity's eternal flame—a light that flickers in the darkest nights of uncertainty and doubt. It is the question that has been whispered to sages in the stillness of deserts, sung to poets in the solitude of mountains, and guided philosophers in their endless search for truth. Why does it captivate us? Because it is not merely about death—it is about life. It is the mirror in which we see the fragility and the magnificence of existence reflected back to us."

He paused, his words settling over the room like a gentle rain nourishing thirsty soil. "Every culture, every tradition, every faith has sought to answer this question, not because they feared death, but because they longed to understand life."

Guruji's hands rested gently on his knees as his voice resonated with calm authority, drawing from the timeless wisdom of the Bhagavad Gita. "Consider this, Roopa," he said. "In Chapter 2, Verse 22 of the *Bhagavad Gita,* Lord Krishna offers Arjuna a profound analogy:"

*vaasansi jirnani yathaa vihaya*
*navaani grihnati naro 'paraani*
*tatha shariraani vihaya jirnanya*
*nyaani sanyati navani dehi*

Meaning: *"As a person discards old, worn-out garments and puts on new ones, so the soul discards worn-out bodies and enters new ones."*

Guruji's eyes scanned the room as the sacred words settled over the group like a gentle breeze, stirring something deep within. "This verse," he continued, "captures the essence of death not as an ending, but as a transformation—a transition from one form to another, much like changing clothes. It reassures us that the soul, the eternal self, is untouched by the decay of the body. What we perceive as death is merely a passage, a step in the soul's journey toward greater evolution and understanding."

He paused, his gaze steady yet tender. "This teaching," Guruji said, "reminds us that fear of death arises from our attachment to the physical form. When we recognise the soul as eternal, *Akshaya,* we free ourselves from that fear and instead see death as an integral part of the divine cycle of life and rebirth."

Here, death is not an end but a transition—a shedding of the temporal to embrace the eternal. The soul is Akshaya, indestructible, and this realisation frees one from the fear of death. It teaches us that life and death are not opposites but partners in an eternal dance.

Guruji continued, "In Christianity, we find a similar thread that speaks of the soul's immortality and the promise of eternal life. Consider the words of Jesus Christ from the Gospel of John, Chapter 11, Verse 25:

*'I am the resurrection and the life. He who believes in me will live, even though he dies.'*

These words are a cornerstone of Christian faith, offering hope and reassurance that death is not the end, but a transition to a higher state of being."

In this passage, Jesus emphasises the power of faith as a bridge between life and death. It speaks to the profound truth that the soul's existence transcends the physical body, echoing the eternal promise of divine union.

Just as Krishna assures Arjuna of the soul's immortality, Christ offers the assurance of eternal life through faith, emphasising that love and trust in the divine are pathways to transcendence.

Here, death is a passage—a doorway to eternal life. The promise of resurrection is not just about the afterlife but about the transformative power of faith and surrender. Death becomes not a wall but a bridge to a realm of love, light, and unity with God."

Guruji said, "The Buddha taught that life and death are two sides of the same coin, bound by the law of impermanence. He said,

*'All conditioned things are impermanent—when one sees this with wisdom, one turns away from suffering.'*

In this teaching, death is not a tragedy but a natural part of existence. It is the cessation of the illusion of permanence, guiding us toward liberation, or Nirvana. The fear of death dissolves when we realise that clinging to life only perpetuates suffering. Death, then, is not an enemy but a teacher, reminding us to live with mindfulness and compassion."

"In Zen," he said, "death is often described with simplicity and clarity. The Zen master Dōgen Zenji once wrote,

*'Life and death are of supreme importance. Time swiftly passes by, and opportunity is lost. Awaken! Awaken! Take heed, do not squander your life.'*

Zen does not dwell on what happens after death. Instead, it urges us to awaken here and now, to live fully in each fleeting moment, for life and death are inseparable—each breath is both a beginning and an end."

Guruji's gaze turned inward. "In Taoism, the Tao Te Ching tells us,

*'Each being in the universe returns to the common Source (One). To return to the Source is to find peace.'*

Here, death is a return to the Tao, the infinite source of all existence. It is not to be feared or mourned but to be accepted as a natural return to the whole. The Taoist view teaches us to flow with life's cycles, to see death not as a disruption but as a continuation of the great rhythm of existence."

He leaned slightly forward, his voice now imbued with the mystical richness of Sufi wisdom. "In Sufism, the great poet Rumi wrote,

*'When I die, I will soar with angels, and when I die to the angels, what I shall become you cannot imagine.'*

For the Sufis, death is a journey of ascent, a shedding of layers until the soul reunites with the Beloved. It is not a loss but a homecoming, an ecstatic return to divine love. Death, in the Sufi tradition, is the ultimate union with the Infinite."

A hush fell over the room as Guruji's words settled into the hearts of his listeners, weaving together the rich tapestry of human understanding.

"Why does this question fascinate us, Roopa?" Guruji said, his voice soft yet resonant. "Because in asking what happens after death, we are really asking, *Who am I? What is the purpose of my life? What lies beyond my fears, my attachments, my illusions?* This question compels us to seek, to explore, to awaken. It is the flame that illuminates the path of self-discovery, urging us to embrace the unknown with courage and wonder."

He paused, his eyes meeting Roopa's with a look of profound compassion. "The answer is not one we can grasp with the mind alone. It is an experience, a surrender, a remembering of our true nature. Death is not the opposite of life—it is the fullness of life, the completion of the circle, the silent whisper of the infinite calling us home."

Explore the universal nature of this curiosity and how it reflects the human quest for meaning and understanding.

*Apeksha asked, "Guruji, how do different philosophical, spiritual, and scientific traditions approach the concept of life after death?"*

Guruji leaned back slightly, his hands resting gently on his knees, and looked at Apeksha with a serene smile.

"Ah, Apeksha," he began, his voice calm yet profound, "you have asked a question that has travelled through millennia, across civilisations, and through the hearts of all who have ever pondered their own existence. Life after death is not just a mystery—it is the thread that binds philosophy, spirituality, and science into one vast, interconnected exploration."

### The Philosophical Lens: The Eternal Inquiry

Guruji gestured toward the ancient banyan tree outside the hall. "Philosophers, like this tree, have stood firm over centuries, contemplating the nature of existence and the soul.

### Socrates' Perspective on Death

Socrates, the ancient Greek philosopher, reflected deeply on the nature of death, particularly in the context of his trial and subsequent execution, as recounted in Plato's *Apology*. Socrates viewed death not as an end but as a transition. He famously said:

*"To fear death, my friends, is only to think ourselves wise without being wise, for it is to think that we know what we do not know." (Plato's Apology, 29a)*

He argued that death could either be a state of nothingness—like a peaceful, dreamless sleep—or a journey of the soul to another realm where it would encounter others who had died. Socrates was unafraid of death because he believed in the immortality of the soul and saw death as a philosophical opportunity to explore a new dimension of existence. His calm acceptance of his death reflects his belief in the continuity of the soul and its liberation from the physical body.

Socrates' philosophy aligns with the idea that fear of death arises from ignorance and that true wisdom lies in embracing the mystery of what lies beyond.

He paused, allowing the group to visualise the metaphor. "Philosophy doesn't give definitive answers, but it offers a framework—a lens through which we can question, reflect, and expand our understanding. It invites us to consider life and death as complementary, not opposing forces, much like day and night."

## The Upanishads on Life and Death

The Upanishads delve deeply into the nature of the soul (*Atman*) and its relationship to the ultimate reality (*Brahman*). They describe the soul as eternal and indestructible, transcending the physical body. A well-known verse from the *Bhagavad Gita* Chapter 2, Verse 22(which is often considered an extension of the Upanishadic teachings) states:

*"As a person discards old, worn-out garments and puts on new ones, so the soul discards worn-out bodies and enters new ones."* (Chapter 2, Verse 22)

This analogy emphasises the soul's immortality and its journey through multiple lives. Death is seen not as an end but as a transition—a shedding of the temporary physical form as the soul continues its eternal journey toward liberation (*moksha*), where it reunites with the divine essence (*Brahman*).

Another powerful teaching comes from the *Katha Upanishad* 1.2.18, which compares the soul's journey to a traveller:

na jayate mriyate va vipascinnaayam kutascinna babhuva kascit |
ajo nityah saasvatoyam purano na hanyate hanyamaane sarire ||
Meaning: "The soul is not born, nor does it die; it has not come from anywhere, nor did it become anything.

Unborn, eternal, constant, and ancient, it is not killed when the body is slain."

This verse underscores the permanence of the soul and the transient nature of the physical body. The Upanishads encourage individuals to transcend the fear of death by recognising their true, infinite nature beyond the physical form.

**Connecting Socrates and the Upanishads**

Both Socrates and the Upanishads approach death with a sense of curiosity and reverence. Socrates' belief that death is either a peaceful nothingness or a journey mirrors the Upanishadic view of death as a transition for the soul. Both perspectives challenge the materialist view of life as limited to the physical body, inviting us to see death as part of a greater cosmic process.

While Socrates approaches the question through philosophical reasoning, the Upanishads offer a spiritual lens grounded in introspection and metaphysical truths. Together, they represent a bridge between Western and Eastern traditions, both emphasising the eternal nature of the soul and encouraging us to embrace life and death with wisdom and courage.

## Spiritual Perspectives: Pathways to the Infinite

Guruji closed his eyes briefly and then opened them, his expression softening as he continued, "Spiritual traditions offer a more experiential approach, emphasising faith, surrender, and personal transformation. Let us look to Buddhism. The Buddha taught that death is not an end but a continuation—a transition shaped by karma.

He turned his gaze toward Apeksha. "In Sufism, the mystics speak of *fana*, the annihilation of the self, and *baqa*, the eternal subsistence of the soul in divine union. Death, for the Sufi, is not a tragedy but a return—a homecoming to the Beloved. Jalaluddin Rumi writes,

*'When I die, I will soar with angels, and when I die to the angels, what I shall become you cannot imagine.'*

Do you see? Death is not an event but a transformation, a reunion with the infinite."

He paused and then added, "In Christianity, Jesus's words about resurrection offer hope—a vision of eternal life where faith bridges the chasm between the finite and the infinite. The teachings of Christ align deeply with the idea that love transcends death, that life is an eternal dance with the divine."

Guruji said, "The teachings of Jesus Christ, particularly as found in the New Testament of the Bible, where He speaks of resurrection and eternal life. A central verse capturing this idea is:

*"I am the resurrection and the life. The one who believes in me will live, even though they die; and whoever lives by believing in me will never die." (John 11:25-26, NIV)*

This passage reflects the Christian understanding of life after death, emphasising faith in Jesus as the path to eternal life. The resurrection of Jesus Christ is viewed as the ultimate victory over death, signifying that life continues beyond the physical world."

In Christianity, resurrection is not merely about life after death; it is a profound statement of hope and transformation. The resurrection symbolises not only the eternal nature of the soul but also the power of divine love to transcend all limitations, including mortality. Jesus's teachings invite believers to see death not as an end but as a transition into a closer union with God.

The idea of love transcending death is also a recurring theme in Christian theology. Paul's epistle to the Romans captures this beautifully:

*"For I am convinced that neither death nor life, neither angels nor demons, neither the present nor the future, nor any powers, neither height nor depth nor anything else in all creation, will be able to separate us from the love of God that is in Christ Jesus our Lord." (Romans 8:38-39, NIV)*

This perspective aligns with the notion that faith bridges the finite and the infinite, offering a vision of eternal communion with the divine. In essence, the resurrection represents a divine assurance that the bonds of love and spirit remain unbroken, even in the face of death.

**Scientific Exploration: The Bridge of Inquiry**

Guruji's tone shifted slightly as he leaned forward, weaving science into the tapestry of his discourse. "And what about science? In its way, it, too, seeks to explore the mystery. Consider near-death experiences studied rigorously by researchers like Dr. Raymond Moody. These accounts—of people seeing the light, meeting loved ones, or feeling an overwhelming sense of peace—cannot be easily dismissed. They challenge us to look beyond the boundaries of materialism."

"Quantum physics adds yet another dimension to the conversation. Some scientists suggest that consciousness is not confined to the brain but is a fundamental property of the universe, much like space and time. If that is so, then perhaps what we call 'death' is merely a shift in the location or expression of consciousness, much like water evaporating into mist."

Guruji's gaze softened as he concluded, "Science approaches the question with caution, seeking evidence where spirituality already offers faith. Yet, when you look closely, they are not so different. Both are driven by a deep curiosity, a desire to understand what lies beyond the visible."

**The Flame and the Lamp**

Guruji leaned back, his voice deepening with metaphor. "Imagine a lamp that burns brightly, its flame lighting the darkness. When the oil runs out, the flame flickers and vanishes. But does it truly cease to exist? No. The heat of the flame merges with the air; its light, however brief, becomes a part of the eternal dance of photons in the universe."

"So too with life and death. The body is the lamp, the soul the flame. When the oil of life is spent, the flame does not die—it transforms, merges, and continues in ways beyond our understanding."

A deep silence fell over the Buddha Hall as the devotees absorbed Guruji's words. Apeksha's eyes glimmered with newfound insight, and the others sat motionless as though held in a sacred stillness.

Guruji spoke again, his voice softer this time. "Whether through philosophy, spirituality, or science, we are all seekers, navigating this vast ocean of mystery. The question of what lies beyond is not just about death; it is about life itself. How we live, how we love, and how we connect with the infinite in each moment—this is what truly matters."

Discuss the diverse perspectives that shape our understanding of death and the possibility of an afterlife.

*Akshatha asked, "Guruji, what role does consciousness play in our understanding of life, death, and what lies beyond?"*

Guruji closed his eyes briefly, allowing the silence in the Buddha Hall to deepen. "Ah, consciousness," Guruji began, his voice a blend of softness and gravitas. "It is both the seeker and the sought, the question and the answer. Consciousness is the lens through which we perceive life and the thread that ties us to the eternal mystery of existence. Without it, life, death, and the beyond would remain incomprehensible."

## The Lamp of Awareness

He gestured toward the flickering oil lamp on the altar nearby. "Think of consciousness as this flame," he said. "The body is the wick, the mind the oil. As long as there is oil to sustain it, the flame burns bright, illuminating the world around it. But what happens when the oil runs out? Does the flame cease to exist, or does it merge into a greater light beyond what we can see? This question has intrigued philosophers, mystics, and scientists alike."

Guruji smiled gently and turned toward Akshatha. "To explore this, let us delve into the perspectives of various traditions."

### Consciousness in the Upanishads

"In the Upanishads," he began, "consciousness is described as the ultimate reality, the *Brahman*. It is not something we possess; it is what we are. The *Mandukya Upanishad* speaks of four states of consciousness: the waking state (*Jagrat*), the dream state (*Swapna*), the deep sleep state (*Sushupti*), and the transcendental state (*Turiya*). This fourth state, *Turiya*, is the foundation upon which all other states rest. It is pure awareness, beyond duality, beyond life and death."

Guruji paused, allowing the profound concept to settle. "When we identify with the body, we see death as the end. But when we experience *Turiya*, we realise that consciousness is eternal. The soul is merely transitioning, much like water evaporating from a pot, only to return to the ocean."

### Socratic Philosophy: The Unexamined Life

He continued, "Socrates, the great Greek philosopher, believed that the soul was immortal and that death was not to be feared. In his words:

*'The unexamined life is not worth living.'*

To Socrates, consciousness was the key to self-awareness and ethical living. He viewed death as the release of the soul from the confines of the body, enabling it to attain a higher state of understanding. He saw it not as an end, but as an opportunity for the soul to explore truth more freely."

Guruji's voice softened. "Socrates, like the sages of India, emphasised that the soul's journey does not end at death—it is the beginning of a new phase in its pursuit of wisdom."

**Buddhist Perspective: The Stream of Consciousness**

"In Buddhism," Guruji said, "consciousness is likened to a flowing river. It is not static but a continuous stream of moments—each one arising, existing, and passing away. This impermanence is called *Anicca*. At the time of death, the stream does not end but merges into another form, guided by the karmic energy we have accumulated in life. The Buddha taught that understanding this flow—this interdependence—frees us from the illusion of a permanent self and the fear of death."

He leaned forward slightly, his expression intent. "To Buddhists, the question is not whether consciousness survives after death but what form it will take. It reminds us that every action, thought, and intention shapes the course of this river, determining whether it flows toward liberation or further entanglement."

**Modern Science: The Frontier of Consciousness**

Guruji's voice softened, taking on a contemplative tone that seemed to mirror the vastness of the subject. He began, "Consciousness, the silent witness of our existence, is one of the greatest enigmas humanity has ever encountered. In the realm of science, it remains both tantalisingly close and endlessly elusive."

He paused for a moment, "Neuroscientists delve deep into the labyrinth of the brain, mapping neural pathways, studying chemical interactions, and attempting to pinpoint the origins of awareness. Yet, they often find themselves confronted by a profound question: Is consciousness merely the product of the brain, or is it something greater—something fundamental to the nature of reality itself?"

Turning his gaze toward Akshatha, Guruji's expression was both curious and serene. "Quantum physicist Erwin Schrödinger once touched upon this mystery when he said,

*'The plurality that we perceive is only an appearance; in truth, there is only one mind.'*

What does this mean? At its heart, Schrödinger was suggesting that consciousness is not confined to individual beings but is instead a universal field—a singular essence that permeates all existence."

He gestured lightly as if tracing the fabric of this interconnectedness in the air. "Consider the concept of quantum entanglement," he said, his voice weaving science and spirituality into one seamless thread. "When two particles interact, they become connected in such a way that their states remain linked, no matter the distance between them. A change in one particle instantaneously affects the other, defying our conventional understanding of time and space."

The room seemed to breathe with awe as Guruji continued, "Now, imagine consciousness not as a byproduct of the brain, but as the universal field in which everything—every atom, every particle, every thought—is entangled. Could this not explain why ancient spiritual traditions speak of oneness? The Upanishads, for instance, proclaim,

*'Sarvam Khalvidam Brahma'—All this is Brahman.*

They remind us that the essence of the universe is interconnected and indivisible."

He leaned forward slightly, his voice tinged with quiet wonder. "This is not unlike the teachings of Buddhism, which view consciousness as the continuum of existence, transcending the boundaries of birth and death. It is also echoed in the mystical traditions of Sufism, where the soul's longing to merge with the divine reflects the eternal unity at the heart of all things."

Guruji smiled softly, his tone shifting to one of gentle inspiration. "If science is the lamp that lights the room, spirituality is the door that opens it to the infinite. Quantum entanglement and the teachings of sages across the ages both whisper the same truth: that separation is an illusion. Whether we call it Brahman, the Tao, or the quantum field, it is the same eternal consciousness that binds us all."

He looked deeply at the gathering, his eyes reflecting the vastness of the cosmos and the intimacy of a shared heartbeat. "And so, the role of consciousness in understanding life, death, and what lies beyond is profound. It is not merely an observer—it is the canvas on which the entire universe is painted. To understand consciousness is to glimpse the infinite, to touch the essence of existence itself."

**Sufism: The Heart's Awareness**

"In Sufism," he continued, "consciousness is experienced through the heart. Rumi writes,

*'Don't be satisfied with stories, how things have gone with others. Unfold your own myth.'*

The Sufi path teaches that awareness is not a mental construct but a direct experience of the divine. Death, for the Sufi, is the ultimate union with the Beloved—a moment when the soul, having shed its earthly coverings, merges with the infinite."

## An Eternal Mystery

Guruji folded his hands together and leaned back slightly. "Across traditions, consciousness is seen as the bridge between the finite and the infinite, the mortal and the divine. Whether it is the *Brahman* of the Upanishads, the river of Buddhism, or the divine love of Sufism, the message is clear: consciousness is not confined by death."

He gestured toward the gathering. "But it is not enough to study these teachings. They are like maps. To truly understand consciousness, you must journey inward and experience it for yourself."

## The Flame and the Wind

"To illustrate this," he said, "let me share a story. Once, a flame asked the wind, 'Why do you always try to extinguish me?' The wind replied, 'I don't extinguish you; I free you. You think you are bound to the wick, but your essence is the light. When I blow, you are not destroyed—you become part of the infinite.'"

Guruji looked at Akshatha, his eyes filled with kindness. "In the same way, death does not extinguish consciousness. It frees it, allowing it to merge with the infinite, where it continues to dance in the great mystery of existence."

The room was silent, and each person was deeply moved. The question lingered in the air, no longer something to be answered but something to be lived.

*Akanksh asked, "Guruji, why is it important to explore the mysteries of life and death in today's world?"*

Guruji's eyes softened with quiet wisdom as he turned to Akanksh. The question lingered in the air, touching something timeless yet urgently relevant in the hearts of all who listened. With a deep breath, he began, his voice resonating like the gentle chime of a bell echoing through the hall.

"In today's world," Guruji said, "we live at an unprecedented pace. Technology has given us tools to connect instantly across the globe, yet many feel more isolated than ever. We are surrounded by distractions, consumed by material pursuits, and driven by deadlines. In this chaos, the mysteries of life and death—the most fundamental questions of existence—often recede into the background, seen as abstractions rather than essentials."

He paused, letting the weight of his words sink in. "But this exploration, Akanksh, is more important now than ever. It is not an indulgence in philosophy or a retreat into mysticism. It is a compass, a map for the soul, guiding us toward a life of purpose and peace. To understand life and death is to understand ourselves—and to live with intention rather than drift in reaction."

Guruji leaned slightly forward, his gaze steady and kind. "Imagine a traveller," he said, "standing at a crossroads with a map in hand but never looking at it. Instead, the traveller stumbles forward, hoping to arrive somewhere meaningful. This is how many of us live today—without truly understanding where we came from, where we are going, or why we are here."

He gestured gently as if tracing the invisible threads of existence. "Exploring the mysteries of life and death helps us unfold this map. It allows us to see that our time on this earth is a chapter, not the entire book. It reminds us that each moment is precious because it is fleeting and that the way we live echoes far beyond our immediate lives."

Drawing from his deep well of wisdom, Guruji continued, "The Bhagavad Gita Chapter 2, Verse 27 reminds us that *'What is born will die, and what dies will be born again.'* This understanding—that life and death are not opposites but two sides of the same coin—frees us from the grip of fear. It gives us the courage to live fully, to love deeply, and to face the unknown with grace."

*jatasya hi dhruvo mrityur dhruvam janma mritasya cha |*
*tasmad apariharye 'rthe na tvam shochitum arhasi | |*
Meaning: *"For one who is born, death is certain; and for one who has died, birth is certain. Therefore, you should not grieve over the inevitable."*

This verse is part of Lord Krishna's counsel to Arjuna during his moment of despair on the battlefield of Kurukshetra. Krishna emphasises the cyclical nature of existence, portraying life and death not as endpoints but as transitions within an eternal continuum. By understanding this eternal rhythm, one can overcome the fear of death and sorrow, embracing life with courage and equanimity.

Guruji's voice grew softer, imbued with emotion. "In Buddhism, the practice of meditating on death is not meant to darken our spirits but to awaken them. It is a call to appreciate the present moment and to cultivate kindness, compassion, and awareness. The Zen tradition likens life to the morning dew—a beautiful, fleeting phenomenon that reminds us to embrace each breath as a gift."

Guruji's gaze swept over the room, connecting with each soul as though he spoke to them individually. "In the modern world, we have developed incredible technologies to extend life, yet we often overlook how to deepen its meaning. We are skilled at accumulating wealth, yet we struggle to nurture inner peace. Exploring life and death is not about answers alone; it is about living with purpose."

Guruji said, "Let me narrate a story: There was once a wise old monk who lived in a monastery atop a mountain. A young seeker climbed the mountain, hoping to learn the secret of life and death. When he arrived, breathless, he asked the monk, 'What is the purpose of life?' The monk smiled and handed him a bowl of water. He said, 'Drink.' The seeker drank. Then the monk asked, 'What do you feel?' The seeker replied, 'I feel refreshed.' The monk said, 'That is life: quenching the thirst of the soul. And death? Death is the reminder that you must drink now, for the bowl will not always be full.'"

The hall grew silent as the profound simplicity of the story sank in. Guruji continued, "This is the relevance of exploring these mysteries. When we understand that death is not an end but a transition and that life is not permanent but precious, we start to live differently. We are kinder to others, more present in our days, and less afraid of letting go."

He glanced at Akanksh with a warm smile. "To explore life and death is to seek wisdom in a world often consumed by knowledge. It is to find peace amid chaos, and it is to cultivate a love for life that is deeper than the fleeting pleasures of the material world. The mysteries of existence are not obstacles; they are doorways—doorways to understanding, to connection, and a life lived in harmony with the infinite."

Guruji, after a long and reflective pause, gently signalled for a short break. The devotees, still immersed in the morning's profound discourse, slowly rose and made their way toward the refreshment counter. The air was filled with the inviting aroma of freshly brewed chai and herbal infusions, mingling with the soft rustle of leaves swaying in the gentle, soothing breeze. The sky stretched wide in a serene shade of blue, a perfect canvas for the bright sun, whose warm rays danced on the tranquil grounds of the ashram.

Some devotees took leisurely strolls along the garden paths, and their footsteps light as they exchanged thoughts from the morning session, their words carrying a mix of wonder and reverence. Others sat quietly in the shade of ancient trees, reflecting on Guruji's teachings or sipping their beverages, the stillness around them echoing the depth of their contemplation. The atmosphere was alive yet peaceful, as though nature itself had harmonised with the seekers' inner journeys.

When the devotees returned to the Buddha Hall, a palpable sense of anticipation filled the air. The hall, with its soft golden light filtering through the high windows, seemed to embrace their presence. The devotees took their seats, their hearts open and ready to absorb the next pearls of wisdom from their revered Guruji. The silence in the room was profound yet comforting, as if the very walls held the echoes of ancient truths waiting to be revealed once more.

In this sacred space, they awaited the continuation of the discourse, their minds prepared to delve deeper into the mysteries of existence, guided by the timeless insights of their beloved teacher.

# SECTION ONE

## Understanding Death and Consciousness

*"After death, the soul returns to the eternal rhythm of nature, like a river merging back into the ocean, endless yet ever-present."*

- *Shree Shambav*

# CHAPTER I

## What is Death? The End or a New Beginning?

*"Death is not the final chapter but the turning of a page—an invitation for the soul to journey beyond the confines of the physical."*

*- Shree Shambav*

**Synopsis:**

*We explore the concept of death from multiple perspectives—biological, philosophical, and spiritual. From a biological standpoint, death is the cessation of vital processes within the body. However, philosophical perspectives question whether death is truly an end or merely a transition to something greater. Meanwhile, spiritual traditions offer varying views on death, often portraying it not as a final conclusion but as a passage to another existence or state of being. The chapter also delves into how different cultures interpret death, embracing it as a natural transition rather than a finality. Through rituals and ceremonies, these cultures shape their collective understanding of death and provide comfort to the living. By examining the diversity of beliefs about death and the afterlife, we open up the possibility that death is not the end of the journey but an invitation to a new chapter.*

Guruji's voice carried the weight of timeless wisdom as he asked, "What is Death? Is it the end or a new beginning?" His words lingered in the silence of the Buddha Hall; a silence so profound that it seemed to echo through the hearts of every devotee present.

After a brief pause, he continued, "From a biological perspective, death marks the cessation of life—the stopping of the heartbeat, the silence of the brain, and the conclusion of cellular functions. Science views it as the point where the body can no longer sustain itself, where life ebbs away into stillness. Yet even within this framework, life persists in another form. The elements of the body return to the earth, nourishing the soil and giving life to new beings. Death is not an annihilation—it is a transformation. In nature, nothing truly dies; it merely changes form, a reflection of the eternal cycle of creation, preservation, and dissolution."

Guruji's gaze swept across the room as he leaned slightly forward, his tone deepening with emotion. "Philosophically, death is a paradox. Socrates, as he faced his final moments, spoke of death not as a loss but as a journey to a greater truth. He said, 'To fear death is nothing other than to think oneself wise when one is not; to think one knows what one does not know.' In his eyes, death was a gateway to deeper knowledge, an opportunity to transcend the illusions of this world and encounter the ultimate reality."

He paused, allowing the depth of these words to settle in the hearts of his listeners before shifting his focus. "Now, consider how spirituality frames death. In the Bhagavad Gita, Lord Krishna reassures Arjuna, 'As a person sheds worn-out garments and wears new ones, likewise, the soul discards its worn-out body and enters a new one.' Here, death is not an end but a transition—a passage for the eternal soul to move from one existence to another, much like a river flowing into the ocean, where it loses its individuality yet becomes part of something vast and infinite."

Guruji's words painted vivid imagery as if death was not an abyss but a doorway to a greater understanding of life itself. "In Buddhism, death is seen as a continuation—a part of the cycle of samsara, the endless cycle of birth, death, and rebirth. Yet, it also offers the chance for liberation. The Buddha taught that by understanding the impermanence of life, one can release attachment and find peace. Death, then, is not a foe to be feared but a teacher guiding us toward enlightenment."

The devotees sat in rapt attention as Guruji gently wove into cultural and spiritual perspectives. "In Christianity, Jesus Christ offers a profound view of death as a resurrection—a promise of eternal life. 'I am the resurrection and the life. He who believes in me will live, even though he dies.' This faith transforms death into an act of trust, a bridge to a realm where love and divine grace prevail."

Guruji's voice softened, yet it carried the weight of cosmic insight as he continued, "Different cultures have beautifully unique ways of honouring this transition. The ancient Egyptians believed death was the beginning of an eternal journey, where the soul would be weighed against the feather of truth. The Native American traditions often view death as a return to the Great Spirit, a merging back into the web of life."

He paused, his expression serene yet contemplative. "And what of modern science? The mysteries of consciousness have prompted some scientists to view death not as an ending but as a transformation of energy. Quantum entanglement—a phenomenon where particles remain interconnected regardless of distance—raises profound questions about the nature of life and existence. Could it be that our consciousness, like those particles, transcends time and space? Might death be not an erasure but a reconnection—a merging back into the infinite web of existence?"

A soft breeze moved through the hall as Guruji leaned back slightly, his voice now tender and compassionate. "Ultimately, death is not a concept to be feared but one to be understood. It is a mirror that reflects the meaning of life. When we recognise that death is a transition, we begin to live with greater awareness, purpose, and peace. We see that every moment is a gift, every relationship sacred, and every breath a step closer to unity with the infinite."

He looked out at the gathering, his eyes radiating both clarity and love. "So, my dear ones, the question is not what death takes from us but what it reveals to us. In understanding death, we learn how to live—not in fear of the end, but in awe of the journey."

*Sam asked, "Guruji, how does the biological definition of death differ from philosophical and spiritual perspectives?"*

Guruji smiled gently. He leaned forward slightly as if inviting everyone to join him in a profound inquiry. "Ah, Sam," he began, "your question touches the heart of the human experience—the interplay between science, philosophy, and spirituality in understanding life and death. Let us explore this deeply, for these perspectives, though distinct, are like threads of a single tapestry, each enriching the other."

He raised his hand slightly, palm open as if holding an invisible idea. "From a biological standpoint," he said, "death is a moment marked by measurable changes—the cessation of a heartbeat, the silence of the brain, the end of metabolic activity. Medical science defines it as the point where the body can no longer sustain itself, where the intricate machinery of life comes to a halt. It is precise, clinical, and rooted in observable facts. Yet, as comprehensive as this view is, it is only the surface of a much deeper ocean."

Guruji's voice softened, drawing the listeners closer. "Philosophy, on the other hand, looks beyond the measurable. It asks, 'What is the essence of being? What does it mean to cease to exist?' Philosophers like Socrates did not view death as an end but as a doorway to deeper truths. When he drank the hemlock, Socrates told his followers, 'Death may be the greatest of all human blessings.' For him, death was not an annihilation but a liberation—a transition from the illusions of the physical world to the reality of the soul's eternal nature."

He paused, letting the weight of these words sink in before continuing. "Consider the wisdom of the Upanishads," he said. "These sacred texts, composed by sages who sought the ultimate truth, speak eloquently of life and death as threads in the same eternal tapestry.

*yatha nadyah syandamanaah samudre'stam gacchanti naamarupe vihaya |*

*tatha vidvan namarupad vimuktah paratparam purusamupaiti divyam ||*

Meaning: "As the rivers flow into the ocean, shedding their names and forms, so too does the wise man, freed from all individuality, merge into the infinite."

Guruji's voice softened. "In this view, death is not a calamity or an end—it is the river's journey home. Just as rivers, despite their diverse paths and origins, ultimately dissolve into the vastness of the ocean, so does the soul, leaving behind the limitations of identity and form, return to the universal consciousness from which it arose."

He gestured toward the devotees as though inviting them to see the rivers within themselves. "Imagine this," he said, weaving an analogy. "Every drop of water in a river carries the memory of the rain, the streams, and the earth it has touched. When it reaches the ocean, it loses its individuality but gains the infinite. It becomes part of something greater, yet it is never truly lost. This is the journey of the soul—leaving the confines of the physical body and the ego to merge with the eternal, to become one with the divine essence."

The devotees sat motionless, captivated by the imagery Guruji painted. He continued, his voice now imbued with a gentle urgency. "This understanding dissolves the fear of death. It teaches us that what we perceive as the end is but a transformation—a homecoming. The wise do not see death as something to dread; they see it as a natural part of existence, as inevitable and as beautiful as the setting sun."

He paused again, allowing the profundity of the Upanishadic teaching to settle in the minds and hearts of his audience. "The Upanishads remind us that life and death are not opposites. They are two sides of the same cosmic coin. Life is the expression of the divine in form; death is the dissolution of that form back into the formless divine. Both are sacred, both are necessary."

Guruji's tone deepened, and his eyes shone with an almost ethereal light. "Spirituality," he began, "offers us a lens through which the mysteries of life and death become clear—not as enigmas to fear but as cycles to embrace. In the *Bhagavad Gita*, Lord Krishna, in his discourse to the anguished Arjuna, reveals a truth so profound it echoes across the corridors of eternity. Krishna says:

*na tvevaaham jaatu nasam na tvam neme janaadhipah* |

*na chaiva na bhavishyaamah sarve vayamatah param* ||

Meaning: "Never was there a time when I did not exist, nor you, nor all these kings; nor will there be a time in the future when we shall cease to be."

Guruji's voice softened. "In this teaching, Krishna dissolves the illusion of death as a finality. Just as the sun seems to set on one horizon only to rise anew in another part of the world, so too does the soul continue its journey. Death, then, is not an end—it is merely a transition, a passage from one state of being to another."

He paused, allowing the imagery to settle. "Think of the body," he continued, "as a garment—clothing for the soul. The Gita reminds us that just as we discard worn-out clothes and don new ones, the soul, too sheds the body when it is no longer needed. This cycle is not random; it is purposeful and guided by karma, lessons, and the evolution of consciousness. It is not a termination but a transformation, much like the caterpillar entering the cocoon, not to end but to emerge as a butterfly, free to explore the skies."

Guruji's gaze swept across the room, resting momentarily on each devotee as if seeking to anchor the teaching in their hearts. "This understanding," he said, "has profound implications. If we truly believe that the soul is eternal and indestructible, as Krishna declares, then what is there to fear? Death is not a thief that robs us of life; it is a sacred doorway, leading us into new realms of existence. It is the soul's pilgrimage—a journey toward higher truths, deeper love, and closer union with the divine."

He gestured toward the bright sunlight streaming through the windows, illuminating the Buddha Hall. "Even now, as the light shifts and dances on these walls, it reminds us that life itself is a dance—a rhythm of beginnings and endings, of births and deaths. But like the light, our essence remains unchanged, moving, transforming, yet eternal."

The room seemed to hold its breath as Guruji continued. "The Bhagavad Gita's teaching is echoed across traditions. Consider the Taoist philosophy, which speaks of the interconnectedness of all things. Death, in the Taoist view, is like a drop of water returning to the ocean—not lost, but becoming part of the greater whole. Or Buddhism, which teaches that the cycle of life and death—*samsara*—is not something to be feared but transcended, as the awakened soul moves toward *nirvana*."

His voice softened to a near-whisper, carrying the weight of a sacred truth. "In embracing this wisdom, we learn to live without clinging and to die without fear. We understand that life and death are not opposites—they are partners in the same eternal dance, guiding us closer to our true essence."

He gestured toward the trees outside the Buddha Hall, their leaves swaying gently in the breeze. "Imagine this tree," he said, his voice taking on a poetic cadence. "When a leaf falls, does it signify the end of the tree? No. The leaf returns to the earth, nourishing the soil and becoming part of something larger. The tree continues to grow, and new leaves take the place of the old. In the same way, biological death is not the end of life—it is a transformation, a return to the source, a continuation in a different form."

Guruji's expression grew contemplative, and he added, "Even modern science, particularly quantum physics, offers insights that blur the lines between these perspectives. Take, for example, the phenomenon of quantum entanglement, where two particles remain connected, influencing each other instantaneously, no matter the distance between them. Could it not be that our consciousness, too, is entangled with the infinite, transcending the boundaries of time and space? If this is so, then biological death may simply be a change in the form of that connection—a shift, not an end."

His gaze swept across the room, meeting the eyes of each devotee as if to draw them into the vastness of the mystery. "And yet," he said softly, "these perspectives are not in conflict. They are like the stages of a journey. Biology gives us the map, philosophy helps us understand the terrain, and spirituality reveals the destination. Together, they show us that death is not a final curtain but a bridge—a bridge between the known and the unknown, between the finite and the infinite."

Guruji leaned back slightly, his smile serene and knowing. "Ultimately, the way we perceive death shapes the way we live. If we see it as an end, we may live in fear. If we see it as a transition, we may live with courage. And if we see it as a return to the infinite, we may live with peace and purpose."

*Rohith asked, "Guruji, in what ways do different cultures interpret death as a transition rather than a definitive end?"*

Guruji listened intently to Rohith's question, his eyes gleaming with a quiet light that hinted at the depth of understanding he carried. He folded his hands in front of him, a gesture both humble and profound, as though preparing to lead the room into the vast ocean of wisdom. After a moment of reflection, he began, his voice measured and rich with emotion.

"Death," he said, "is one of the few experiences every culture, every human being, must eventually confront. And yet, it is interpreted so differently across the world. Why? Because the way we view death is deeply entwined with how we view life, the soul, and the infinite mystery of existence."

He glanced around the hall as if inviting everyone to join him in the unfolding exploration. "Let us begin with ancient Egypt. To the Egyptians, death was not an end but a continuation of life in another realm. The soul, or *ka*, was believed to journey to the afterlife, where it would be judged. If found pure, it would join the eternal, harmonious field of reeds—a land free from pain and filled with light. The elaborate rituals of mummification and tomb preparation were not acts of fear but of love and reverence for the journey that lay ahead. Death, for them, was like embarking on a sacred voyage, with the body as the vessel and the heart as the compass."

Guruji's voice softened as he moved to another example. "In the East, the cyclical nature of existence is a cornerstone of many traditions. Consider the teachings of the Bhagavad Gita, where Lord Krishna tells Arjuna, 'As the soul sheds its body, it takes on a new one, like garments replaced when they wear out.' This concept of reincarnation is not a metaphor but a deeply held belief that life and death are part of an endless cycle of learning and growth. The soul is not bound by the body; it merely inhabits it for a time, much like a traveller stopping at an inn on their journey."

He smiled gently. "And what of the Buddhists? They speak of *samsara*, the cycle of birth, death, and rebirth. For them, death is not a tragedy but an opportunity—

a moment of transition where the accumulated karma of one life influences the next. It describes this journey as a sacred process, where the soul has the potential to attain liberation if it can transcend fear and recognise its true nature."

Guruji paused, allowing his words to sink in before continuing. "In Christianity, we find the promise of resurrection and eternal life. Jesus Christ said, 'I am the resurrection and the life. Whoever believes in me will live, even though he dies.' For Christians, death is not an end but a passage into a new existence, a reunion with God and a continuation of the soul's eternal journey. The image of Christ's resurrection serves as a beacon of hope, reminding us that love and faith conquer even death."

He leaned slightly forward, his tone growing more introspective. "Then there is the Taoist philosophy, which sees death as part of the great flow of the Tao—the universal way. Life and death are not opposing forces but complementary aspects of the same reality. Just as day transitions into night and spring into summer, life transitions into death and death back into life. The Taoist accepts this with grace, seeing death not as an interruption but as a continuation of the cosmic rhythm."

Guruji's eyes swept across the room, catching the attentive gaze of each devotee. "In Sufism," he continued, "death is seen as a return to the Beloved, a reunion with the Divine. The Persian poet Rumi wrote, 'Don't grieve. Anything you lose comes around in another form.' For the Sufi, death is not a loss but a homecoming—a moment of ecstatic union with the Creator, where the soul sheds its separateness and becomes one with the infinite."

The devotees sat motionless as though they were not just listening but absorbing his words on a deeper level. Guruji, noticing their rapt attention, spoke again, this time with an almost story-like tone.

"Imagine a drop of water falling from the sky. To the unknowing eye, it seems to vanish as it hits the ocean. But does it truly disappear? No. It becomes part of something vast and immeasurable, losing its individual form but gaining infinity. This is how many traditions see death—not as an end, but as a merging, a transition into a greater reality."

His voice softened, his words carrying the weight of compassion. "In today's world, with its rush and noise, we often fear death because we see it as an interruption to the life we know. But these traditions remind us to shift our perspective. Death is not an adversary to conquer but a guide, a moment of transformation that leads us to our truest essence. It teaches us to live more deeply, to love more fiercely, and to release our attachments with grace."

He closed his eyes for a moment, then said, "The ways cultures interpret death reflect their understanding of life itself. And when we embrace these perspectives, we discover that death is not the opposite of life but its continuation—like the next chapter of a book we have yet to read, one that promises wisdom, wonder, and reunion with the eternal."

*Nita asked, "Guruji, what role do rituals and ceremonies play in shaping cultural understandings of death?"*

Guruji looked at Nita, his gaze steady and filled with a depth of compassion. He gently clasped his hands as if holding the question itself with reverence. After a moment of silence, his voice resonated with a calm yet profound tone.

"Rituals and ceremonies," he began, "are humanity's way of giving structure to the mystery of death—a mystery that often feels too vast, too incomprehensible, to face alone. They are the bridges we build between the known and the unknown, the tangible and the intangible. Through them, we give meaning to endings, honour the departed, and find solace in community."

He paused as though to invite everyone to step into the shared wisdom he was about to reveal. "Consider," he continued, "the fire rituals of the Hindus, where the body is returned to the elements through cremation. The act of offering the body to Agni, the god of fire, is not simply a physical process. It is a profound acknowledgement that the soul has completed its earthly journey. The fire symbolises purification, transformation, and the release of the soul from its mortal vessel. As the flames rise, so too does the soul, embarking on its journey toward the next phase of existence. The chanting of mantras during this ritual is like a sacred thread, weaving the earthly and the divine into one harmonious whole."

Guruji's eyes shone with quiet intensity as he continued. "In Christianity, rituals surrounding death are imbued with a deep sense of hope. The funeral service, often accompanied by hymns and prayers, is not just a farewell but a celebration of eternal life. The lighting of candles, the reading of scripture, and the solemn ringing of bells—all these acts are symbols of light in the face of darkness, of faith in the promise of resurrection. When the priest declares, 'Ashes to ashes, dust to dust,' it is not a lament but a reminder of our cyclical nature—of returning to where we came from, with the assurance of a new beginning in the presence of God."

He leaned forward slightly, his voice taking on a gentler tone. "In Tibetan Buddhism, the *phowa* ceremony is performed to help guide the consciousness of the deceased into higher realms. This ritual, filled with chants and visualisations, serves as a compass for the soul navigating the *bardo*—the intermediate state between death and rebirth. It is an act of love and guidance, a way of ensuring that the soul is not lost but led toward liberation. Imagine a parent holding a child's hand as they cross a busy street—that is the essence of the *phowa* ceremony: a hand extended to the soul as it transitions."

He let those words linger before continuing. "In African traditions, rituals often focus on the idea of ancestral connection. The deceased are not seen as gone but as having moved into a realm where they become guardians of the living. Libations are poured, prayers are offered, and their names are spoken aloud to keep their presence alive. These rituals remind us that death is not a severance but a strengthening of ties—a bridge that allows the living and the dead to coexist in mutual care and reverence."

Guruji paused again, letting his words settle like leaves on a still pond. "In the Taoist tradition, death is embraced as part of the great flow of life. Rituals are often designed to harmonise the energies of the departed with the natural world. Offerings of food, incense, and symbolic items are made not just for the deceased but to honour the cosmic balance. The Taoist approach is like standing at the edge of a river, knowing that the water flowing away will eventually return as rain. Their rituals remind us that nothing is truly lost—it merely changes form."

A faint breeze drifted through the hall, carrying the sound of distant chimes. Guruji smiled, his eyes glistening with empathy. "Rituals, at their core, are stories. They tell us where we've come from, where we are, and where we are going. They give us a sense of continuity when faced with the finality of death. Imagine standing at the edge of a vast, unknown ocean. The rituals are like lighthouses, illuminating the path, offering comfort in the face of uncertainty."

He then told a story, his voice wrapping the devotees in its warmth. "There's an ancient tale of a monk who, upon his deathbed, told his disciples, 'When I die, bury me under a tree, without a marker, and let nature take its course.'"

His disciples were bewildered and asked, "But, Master, what of your legacy? What of your memory?"

The monk smiled and said, "My legacy is in the way you live your lives, not in how you remember my death."

Guruji let the tale settle in the room before saying. "Rituals, you see, are not just for the dead. They are for the living—to guide, to heal, to remind us that death is sacred. Through them, we transcend the fear of endings and embrace the beauty of transitions. They connect us to something greater than ourselves, to the timeless truth that life and death are but two movements in the eternal dance of existence."

The room was silent, but it was not a silence of emptiness—it was a silence filled with awe, understanding, and a sense of shared humanity. The rituals of death, they realised, were not just acts—they were bridges, leading them closer to the infinite.

*Alice asked, "Guruji, how do philosophical views on death challenge or support the idea of an afterlife?"*

Guruji listened intently to Alice's question, his serene expression reflecting the depth of thought the inquiry deserved. "Alice," he began, "philosophy, at its core, is humanity's attempt to navigate the great unknown, and death has always been one of its central mysteries. Philosophical views on death often oscillate between the finite and the infinite, between what we know and what we hope for. These perspectives can challenge or support the idea of an afterlife depending on the lens through which we view existence."

He paused as though to allow the weight of his words to sink in before continuing. "Consider the existentialists, such as Jean-Paul Sartre and Albert Camus. They viewed death as the ultimate end—an event that underscores the absurdity and fragility of human life. Sartre famously said, 'Man is a useless passion,' emphasising the finality of death. For them, there is no afterlife, no grand design—only the here and now, and it is up to us to create meaning in the face of our mortality. This view, while stark, can also be liberating. It challenges us to embrace life fully, to live authentically, knowing that this moment is all we truly have."

Guruji's voice softened, drawing the room into a more introspective space. "On the other hand, philosophers like Plato saw life and death as part of an eternal cycle, much like day and night. In *Phaedo*, one of his most influential works, Plato depicted Socrates, his teacher, discussing the immortality of the soul before his death. For Plato, the soul was not only eternal but divine, untouched by the frailty of the physical world. He used the analogy of the charioteer to explain this: the soul is the charioteer, guiding the body, which is like the horses. While the horses—representing physical desires and instincts—can tire or falter, the charioteer remains constant, steering the path forward.

"When the body, like a worn-out chariot, breaks down, the charioteer—the soul—is set free to continue its journey, unbound by earthly constraints. Plato believed that this journey was not random; it was a process of growth and learning. To him, earthly life was but a shadow of a greater, eternal reality—a stepping stone on the soul's path to ultimate truth.

This aligns beautifully with spiritual ideas of liberation, where death is seen not as a loss but as a return to a more profound, infinite existence."

Guruji paused, his gaze sweeping across the room as if inviting each devotee to reflect on the timelessness of Plato's vision. Then he continued, his tone deepening with a quiet gravity.

"Immanuel Kant offers us another perspective, one rooted in morality and justice. Kant, as a philosopher of reason, did not claim to know the nature of the afterlife, but he argued for its necessity. He believed that the moral law within us—the deep-seated sense of right and wrong—points to a realm beyond our physical existence. Why? Because in our earthly lives, justice is often incomplete. The virtuous may suffer, and the wicked may prosper. If this life were all there is, it would undermine the very essence of morality.

"Kant suggested that the existence of an afterlife and the immortality of the soul are necessary assumptions for the moral order of the universe. He viewed these ideas as postulates of practical reason—things we must believe in for our ethical actions to have ultimate meaning. In this way, Kant's philosophy doesn't directly describe an afterlife but rather supports its necessity. It's as if he's saying,

'There must be a place, a realm, where justice is fulfilled, where the good are rewarded, and wrongs are righted.'"

Guruji leaned forward slightly, his eyes seeming to shine with a deeper light. "Think of it this way: Plato's vision of the soul's journey is like a bird flying home after a long sojourn, free and unencumbered. Kant's perspective, on the other hand, is like the scales of justice, balancing the universe by ensuring that the efforts and sacrifices of goodness do not go unnoticed or unrewarded."

He smiled gently, allowing the room to absorb these profound thoughts. "These two views, though different in approach, offer us profound insights. Plato invites us to see death as liberation, a return to the eternal, while Kant reminds us of the moral fabric of the universe and the importance of a realm where justice reigns supreme. Together, they remind us that death, far from being an end, is a gateway—one that leads to deeper truths, greater understanding, and the fulfilment of life's ultimate purpose."

Guruji's voice grew softer, yet more profound, as he introduced an ancient lens through which to view death and the afterlife. "In the wisdom of the East," he began, "death is not seen as a final curtain call nor as an interruption in the continuity of life. It is a transition—a sacred return to the origin of all existence, the ultimate merging with the infinite."

He paused, letting the room absorb his words, before continuing.

"From the unreal, lead me to the real. From darkness, lead me to light. From death, lead me to immortality."

This verse from the *Brihadaranyaka Upanishad* is a prayer, a yearning for liberation, but it is also a declaration of truth. The 'unreal' refers to the transient, the illusory world of form and ego. The 'real' is the unchanging essence—the Atman, or soul—that exists beyond the body. This prayer is not merely about an afterlife; it is an invitation to transcend the illusion of separation and awaken to the eternal reality that we are.

Guruji's gaze swept across the hall, resting briefly on each devotee. "The Upanishads teach that the soul, like a drop of water, does not cease to exist when it falls into the ocean. Instead, it becomes one with the vastness. Death, in this sense, is not an ending but a homecoming. It is the shedding of the finite to merge with the infinite. This is the soul's journey—a pilgrimage beyond form, beyond time."

Guruji's voice takes on an even deeper resonance. "This perspective is not limited to the Upanishads. In Buddhism, too, the concept of *nirvana* points to a similar truth. To attain *nirvana* is to extinguish the flames of desire, to transcend the cycle of birth and death, and to merge with the boundless. In Zen, death is often described not as the end but as the dissolution of duality—the dropping of the veil that separates us from ultimate reality. 'The wave returns to the ocean,' as the Zen masters say."

He glanced at Alice, who had asked the earlier question about the afterlife and continued, "Even in Taoism, death is viewed not as a tragedy but as part of the natural flow of the Tao. The Tao Te Ching tells us,

*'Life and death are one thread, the same line viewed from different sides.'*

Death is not an aberration; it is as natural as the setting of the sun, which makes way for the moon to rise."

Guruji's expression softened, a gentle smile playing on his lips. "What unites these teachings is the understanding that death is not an annihilation, but a transformation. The body may perish, but the essence—call it Atman, soul, energy, or consciousness—remains. Just as the wind carries the fragrance of a flower even after the petals fall, so does the soul carry its essence forward, beyond the boundaries of the physical."

He smiled gently. "In Buddhism, the idea of an afterlife is less about the continuity of the self and more about the continuity of consciousness. The Buddha taught that what we think of as the 'self' is a collection of ever-changing elements. At death, these elements disperse, and a new being arises based on the karma of past actions. This is not reincarnation in the sense of a fixed soul moving from one body to another, but rather a dynamic process of cause and effect. Death, in this view, is both an end and a beginning—a dissolution and a rebirth."

Guruji paused and then added, his voice tinged with awe, "Even modern science offers intriguing perspectives. Quantum physics, for example, challenges our conventional understanding of life and death. Quantum entanglement suggests that particles, once connected, remain intertwined regardless of distance or separation. If we view consciousness as a fundamental part of the universe, could it not also transcend the boundaries of physical death? Scientists like Erwin Schrödinger have hinted at this possibility, suggesting that consciousness may not be confined to the body but is instead woven into the very fabric of reality."

He leaned back slightly, allowing the devotees to absorb his words. "Philosophy, you see, acts like a prism, refracting the light of truth into its many colours. It challenges us to question, to doubt, to explore. But it also supports us, offering frameworks and perspectives that help us make sense of the unfathomable. Whether it affirms or denies the afterlife, it ultimately points us back to the same profound truth: the importance of living fully, authentically, and with purpose."

The hall was utterly silent, each devotee immersed in Guruji's words. He leaned forward slightly, his tone growing even more reflective. "In the West, death is often feared, resisted, or seen as the ultimate unknown. But these Eastern traditions invite us to embrace it as a natural, even sacred, part of existence. To meditate on death is not to dwell on loss but to deepen our understanding of life. For in recognising the impermanence of the body, we begin to grasp the timelessness of the soul."

He said with a gentle sigh, his voice almost a whisper. "The Upanishads, Buddhism, Taoism—they do not promise an afterlife in the sense of continuation as we know it. Instead, they offer a greater truth: that what we are, in our essence, has no beginning and no end. Death, then, is not the opposite of life. It is the opposite of birth. And beyond both is something eternal, something real. That is what we are called to realise."

A warm breeze stirred the air, carrying with it the faint rustle of leaves as if nature itself were nodding in agreement. Guruji's voice softened to a near-whisper. "Philosophy reminds us that death is not merely an end, nor is it merely a beginning. It is a mirror reflecting the essence of life itself, urging us to look within, to question deeply, and to embrace the mystery with open hearts."

Guruji sat in stillness for a long moment. Then, with a serene nod, he signalled for a midday break. The devotees slowly rose, their minds still echoing with the wisdom they had just received. They moved from the Buddha Hall to Annapoorneshwari, where the air carried the warm, rich aroma of freshly prepared food.

After the meal, the ashram took on a quieter rhythm—some returned to their rooms to rest, others wandered into the gardens, drawn by the scent of blooming jasmine and the rustling whispers of ancient trees. A few made their way back to the Buddha Hall, seeking the comfort of its silent embrace.

Beneath the large Banyan tree, its sprawling roots like the arms of an old sage holding space for seekers, a small group gathered. Akshaya, Vasudeva, Padma, and others settled under its shade, while Nita, Lalitha, Rohith, Sujitha, Espen, Astyn, and Kieron soon joined them. Conversations unfolded in quiet reverence—Rohith introduced himself to those he hadn't met before, and Nita shared a profound experience from her last retreat, her voice carrying both wonder and gratitude.

After a moment, Vasudeva turned to Sam, his eyes searching for something deeper.

"Sam, I've seen you in many retreats. What first brought you to Guruji, and what compels you to return again and again?"

Sam smiled, but there was something in his eyes—an unspoken weight, a story waiting to be told.

"Vasudeva," he said softly, "you already know the answer. Maybe the details are different, but the essence is the same for all of us."

Vidyarthi leaned forward. "That may be true, Sam. But still, something must have made you bond with Guruji in a way that keeps calling you back."

Padma, Kiran, and others nodded in silent agreement. Each of them had a reason for being here—a thread of longing, pain, or seeking that had woven them into this journey.

Vasudeva placed a hand on Sam's shoulder. "Brother, we all carry stories. And these stories, even the painful ones, help us understand who we are. Every sorrow, every loss—if we allow it—guides us toward surrender, toward something greater than ourselves."

Sam lowered his gaze. His breath trembled as if something deep within him was stirring after being buried for too long. He hesitated, then whispered, "I do want to share. To lighten myself. You are my family, after all. Who else would I share with?"

A single tear slipped down his cheek. He let it fall, unashamed.

Vasudeva gently squeezed his hand. "We are here, Sam. You don't have to carry it alone."

Sam exhaled slowly. "Thank you, Vasudeva… for asking, for seeing what I was afraid to open. I've been holding onto this darkness for so long, not knowing how to release it."

A soft rustling of leaves filled the silence as if the Banyan tree itself had witnessed his surrender.

Just then, Kiran glanced at his watch and signalled—it was time for the next session.

One by one, they rose, the air between them now charged with unspoken understanding. As they walked toward the Buddha Hall, Sam's steps felt lighter, as though, for the first time in a long while, he was no longer walking alone.

# CHAPTER II

## Consciousness: The Key to the Unknown

*"Consciousness is the key that unlocks the door to the infinite; it is not confined to the mind but reaches into realms unknown, where time and space dissolve."*

*– Shree Shambav*

### Synopsis

*Delves into the intriguing nature of consciousness, examining its deep connection with the physical body and exploring whether it survives the death of the body. It begins by reviewing the leading theories on the relationship between consciousness and the brain, questioning whether consciousness is simply a product of neural activity or something more profound. The chapter also addresses the phenomenon of near-death experiences (NDEs), where individuals report vivid experiences while clinically "dead," providing compelling evidence for the possibility of consciousness beyond the body. Additionally, the exploration of past-life memories and anecdotal evidence challenges conventional scientific understanding of consciousness, suggesting that it may persist after death. Finally, we look at how different academic fields—*

*neuroscience, psychology, and philosophy—approach the mystery of consciousness and its potential to survive physical death. This chapter invites readers to reflect on the nature of their own consciousness and its role in life and death.*

Guruji turned his gaze toward Padma, and with a knowing smile, he began, "Consciousness: The Key to the Unknown."

He took a measured breath before continuing. "For centuries, sages, philosophers, and scientists alike have sought to unravel the enigma of consciousness. What is it? A mere byproduct of neural activity? Or something far greater—something that transcends the physical and touches the infinite?"

The hall was silent, the weight of the question hanging in the air like mist on a still lake. "In modern science, consciousness is often studied within the confines of the brain," he said. "Neuroscientists tell us that consciousness arises from complex neural networks, an emergent property of biochemical reactions. And yet," he paused, his eyes gleaming with mystery, "if that were true, then why do so many accounts challenge this view? Why do near-death experiences, past-life memories, and inexplicable moments of heightened awareness suggest that consciousness exists beyond the physical form?"

He glanced around at the gathered devotees, some leaning forward, hanging onto his every word. "Consider the stories of those who have stood at the threshold of life and death—those who have clinically 'died' and yet returned with visions of what lies beyond. Near-death experiences (NDEs) are often dismissed as hallucinations of a dying brain. Yet, time and again, individuals report vivid encounters—journeys through tunnels of light, encounters with departed loved ones, and a feeling of expansion beyond the self. And more remarkably, some recall details from beyond the operating table—conversations in adjacent rooms, objects that could not have been seen from where their body lay."

He let his words settle before adding, "How do we explain this? If consciousness is merely a function of the brain, then it should cease when the brain stops functioning. And yet, something remains. Something watches. Something *knows*."

The air was thick with contemplation. Guruji then drew upon an ancient parallel. "In the Upanishads, consciousness is not a fleeting phenomenon but the very essence of existence itself. The *Mandukya Upanishad* declares,

'The Self is beyond the waking, dreaming, and deep sleep states; it is pure awareness, unchanging, eternal.'

What the sages realised thousands of years ago, science is only beginning to grasp: that consciousness may not originate *from* the body, but instead may use the body as a vessel—a temporary dwelling."

He then turned to another profound analogy. "Imagine consciousness as a vast ocean and the body as a wave. The wave appears, rises, moves, and eventually dissolves back into the ocean. But does the ocean cease to exist when the wave disappears? No. The water remains. The essence of the wave is never lost—it simply returns to its source. Likewise, when the body perishes, does our consciousness dissolve into nothingness? Or does it return to its boundless, original nature?"

A gentle breeze drifted through the hall, stirring the incense smoke into ethereal patterns. "And then, there are the accounts of past-life memories," he continued, his voice steady, deep. "In many cultures, particularly in Hinduism and Buddhism, reincarnation is not a belief—it is an observed reality. Dr. Ian Stevenson, a psychiatrist, spent decades documenting children who recalled past lives with astonishing accuracy—details of names, places, and deaths they could not have possibly known. Science hesitates to accept these accounts, yet it struggles to dismiss them."

Guruji's gaze swept across the hall, his voice resonating with both the depth of ancient wisdom and the precision of modern discovery. “Science, in its relentless pursuit of understanding, has unveiled mysteries that echo the very truths expounded by sages thousands of years ago. Among these discoveries, quantum entanglement stands as one of the most profound.”

He paused for a moment, allowing the weight of his words to settle before continuing. “Quantum entanglement is a phenomenon where two particles, once connected, remain linked regardless of distance. No matter how far apart they are—whether across a room or on opposite ends of the universe—when one particle is affected, the other responds instantaneously. This defies our classical understanding of space and time, challenging the notion that information or influence requires a medium to travel. Albert Einstein himself called this ‘spooky action at a distance,’ unable to fully reconcile it with conventional physics.”

A hush fell over the hall as the devotees contemplated this invisible thread that wove together the fabric of existence. Guruji leaned forward, his voice carrying a quiet intensity. “If the very essence of the universe is interconnected at a fundamental level, then can we not extend this understanding to consciousness itself? Could it be that our awareness, our very being, is not confined within the biological shell of the brain, but is instead part of a vast, interconnected field—entangled with the infinite?”

He gestured toward the open sky. "Imagine consciousness not as an isolated flame but as a spark from an eternal fire. Just as entangled particles remain connected across unfathomable distances, what if our awareness, too, transcends the limitations of time and space? What if death is not the severing of consciousness but merely the dissolution of the vessel that carries it—while the essence of our awareness remains entangled with the great cosmic intelligence?"

"This is not mere speculation," he continued. "Some of the greatest scientific minds have suggested that consciousness may not be a byproduct of the brain, but rather a fundamental aspect of reality itself. Erwin Schrödinger, a pioneer of quantum physics, once wrote:

*"Consciousness is a singular of which the plural is unknown; … there is only one thing, and that, what seems to be a plurality, is merely a series of different aspects of this one thing, produced by a deception (the Indian MAYA); the same illusion is produced in a gallery of mirrors …"*

*'The overall number of minds is just one. It is the singular of which plural is unknown.'*

What did he mean by this? That our sense of individuality is an illusion, a temporary reflection within the vast ocean of universal consciousness."

The devotees sat in contemplative silence, their minds expanding with the implications. Guruji's voice softened yet carried the depth of ages. "The sages of the Upanishads spoke of the same truth long ago. They declared, 'The knower of the Self sees all beings in the Self, and the Self in all beings. There is no separation.' Modern science and ancient wisdom—both point to the same reality: that we are not separate entities but interconnected expressions of the 'One'."

He closed his eyes briefly as if touching the fabric of the unseen. "Thus, when we ask whether consciousness survives death, we must first ask—was it ever truly confined to this body in the first place? Or have we always been, and will always be, part of the eternal, indivisible whole?"

A moment of stillness followed the only sound: the distant rustling of leaves in the garden beyond. Guruji's voice softened as he concluded, "Padma, consciousness is not bound by the flesh nor confined to the brain. It is the silent witness, the eternal observer. Whether we call it Atman, spirit, or pure awareness, it remains untouched by birth and death. The body may fade, the mind may quiet, but consciousness—like the sky above—remains vast, limitless, and free."

The devotees sat in quiet reverence as though the very nature of reality had shifted before their eyes.

*Kieron asked, "Guruji, what are the leading theories about the relationship between consciousness and the physical brain?*

Guruji's eyes reflected a quiet knowing as he turned his gaze towards Kieron, his voice carrying the weight of both inquiry and insight. "Ah, the great question—does the brain create consciousness, or is consciousness something greater, merely using the brain as an instrument? This question has puzzled scientists, philosophers, and mystics alike, for to understand it is to unravel the very nature of existence itself."

He let the thought linger before continuing, "There are two dominant schools of thought. The first is materialism, which asserts that consciousness is simply an emergent property of the brain—a byproduct of complex neural activity. In this view, the firing of neurons, the intricate web of electrical and chemical processes, gives rise to our thoughts, emotions, and sense of self. When the brain ceases to function, consciousness, too, fades into nothingness. This is the perspective of much of modern neuroscience."

Guruji paused, allowing the gravity of this perspective to settle. Then his tone shifted, carrying a quiet reverence. "And yet, there is another view—one that aligns more closely with the wisdom of the ancients. This is the idea that consciousness is fundamental, not derivative. The brain does not produce consciousness but rather receives and filters it—like a radio tuning into different frequencies. The radio does not create the music; it only allows it to be heard. Similarly, the brain may be an instrument that channels a consciousness that exists beyond it."

A gentle breeze swept through the hall as he continued, his words painting vivid imagery. "Consider a vast ocean. If you scoop up a handful of water, it may appear separate from the ocean for a time, contained within your hands. But when you release it, it merges back into the whole. Is the water in your hands different from the water in the sea? No—it is the same, only temporarily contained. Likewise, consciousness, which we perceive as 'ours,' may only be a fragment of an infinite awareness, temporarily residing in the body, only to reunite with the whole upon death."

He smiled. "This idea is not new. The Upanishads declared thousands of years ago,

*'The Self is not born, nor does it die. It was not produced from anything, nor was anything produced from it. It is unborn, eternal, everlasting, and ancient. It is not slain when the body is slain.'*

The sages understood that the body is transient, but consciousness—the Self—is eternal."

Guruji then gestured towards the flickering oil lamp beside him. "Imagine consciousness as this flame. If you place a glass over it, the light seems confined and limited. But when the glass is lifted, the flame continues—it is not extinguished. The body, like the glass, may hold the light for a time, but it does not create it. And when the body is no more, the light—consciousness—remains, boundless and free."

Guruji's expression grew contemplative, "Even modern physics," he began, his voice steady yet filled with wonder, "offers glimpses into the nature of consciousness—glimpses that challenge our long-held assumptions. Classical science has long suggested that consciousness arises from the brain, that it is a mere byproduct of chemical and electrical processes. But quantum mechanics, with its paradoxes and mysteries, tells a different story—one that suggests consciousness is not simply an effect of the physical world but is, perhaps, woven into the very fabric of reality itself."

He paused, allowing the thought to settle before continuing. "Take, for instance, the famous *observer effect*—a phenomenon that defies our everyday understanding of existence. In quantum experiments, particles such as electrons exist in a state of probability, a cloud of potential outcomes, until they are observed. The moment an observer measures them, they 'choose' a definite state. This suggests that observation—the act of conscious awareness—plays a fundamental role in determining reality itself."

Guruji's gaze swept across the hall, his voice carrying both reverence and curiosity. "This discovery shakes the very foundation of materialist thought. If matter itself does not take a definitive form until it is observed, then what does that say about the relationship between consciousness and the universe? Could it be that consciousness is not merely a byproduct of the brain, but rather a fundamental force—one that gives shape and meaning to existence?"

"Now, consider this," he continued, leaning forward slightly. "If the simple act of observing changes the outcome of a quantum event, then how can we claim that consciousness is passive? It is not merely a witness—it is a participant, an active force that shapes reality. And if consciousness holds such power over the smallest particles of existence, then can we truly say that it ceases to exist when the body dies?"

He let the question linger, inviting his audience into the depths of contemplation.

"Think of it this way," he said, picking up a small brass bowl from beside him. "Imagine this bowl is your brain. Materialists would say that consciousness is like the sound produced when you strike it—a temporary resonance, fading as the vibrations stop. But what if consciousness is not confined to this vessel? What if, instead, the bowl is merely a receiver, an instrument that tunes into an already existing field of awareness?"

He struck the bowl gently with a wooden mallet, and a soft, resonant hum filled the hall. "When the bowl is struck, the sound emerges. But even if the bowl were to break, would the possibility of sound disappear? No—the vibration remains, simply awaiting a new vessel to manifest through. In the same way, if the brain ceases to function, does that mean consciousness itself ceases? Or does it merely shift, waiting to be expressed in another form?"

He set the bowl down and looked toward his students, his voice now filled with quiet conviction. "This is not just spiritual speculation. Even physicists like Max Planck, the father of quantum mechanics, recognised this truth. He once said, *'I regard consciousness as fundamental. I regard matter as derivative from consciousness.'* That is, consciousness is not something that arises from the material world—rather, the material world arises from consciousness."

A hush fell over the hall as his words sank in, stretching the limits of perception.

"So," Guruji continued, his voice now soft yet potent, "if consciousness is more than the activity of neurons—if it is, as many quanta physicists suspect, a fundamental aspect of reality—then what does that mean for death? If we, at our core, are consciousness, and consciousness is not bound by space and time, then can we truly say that we end when the body ceases?"

His eyes shone with deep knowing as if he had glimpsed the vastness beyond form and time. "Perhaps death is not the extinguishing of consciousness, but its expansion—like a river merging into the ocean, no longer confined by its banks, but now part of something far greater."

He leaned forward, his voice carrying a quiet intensity. "Consider near-death experiences—countless accounts of individuals who, though declared clinically dead, describe seeing and feeling beyond the body. They speak of hovering above their lifeless forms, of entering realms of profound light and love, of experiencing a reality more vivid than anything on Earth. If consciousness were purely a function of the brain, how could these experiences occur when brain activity has ceased?"

Silence enveloped the hall as the devotees absorbed his words. The boundaries between science, philosophy, and spirituality seemed to blur, revealing glimpses of something beyond ordinary perception.

Guruji's voice softened. "The truth of consciousness cannot be fully captured in words. The intellect can only take us so far. It is like trying to grasp the ocean in one's hands—the moment you close your fingers, it slips away. But through deep meditation, through silence, through inner stillness, we can begin to touch the infinite within ourselves. We do not *have* consciousness. We *are* consciousness."

He closed his eyes for a brief moment as if touching that infinite expanse himself. Then, with a serene smile, he said, "And so, I leave you with a thought—if the brain is but an instrument and consciousness is the eternal musician, then perhaps death is not the end of the music… but merely the changing of the tune."

*Kiran asked, "Guruji, how do near-death experiences (NDEs) challenge or support the concept of consciousness surviving after death?"*

Guruji closed his eyes for a moment. "Kiran," he said gently, "near-death experiences, or NDEs, stand at the crossroads of science and spirituality, challenging everything we think we know about life, death, and consciousness itself. They emerge from the threshold between worlds, offering us glimpses of something beyond the confines of the physical."

The hall was silent, the devotees leaning in, drawn by the depth of his words.

"In countless accounts," he continued, "those who have stood at death's door and returned describe something extraordinary—a moment when the body lay lifeless, but awareness remained. Many speak of floating above their bodies, seeing and hearing things they could not possibly have perceived with closed eyes and silent ears. Some recount travelling through tunnels of light, meeting departed loved ones, or being enveloped in an overwhelming sense of peace, love, and unity."

He paused, his gaze steady. "Science has long struggled to explain this. Some researchers argue that NDEs are simply hallucinations—chemical reactions in a dying brain. They suggest that a lack of oxygen, or surges of neurotransmitters, creates these experiences. But can chemical activity alone account for the accuracy of details perceived outside the body? Can it explain why people blind from birth report seeing for the first time in their NDEs? Can it explain why so many describe the same journey—the tunnel, the radiant light, the presence of an all-encompassing love—regardless of their cultural or religious background?"

A hush fell over the room, the question hanging in the air like the final note of a sacred chant.

Guruji's voice softened yet held the weight of timeless truth. "Imagine, Kiran, a clay pot filled with air. When the pot breaks, does the air inside cease to exist? No—it simply merges with the vastness that was always there. In the same way, NDEs suggest that consciousness is not confined to the brain but exists beyond it, just as a wave is not separate from the ocean but part of its endless rhythm."

He leaned forward, his hands resting gently upon his knees. "The Upanishads echo this truth, teaching us that 'the self is never born and never dies.' Even in Christianity, those who have had NDEs often speak of encountering a loving presence they recognise as Christ. In every tradition, across time and geography, we find this profound commonality."

Guruji's eyes shimmered with something unspoken, something vast. "But let us not only look at ancient wisdom. Modern science itself is beginning to take notice. Dr. Bruce Greyson, one of the foremost researchers on NDEs, has documented cases where people have correctly described events happening outside their hospital rooms while their bodies were clinically dead. Dr. Eben Alexander, a neurosurgeon, once doubted the existence of an afterlife—until he had an NDE himself. When his brain was severely damaged by meningitis, he experienced a consciousness so vivid, so expansive, that he emerged with an unshakable certainty: awareness does not end with death."

A cool breeze rustled the leaves outside as if the very air carried the whispers of those who had crossed the veil and returned.

Guruji's voice took on a note of reverence. "Consider this: If NDEs were mere illusions, why do they transform people so profoundly? Many who return speak of losing their fear of death. They live with greater compassion, with a sense of interconnectedness, as if they have touched something far greater than themselves. If these were simply dreams of a dying mind, why would they lead to such lasting spiritual awakenings?"

He spread his hands, palms open to the sky. "The wise do not dismiss the whispers of the unknown simply because they challenge what we can measure. Science seeks to understand reality through observation and analysis—but what if consciousness itself is beyond measurement, beyond the grasp of instruments? What if it is, as the ancient texts have long said, the very foundation of existence?"

The devotees sat in rapt silence, the weight of the question pressing upon their souls.

Guruji smiled gently. "Perhaps, Kiran, the real question is not whether consciousness survives death—but whether we are ready to embrace the possibility that we are far more than we have ever imagined. Perhaps, just like those who return from the brink of death, we too must awaken—to the truth that life and death are not two but one. That in passing, we do not vanish but return to the vast, eternal embrace of existence itself."

The air in the hall felt different now, charged with an unspoken knowing. And at that moment, as they sat before their Guru, each devotee felt it—not as a theory, not as a belief, but as a quiet stirring deep within:

That consciousness, like the light of the sun, does not end when it disappears from sight. It only continues its journey beyond the horizon into the infinite.

*Akshaya asked, "Guruji, what evidence exists to suggest consciousness may persist beyond the death of the body?"*

"Akshaya, this question—perhaps the most ancient of all—has whispered through the corridors of human thought since the dawn of civilisation. And yet, for all our progress, for all the vastness of our knowledge, we stand before it as children before the ocean, gazing at a mystery far greater than ourselves."

The devotees sat motionless, drawn into his words as if time itself had paused.

"In our search for evidence," he continued, "we must look in many directions—science, spiritual traditions, and even the lived experiences of those who have walked the edges of life and returned to tell the tale. Let us begin with what the modern world considers most reliable: empirical evidence."

He leaned forward, his gaze unwavering. "The field of near-death experiences (NDEs) has given us thousands of accounts from individuals who were clinically dead—no heartbeat, no brain activity—yet returned with vivid memories of an existence beyond the body. Some recount floating above their lifeless forms, witnessing doctors struggling to revive them. Later, they describe events and conversations that they could not possibly have perceived with their physical senses. In some cases, these details have been verified with astonishing accuracy."

A quiet murmur spread through the hall.

"Consider the work of Dr. Pim van Lommel, a cardiologist who studied NDEs in patients who had suffered cardiac arrest. He found that even when brain activity had completely ceased, many patients reported experiences of light, overwhelming love, and encounters with beings they recognised—even deceased loved ones. How does one explain awareness when the brain, the supposed seat of consciousness, is no longer functioning?"

Guruji's voice grew softer, more intimate, as if drawing them closer to a great truth.

"And then there are the children," he said, "those who speak of past lives with details so precise that researchers have traced their stories to real individuals who lived and died before they were born. Dr. Ian Stevenson, a psychiatrist, spent decades investigating such cases. He documented young children who recalled names, places, and events from past existences—sometimes even bearing birthmarks in the exact locations of fatal wounds from their previous lives. How does one explain this?"

The room was utterly still as if the very air were listening.

"But science alone does not hold the key," Guruji continued. "For thousands of years, the wisdom of the ancients has spoken of this truth—that consciousness is not bound by the body, that it is eternal, flowing through birth and death like a river that never ceases. The Bhagavad Gita tells us, *'The soul is neither born nor does it die. It is eternal, indestructible, and beyond time.'* And the Upanishads declare, *'As a caterpillar, having reached the end of a blade of grass, draws itself onto the next, so does the soul move from one life to another.'"*

He paused, letting the sacred words settle within them before he continued.

"In Buddhism, the Tibetan Book of the Dead speaks of the *Bardo*—the intermediate state between death and rebirth, where consciousness lingers before it moves into a new existence. In Christianity, Jesus speaks of eternal life, of the soul transcending death. The Sufis tell us that *we do not die but merely awaken from a dream.* In every tradition, in every corner of the world, this idea resounds like a celestial echo—whispering that we are more than flesh and bone, more than the sum of our days upon this earth."

He looked at Akshaya, his expression both tender and knowing. "And what of quantum physics?"

A flicker of curiosity crossed her face.

"Even modern science now hints at what the sages have known for millennia. Quantum entanglement reveals that particles can be connected across vast distances, responding to each other instantaneously, defying space and time. If the very fabric of reality is interconnected beyond physical constraints, then could consciousness, too, exist beyond the limits of the body?"

The devotees exchanged glances as if sensing the enormity of this thought.

Roger Penrose, the renowned physicist, and Stuart Hameroff, an esteemed anaesthesiologist, put forth a groundbreaking theory of consciousness known as

*Orchestrated Objective Reduction* (Orch-OR). This model challenges conventional neuroscience by proposing that consciousness is not merely a byproduct of neural activity but a fundamental quantum-mechanical phenomenon.

According to their theory, consciousness emerges from quantum processes occurring within the microtubules—tiny structural components within brain cells that play a crucial role in cellular functions. These microtubules, they suggest, serve as the stage for quantum computations, orchestrating the very essence of awareness.

Most profoundly, Penrose and Hameroff argue that at the moment of death, these quantum processes do not simply cease; rather, they dissipate into the fabric of the universe itself. Like a wave merging back into the vast ocean, consciousness does not vanish but transitions—returning to a deeper, more fundamental level of reality. If true, this would mean that our awareness is not bound to the physical body but is instead woven into the very structure of existence, interconnected with the cosmos in ways we are only beginning to understand.

Guruji closed his eyes briefly, his presence filling the space like a steady flame in the wind.

"So, Akshaya, what does this evidence suggest? It tells us that consciousness is not a mere accident of biology. It is not simply a byproduct of neurons firing in the dark. It is something deeper, something vast—perhaps the very essence of reality itself. Whether through science or scripture, through experience or intuition, we arrive at the same truth:

"*We are not the body. We are not the mind. We are something far greater, something eternal.*"

A profound hush settled over the room. It was not silence—it was a reverence, a stillness filled with the weight of understanding.

Then, with a smile that carried both warmth and infinite depth, Guruji spoke once more.

"So, tell me—if a dream ends, does the dreamer cease to exist?"

And in that moment, each devotee felt it—not as a concept, not as a belief, but as a knowing that stirred deep within:

Consciousness does not end. It only moves beyond the horizon into the infinite expanse of existence itself.

*Sujitha asked, "Guruji, how do different fields of study (neuroscience, psychology, philosophy) contribute to the debate about consciousness after death?"*

Guruji's eyes gleamed with quiet intensity as he listened to Sujitha's question, allowing the depth of inquiry to settle into the sacred space of the hall. The air was thick with contemplation, and for a moment, there was only silence—the kind that precedes revelation.

He finally spoke, his voice carrying the weight of both ancient wisdom and modern discovery.

"Consciousness, the essence of our being, has long perplexed seekers and scholars alike. Across the vast landscape of human knowledge, different disciplines attempt to decode its mysteries, each offering a fragment of a greater truth. Like blind men describing an elephant, neuroscience, psychology, and philosophy, each touches a different aspect of consciousness—yet the whole remains elusive."

He turned his gaze toward the devotees, his words weaving together the perspectives of science and spirituality.

**Neuroscience: The Mechanistic Lens**

"The neuroscientist, armed with tools like fMRI scans and EEG readings, seeks consciousness in the intricate dance of neurons and synapses. They map electrical activity in the brain, observing how thoughts flicker, and emotions surge like waves upon the shore. Some claim that consciousness is an emergent property of complex neural networks—a mere illusion arising from biological processes. When the brain dies, they argue, so too does awareness.

But does the flickering flame of a lamp truly *cease* when the oil runs dry? Or does light exist beyond the vessel that once contained it? Some neuroscientists, like Christof Koch and Giulio Tononi, propose that consciousness is not just a byproduct of the brain but a fundamental property of the universe—much like space, time, and energy itself. Their *Integrated Information Theory* (IIT) suggests that awareness does not arise *from* matter, but rather, that matter is imbued with awareness at its core."

## Psychology: The Bridge Between Science and the Self

"Psychology, on the other hand, approaches consciousness through the lens of experience—the subjective reality of thoughts, emotions, and memories. Carl Jung, the great psychologist, spoke of the *collective unconscious*—a vast reservoir of archetypes and ancestral wisdom that transcends individual lives.

How, then, do we explain cases where young children, with no prior exposure, recall vivid details of past lives—stories that, when investigated, reveal startling accuracy? Many psychologists studying reincarnation, like Dr. Ian Stevenson, have meticulously documented thousands of such cases, challenging the notion that memory and identity are bound to a single lifetime."

## Philosophy: The Eternal Question

Guruji's voice softened as he shifted to a more reflective tone.

"And then, there is philosophy—the realm where reason dances with the unknown. The great Greek philosopher Plato likened the soul to a charioteer, guiding the body through the transient world of forms. To him, death was not an end but a return—a release from the limitations of flesh into the boundless truth beyond.

Immanuel Kant, centuries later, argued that the afterlife was not merely a hopeful idea but a moral necessity. If justice is to have meaning, if virtue is to hold weight, then there must exist a realm where the soul's journey continues beyond the boundaries of mortality."

## The Unifying Thread: A Conscious Universe?

Guruji paused, allowing his words to settle like ripples in a still pond. Then, his voice took on a contemplative tone.

"Even quantum physics whispers of a truth beyond materialism. The phenomenon of *quantum entanglement* suggests that particles, once connected, remain instantaneously linked across infinite distances. If the building blocks of reality defy space and time, then why should consciousness—our deepest essence—be any different?

Perhaps consciousness does not reside *within* the brain but uses it as a vessel, much like a musician playing an instrument. When the instrument is broken, the music does not cease—it simply returns to the silence from which it arose, waiting for another form through which to sing."

The hall was hushed, each devotee lost in thought, as Guruji concluded, "The question of consciousness after death is not a puzzle to be solved, but a doorway to be entered—a journey that invites us to look beyond what we *see* and into what we *are*."

Guruji, after a long, contemplative pause, gently signalled for the evening break. The golden sun dipped behind the horizon, its last rays stretching like delicate fingers over the landscape, reluctant to leave. The birds, weary from their day's endless flight, fluttered back to their nests, their calls softened into a lullaby. The air, once thick with the heat of the day, cooled into a soothing embrace as a gentle breeze meandered through the trees, carrying with it the hushed whispers of rustling leaves.

Darkness began its slow descent, painting the sky in deep indigo, where the first stars blinked into existence like scattered fragments of ancient, celestial memory. There was a melancholy in the air—neither sorrowful nor heavy, but the kind that comes with deep reflection when the heart stirs with unspoken questions.

The aroma of freshly brewed tea and spiced beverages wafted through the ashram, blending with the earthy scent of nightfall. The devotees gathered, sipping from their cups, their bodies warm but their minds restless. The day's sessions had left ripples in their consciousness—new insights clashing with long-held beliefs, an inner stirring that was both unsettling and profound. Some sat in silence, staring at the flickering lights placed along the path. Others gazed at the sky as if the answers to their questions might be written among the stars.

The hush of the moment was finally broken when Akshaya turned to Bhavya with quiet curiosity.

"Bhavya, I have always wanted to ask you—how did you meet Guruji? We've known you for years, yet we hardly know your story."

Bhavya smiled, but there was a distant look in her eyes as if she were seeing something long past, something that had once been tucked away in the quiet corners of her soul.

She took a slow breath, allowing the moment to settle before she spoke.

"The time has come to tell you…" she murmured.

There was a pause, a fragile silence stretching between them, filled with unspoken anticipation.

"We will talk after dinner."

Padma, Apeksha, and Roopa exchanged glances before nodding in quiet agreement. Some stories were meant to be shared at the right time—when the night had deepened, when hearts were ready to listen, and when words could flow freely like water breaking through a long-held dam.

Just then, Kiran glanced at his watch and gestured.

"It's time for the next session."

The spell of the moment broke, and the devotees slowly rose, their footsteps light against the cool earth. But even as they made their way toward Guruji's hall, the air between them held an unspoken promise—tonight, a story would be told, and something hidden in Bhavya's past would finally come into the light.

.

# CHAPTER III

## The Soul's Journey

*"The soul's journey is not a path of distance but of awakening—a return to the divine, guided by the wisdom of countless lifetimes and the teachings of the spirit."*

*– Shree Shambav*

### Synopsis

*Explores how different spiritual traditions understand the soul's journey after death, offering a rich tapestry of perspectives on what happens beyond the physical realm. It delves into the contrasting views of reincarnation, heaven, hell, moksha, and nirvana across religions, such as Hinduism, Buddhism, Christianity, and Islam. Hinduism and Buddhism emphasise the cycle of birth, death, and rebirth, with the ultimate goal of liberation through moksha or nirvana. In contrast, Christianity and Islam typically offer concepts of heaven and hell, where souls are judged and rewarded or punished based on their earthly actions. The chapter also explores how these diverse views influence ethical behaviour and moral decisions, encouraging individuals to live in accordance with spiritual teachings to shape their soul's destiny. Through examining these varying beliefs, readers are invited to reflect on their own understanding of life, death, and the soul's ultimate purpose.*

Guruji turned to Apeksha, his voice resonant yet gentle.

## The Soul's Journey: A Universal Inquiry

"Apeksha, the journey of the soul, has been the most enduring mystery of human existence. Across cultures, civilisations, and millennia, seekers have looked toward the heavens, the scriptures, and the depths of their own hearts to understand what lies beyond the veil of death.

Like rivers flowing toward the ocean, each spiritual tradition describes this journey in its own way, yet all point to the same eternal truth—that life is not a single fleeting moment but part of an infinite, cyclical, or transcendent existence."

## Hinduism: Reincarnation and the Path to Moksha

Guruji said, "In the vast tapestry of Hindu philosophy, the soul, or *Atman*, is eternal. The Bhagavad Gita Chapter 2, Verse 22 tells us:

*'Just as a man discards worn-out clothes and puts on new ones, so does the soul discard a worn-out body and take on a new one.'*

This profound metaphor likens the soul (*Atman*) to a person changing garments, emphasising that death is not an end but merely a transition. The physical body is temporary, but the soul is eternal, passing from one life to another according to its karma, until it attains *moksha*—liberation from the cycle of birth and rebirth (*samsara*).

This understanding gives rise to the concept of *samsara*, the cycle of birth, death, and rebirth. But this cycle is not random; it is shaped by *karma*, the law of cause and effect. Every action, every thought, every intention we carry in this life plants seed for the next.

Yet, the ultimate goal is not endless rebirth but *moksha*—liberation from the cycle. Just as a drop of water merges back into the ocean, so too does the realised soul dissolve into the infinite, becoming one with the divine."

The verse reassures seekers that death is not to be feared, for just as we do not mourn the loss of old clothes, the wise do not grieve for the departure of the physical body. Instead, they understand that the soul continues its journey, evolving, learning, and ultimately merging with the divine.

**Buddhism: The Illusion of Self and Nirvana**

Guruji's eyes softened as he continued.

In Buddhism, the nature of the self and the cycle of life and death are viewed through a unique lens. While Hinduism emphasises the eternal soul (*Atman*), Buddhism rejects the concept of a permanent, unchanging self. The Buddha taught that what we consider the "self" is an illusion, an ever-changing collection of mental and physical processes, including thoughts, memories, desires, and sensations. This concept is encapsulated in the Buddhist teaching of *anatta*, or "non-self."

To illustrate this, imagine the ocean. We often speak of waves, but each wave is not an entity in itself—it's a temporary formation of water that rises and falls, constantly changing and never the same from one moment to the next. Similarly, the "self" in Buddhism is like a wave, constantly in flux, never fixed, and never permanent. The "self" you identify with today is different from the one you were yesterday, and it will change again tomorrow. In this light, death is not the departure of a permanent soul but the cessation of the physical body and the dissolution of the illusion of a fixed identity.

Buddhism also embraces the concept of reincarnation, but rather than a fixed soul being reborn, it is the karmic momentum—the accumulated actions, thoughts, and intentions—that continues from one life to the next. This is like a candle passing its flame to another candle: there is continuity but no permanence of the original flame. The "self" is not what reincarnates; rather, the energy of one's actions and choices—good or bad—creates conditions for the next life.

The ultimate goal in Buddhism is to transcend the cycle of birth, death, and rebirth, known as *samsara*. This cycle is driven by desires, attachments, and ignorance, which perpetuate suffering. The Buddhist path leads to *nirvana*, which is not a place but a state of being—liberation from all attachments, desires, and suffering. It is the cessation of craving and the extinguishing of the ego, where one no longer identifies with the transient phenomena of life.

To understand *nirvana*, imagine a flame gradually burning itself out. It is not the flame disappearing into nothingness but rather its natural extinguishing—a return to stillness, peace, and calm. In this state, there is no more desire, no more fear, and no more suffering. It is the end of the "cycle of becoming," where one is no longer bound by the illusions of individuality and the impermanence of the material world.

In this way, Buddhism views death not as an end but as a part of the ongoing process of liberation. The ultimate goal is to break free from the illusion of the self and to experience the ultimate peace of *nirvana*, where there is no longer any distinction between life and death, self and other, suffering and peace. This is the culmination of the path—an eternal peace, where the flame of desire is extinguished, and only the tranquillity of being remains.

### Christianity: The Promise of Resurrection and Eternal Life

Guruji's voice took on a note of reverence.

In Christianity, the concept of the soul's journey after death is intricately woven into the fabric of faith, redemption, and divine grace. Central to Christian belief is the idea of eternal life, made possible through faith in Jesus Christ. His teachings offer a profound perspective on death, not as a finality but as a transformative passage.

In the Gospel of John, Jesus says:

*"I am the resurrection and the life. Whoever believes in me will live, even though he dies."*

This statement encapsulates a core Christian belief: death, while inevitable, is not the ultimate end of existence. Rather, it is a transition into eternal life with God. Jesus' words offer hope, emphasising that faith in Him brings the promise of resurrection—a return to life after physical death. Through His death and resurrection, Christians believe that the power of sin and death is broken, offering all believers the opportunity for eternal life, where the soul is reunited with the divine presence of God.

In Christianity, the soul's journey after death depends significantly on one's relationship with God, which is shaped by faith, love, and deeds throughout life. According to Christian doctrine, those who accept Christ and live according to His teachings are promised a place in heaven, a realm of divine communion. Heaven is seen as a paradise where the soul enjoys eternal peace, joy, and closeness with God. It is often described as a state of perfect fulfilment, where the soul finds rest in the unbroken presence of

God, free from the suffering and pain of earthly existence.

On the other hand, for those who reject God or live in opposition to His teachings, the destination after death is described as hell—a state of separation from God. Hell is often viewed not as a place of physical torment but as a spiritual and emotional anguish, a profound sense of loss and alienation from the divine source of life. The concept of hell underscores the Christian teaching that our choices in life have eternal consequences, particularly in relation to our relationship with God.

But at the heart of Christianity is the central promise of resurrection—one of redemption and transformation. The belief in the resurrection is deeply rooted in the life, death, and resurrection of Jesus Christ. Christians believe that through Christ's resurrection, death itself is defeated. In the Christian narrative, Jesus' rising from the dead signifies the possibility of new life for all who believe. This resurrection is not just a return to earthly life but a transformation—a spiritual rebirth that leads to eternal union with God.

In Christian theology, this is not just an abstract concept but a hope and an assurance. The resurrection is seen as a cosmic event that will one day unfold for all of humanity. Those who have died in Christ are expected to rise again, with their bodies transformed into glorified, eternal bodies, no longer bound by the limitations of earthly existence. This resurrection is described as the ultimate victory over death, where all believers will experience a perfect and eternal existence in the presence of God.

In this sense, Christianity teaches that death is not the end of the soul's journey. Rather, it is a moment of transition into a new and eternal reality, where the soul, having been redeemed through Christ, will live forever with God. Through faith, repentance, and divine grace, death is transformed from a fearful event into a hopeful passage, offering the promise of eternal life in communion with the divine.

Thus, the Christian view of the soul's journey after death is one of profound hope, where the soul's ultimate destination is determined by its relationship with God and where the promise of resurrection ensures that death is not the final word but a step towards eternal life and divine fulfilment.

### Islam: The Final Judgment and the Garden of Bliss

Guruji's hands rested on his knees as he continued.

"In Islam, too, the soul's journey is guided by divine justice. The Qur'an speaks of *Akhirah*, the afterlife, where every soul stands before God on the Day of Judgment.

Here, deeds are weighed—good and bad—and the soul is guided toward *Jannah* (Paradise), a garden of bliss, or *Jahannam* (Hell), a realm of purification and consequence. Yet, Islam also teaches of divine mercy, that no soul is beyond redemption, and that ultimately, the journey of the soul is toward reunion with the Creator."

## Sufism: The Soul's Yearning for the Divine

Guruji's eyes glowed with a mystical light.

"Sufism, the mystical heart of Islam, speaks of death not as a fearsome end but as the return of the lover to the Beloved. The great Sufi poet Rumi wrote:

*'When the soul leaves the body, it soars toward its origin, like a falcon returning to the hand of the king.'*

For the Sufi, life is a journey of love, and death is merely the moment of reunion with the divine. They do not mourn death; they celebrate it as the homecoming of the soul."

## The Universal Truth: A Journey Beyond Form

Guruji paused, allowing his words to settle into the hearts of those listening.

"My dear ones, whether it is Hinduism's *moksha*, Buddhism's *nirvana*, Christianity's *eternal life*, or Islam's *paradise*, all traditions speak of a journey beyond the physical, beyond time. Some see it as a cycle, some as a judgment, some as a dissolution, and some as a homecoming.

But all remind us of one thing: that what we do here, how we live, how we love, and how we seek truth—all shape the journey ahead."

The hall was silent, the weight of the moment pressing upon every soul present. It was as if, for a brief moment, they had glimpsed the infinite.

*Abhilasha asked, "Guruji, how do Hindu and Buddhist views on reincarnation differ from Christian and Islamic views of an afterlife?"*

Guruji's gaze softened as he looked at Abhilasha, aware of the depth of the question she posed. "Ah, the journey of the soul," he murmured, a distant glimmer in his eyes as if he were looking beyond time itself. "In every tradition, the nature of existence, life, and death are central. And the views on reincarnation and the afterlife offer profound insights into the way we see ourselves and the divine."

He paused for a moment, allowing the weight of the question to settle, before continuing with a voice rich in the echoes of ancient wisdom.

"In Hinduism," Guruji began, "the journey of the soul is cyclical. Life is a constant process of birth, death, and rebirth, a wheel of samsara until the soul achieves liberation—moksha. The Upanishads describe this beautifully:

*'From the unreal, lead me to the real; from darkness, lead me to light; from death, lead me to immortality.'*

In this view, death is not an end but a transition, a shedding of the old to make way for the new. The soul is eternal, never dying, merely changing forms, like the rivers that merge into the ocean, losing their individual identity but becoming one with the vast, infinite water. Reincarnation is the soul's journey through different lives, driven by karma—the actions of our past lives—that shape our future existence."

Guruji smiled softly, his words woven with compassion and understanding. "Reincarnation is the soul's ongoing learning process. Each life presents opportunities for spiritual growth, for overcoming attachments, desires, and ignorance. Eventually, after countless cycles, the soul attains moksha, or liberation, and merges with the ultimate reality, the Brahman, beyond birth and death. This idea of reincarnation allows for the belief that our actions have meaning across lifetimes. If we don't reach liberation in one life, we have many more chances to try again."

He looked at the gathered devotees, their faces reflecting both curiosity and contemplation. "In Buddhism, the journey is similarly cyclical. The Buddha taught that life is dukkha—suffering—and this suffering arises from our attachments and desires. Reincarnation is seen not as a passage to better lives but as an endless cycle of birth, death, and rebirth, known as samsara. What reincarnates, however, is not a permanent soul but the karmic momentum of one's actions. The Buddha described it as a flame being passed from one candle to another. The flame is not the same, but it carries the energy of what came before."

Guruji continued, his voice becoming quieter, more introspective. "The goal of Buddhism is to transcend this cycle of samsara by attaining nirvana—the cessation of suffering. Nirvana is not a place or an afterlife but a state of awakening, a realisation of the impermanence of all things and the end of attachment. It is like a fire burning itself out, no longer feeding on the fuel of desire or ignorance. This is the ultimate freedom—the extinguishing of the self, the end of the cycle, and the liberation from all rebirths. In this view, there is no eternal soul; there is only the illusion of the self that must be overcome."

He paused again, letting the depth of these two perspectives settle in the minds of his listeners. Then, he shifted to the perspectives of Christianity and Islam—two traditions rooted in the belief of a single life and an afterlife.

"In Christianity," Guruji said, "the focus is on the soul's eternal fate after this one life. There is no cycle of rebirth. The afterlife is seen as a permanent destination, depending on how one lives and one's relationship with God. The Christian view offers two main possibilities: heaven, a place of eternal communion with God, and hell, a state of separation from the divine presence. Heaven is described as a paradise where the soul experiences eternal peace and joy, while hell represents a spiritual death, a separation from the divine. The teachings of Jesus emphasise faith and redemption as the keys to salvation, and through belief in Christ, the soul can be saved from eternal separation from God. The resurrection is central to Christianity—the belief that, after death, the body will rise again in a transformed, eternal form, reuniting the soul with the divine presence."

Guruji's eyes softened as he continued, "In Islam, there is also a belief in the afterlife, but it is framed within the context of one's deeds in this life. Like Christianity, Islam teaches that after death, the soul faces judgment and is directed to either paradise or hell. The Quran describes paradise as a garden of eternal bliss, where the righteous are rewarded with divine presence, while hell is a place of torment for those who have led lives of sin and rejection of God's will. The soul's journey in Islam is shaped by submission to Allah, righteousness, and devotion. The belief in resurrection is also central, as the body and soul are reunited on the Day of Judgment, where every person's deeds are accounted for."

Guruji's gaze drifted far away as if he were seeing beyond time, beyond life and death. "In these traditions, death is a final moment, a decisive turning point. It is the end of this physical journey and the beginning of something eternal. There is no reincarnation; rather, the soul's actions in this life determine its ultimate destiny—either eternal life in the presence of God or eternal separation from it. This view emphasises moral responsibility and divine grace as the guiding forces of the soul's journey."

He closed his eyes for a moment as if reflecting on the vastness of the journey he had just described. "In Hinduism and Buddhism, the soul's journey is ongoing, a process of learning, evolving, and liberation across countless lifetimes. In Christianity and Islam, the focus is on a single lifetime, where the soul's choices lead to either eternal unity with the divine or eternal separation. The contrast is striking, but the common thread among all of these traditions is the profound mystery of the soul's journey and the quest for meaning beyond this life. The question of what happens after death is one that has lingered in the hearts of all human beings for millennia, guiding our actions, our faith, and our search for truth."

He opened his eyes and looked at Abhilasha, who was deep in thought. "Ultimately, the soul's journey is a reflection of the deepest yearnings of the human spirit—to understand, to transcend, and to connect with the divine. Each tradition offers its own lens through which we can view this profound journey, and while the details may differ, the essence remains the same: we are all on a quest for the eternal, seeking to make sense of our brief yet meaningful existence in this vast, mysterious cosmos."

*Akshatha asked, "Guruji, what concepts, such as moksha or nirvana, do spiritual traditions offer as ultimate goals after death?"*

Guruji sat in serene silence for a moment, allowing the question to resonate deeply in the room as though it echoed through the fabric of existence itself. His gaze softened, and he leaned forward. "Ah, Akshatha, the ultimate goal after death. The question itself reveals a deep yearning within every human heart—the search for freedom, peace, and unity with the divine. Across spiritual traditions, this quest takes on different forms, each a reflection of humanity's deepest longings."

He paused, letting the weight of the question settle. "In Hinduism, the concept of moksha stands as the pinnacle of spiritual realisation. Moksha is not just the cessation of suffering but the ultimate liberation from the cycle of birth, death, and rebirth—samsara. It is the realisation that the soul, or Atman, is one with the supreme consciousness, Brahman, and that the apparent separation we experience in our individual lives is an illusion—a veil that hides our true nature."

Guruji, after a pause, said, "Imagine a drop of water, seemingly separate, falling from the sky. It may feel distinct, but when it merges with the ocean, it loses its individual identity and becomes one with the vastness of the sea. Similarly, moksha is the merging of the individual soul with the divine, a return to the ocean from which we came. It is a state beyond desire, beyond fear, where the self is dissolved into the infinite. In moksha, there is no rebirth, no cycle—only eternal peace and oneness with all that is."

He let the silence linger, allowing the analogy to take root. Then, with a gentle smile, he continued. "In Buddhism, the goal is nirvana, which, like moksha, represents liberation from suffering. But unlike the Hindu concept of moksha, nirvana is not seen as a merging with a universal self but as the extinguishing of the self altogether. The Buddha taught that all suffering arises from attachment and desire, and that the self is an illusion—a fleeting collection of thoughts, feelings, and sensations."

Guruji's voice became quieter, more intimate. "Think of a flame. It burns brightly as long as it has fuel, but when the fuel is exhausted, the flame goes out. Similarly, nirvana is the extinction of the flame of desire, the cessation of the cycle of becoming. It is not a place or a state but a realisation—a profound insight into the impermanence of all things. When the attachment to self and the illusion of ego are extinguished, suffering ceases, and the soul is freed. Nirvana is not a goal to attain but a truth to realise, an awakening of the boundless peace that lies beyond the illusions of this world."

He looked around at the devotees, their faces reflecting the depth of the teachings. "Now, in Christianity, the ultimate goal is eternal life with God—what Jesus described as the Kingdom of

Heaven. For Christians, the soul's journey after death is determined by one's faith in Christ, repentance, and the grace of God. Jesus said, 'I am the resurrection and the life. He who believes in me will live, even though he dies.' The belief in the resurrection of the body and the soul's eternal communion with God is central to Christianity. Heaven, in this view, is a place of eternal peace, joy, and closeness to the divine presence, where there is no suffering, no sin, and no separation from God. Hell, on the other hand, represents an eternal separation from God, a state of spiritual death."

Guruji paused, his eyes closing as he reflected on the profound nature of Christian teachings. "In Christianity, the goal is not to escape the world or the self but to be transformed and reconciled with the divine through love and faith. It is a return to the source but through a path of redemption and grace. The ultimate goal is union with God—eternal life in His presence, where the soul finds its true home."

Guruji opened his eyes and, with a soft sigh, continued, "In Islam, the ultimate goal is also eternal life, but in a context that emphasises submission to Allah's will and the righteous living of one's life according to the teachings of the Quran. The afterlife in Islam is a place of divine reward or punishment, determined by one's actions and faith during this life. Jannah, or Paradise, is a realm of eternal bliss, a garden of peace, where the soul is rewarded with the ultimate closeness to Allah. But there is also Jahannam, or Hell, where those who have rejected Allah's guidance suffer eternal separation from the divine presence."

Guruji's voice became more solemn. "The goal in Islam, like in Christianity, is to attain closeness to the divine, but it is a journey of righteous deeds, submission, and devotion. It is a path of moral and spiritual discipline, where the soul strives to live in accordance with Allah's will, seeking the ultimate reward of Paradise."

He then leaned back slightly, his face illuminated by a soft inner light. "The common thread that runs through these traditions is the longing for liberation, for the end of suffering, and for union with the divine. Whether it is moksha, nirvana, eternal life in heaven, or the reward of Jannah, these goals represent the deepest desires of the human soul—to transcend the limitations of the body, to overcome fear and suffering, and to return to the ultimate truth from which we came."

Guruji's words hung in the air, each syllable a thread weaving through time and space, as the devotees sat in silence, deeply moved by the vastness of the journey he had described.

"But remember," Guruji continued, his voice filled with compassion, "these goals are not just destinations after death—they are ways of living, ways of being in the world. Moksha, nirvana, eternal life—these are not things to be grasped in the future. They are the truths we must live with now. How we live each moment with love, with awareness, with faith will shape our soul's journey. The goal is to live with purpose and peace, for in the end, the destination is not separate from the journey."

*Padma asked, "Guruji, how does the idea of the soul's journey shape ethical behaviour and decisions in various religious traditions?"*

Guruji's gaze swept across the hall, his eyes reflecting the depth of the question Padma had asked. "Ah, Padma, this question touches upon something very fundamental—the connection between belief and action, between our understanding of the soul's journey and the way we choose to live. Every religious tradition offers a vision of what happens after death, but more importantly, it teaches us how to live before that moment arrives."

He took a deep breath, allowing the silence to draw everyone inward before continuing.

**The Law of Karma: A Mirror to Our Deeds**

"In Hinduism, the concept of karma governs the soul's journey. Every thought, every action, every intention plants a seed that will bear fruit in this life or the next.

*'As a man sows, so shall he reap. Bound by karma, the soul takes birth again and again until it attains liberation.'*

Just as a farmer tends to his field, knowing that the quality of his harvest depends on the seeds he sows, so too must a person tend to their actions. Ethical behaviour is not just about following rules—it is about ensuring the soul moves toward **moksha**, liberation from the cycle of birth and rebirth. Dishonesty, cruelty, and greed weigh the soul down, pulling it back into suffering. Compassion, truth, and selflessness free it from bondage.

The Bhagavad Gita Chapter 2, Verse 27 reminds us:

*jaatasya hi dhruvo mrityur dhruvam janma mritasya cha |*

*tasmaad aparihaarye 'rthe na tvam shochitum arhasi ||*

Meaning: "One who has taken birth is sure to die, and after death, one is sure to be born again. Therefore, in the unavoidable discharge of your duty, you should not lament."

Imagine a potter shaping clay. If his hands are careless, the pot will crack. If he works with patience and care, it will be strong and beautiful. In the same way, our actions shape our destiny, crafting the path the soul must walk."

**Buddhism: The Ripple Effect of Our Choices**

Guruji's voice softened as he transitioned into another tradition.

"In Buddhism, the idea of an immortal, unchanging soul is not the focus. Instead, the Buddha taught that our actions create ripples—what we do today shapes the world tomorrow. The concept of karma and rebirth still applies, but instead of an eternal soul, what continues is the momentum of our actions, like a flame passing from one candle to another.

A story is often told of a traveller who comes across two paths—one covered in thorns, the other in soft grass. If he chooses the thorny path, he will suffer. If he chooses the smooth path, he will walk with ease. But the paths were not created by chance—they were laid by those who walked before him. Our choices, too, carve the road ahead. A kind heart leaves a path of peace; a selfish mind leaves a path of suffering.

Ethical behaviour, then, is not just about a future reward but about transforming suffering into compassion, ignorance into wisdom, and greed into generosity. The soul's journey is shaped not by an external judge but by the very nature of cause and effect."

**Christianity: The Weighing of the Soul**

Guruji's expression grew contemplative, his words imbued with deep reverence.

"In Christianity, the soul's journey after death is often understood through the lens of faith, grace, and divine judgment. The idea of heaven and hell does not exist merely as a reward or punishment—it serves as a moral compass guiding one's choices. Jesus taught:

*'Whatever you do for the least of my brothers, you do for me.' (Matthew 25:40)*

Meaning: "This highlights the importance of showing compassion and kindness to all, regardless of their social status. It conveys that serving those in need is a reflection of true humanity and is regarded as serving Jesus himself."

Ethics in Christianity are deeply tied to love, mercy, and righteousness. Acts of kindness, forgiveness, and faithfulness shape the soul's path toward heaven, where it finds eternal communion with God. But those who walk the path of cruelty and selfishness risk separation from this divine presence.

It is said that when a person dies, their deeds are weighed not by external gold or riches but by the love they have given and the truth they have lived. Imagine a tree—if it has been nourished with care, it bears sweet fruit. If neglected, it withers. The soul, too, is shaped by its choices."

## Islam: The Bridge of Justice

Guruji's voice took on a steady rhythm, echoing the certainty of divine justice.

"In Islam, the soul's journey is marked by accountability. The Quran speaks of Yawm al-Qiyamah, the Day of Judgment, where each person's deeds are weighed. The righteous are granted entrance to Jannah, a paradise of peace, while those who have acted unjustly face Jahannam.

But divine justice is tempered with mercy. A single act of kindness can tip the scales in a person's favour, just as a single drop of water can revive a dying plant. Islam teaches that life is a test—our actions write the book that will be read on the Day of Judgment. The Prophet Muhammad (peace be upon him) said:

'The best among you are those who have the best manners and character.'

Thus, ethical behaviour is not merely about avoiding punishment but about striving toward righteousness, honesty, and service to others. The soul's journey is determined by how we live in submission to the divine will."

**A Common Thread: The Road We Walk Together**

Guruji leaned back slightly, his eyes sweeping across the devotees as if drawing them closer to the vast, interconnected story of human belief.

"What do we see here? Across religions, the soul's journey is not merely about what happens after death—it is about the choices we make now. Whether through karma, moral judgment, or divine grace, every tradition teaches us that ethical behaviour is the key to liberation, peace, and union with the divine."

He smiled, his expression serene.

"Imagine a river flowing to the ocean. Some believe the river carries the same drop of water until it reaches the sea. Others believe the water constantly changes, yet the river still flows. Some believe the river's course is set by its actions; others believe it is guided by divine hands. But in the end, all rivers seek the same destination—the vast, boundless ocean.

So, too, all paths of the soul's journey, no matter how different they may seem, lead us toward truth, toward peace, toward love. And the way we walk that path, the way we treat others, the way we nurture wisdom and compassion—that is what truly shapes our destiny."

A hush fell over the hall. The weight of Guruji's words settled deep into the hearts of the devotees like seeds waiting to blossom.

And in that sacred moment, they understood—the soul's journey was not about where one went after death.

It was about how one chose to live.

*Astyn asked, "Guruji, what similarities and differences exist in how different religions perceive the existence of heaven, hell, or other realms after death?"*

Guruji closed his eyes for a moment, as if peering beyond the veil of time into the vast tapestry of human belief.

## The Universal Longing for Beyond

"Across cultures and centuries, humanity has gazed at the stars and wondered—what lies beyond this fleeting existence? Whether in the sacred verses of Hinduism, the sutras of Buddhism, the revelations of Christianity and Islam, or the mystical poetry of Sufism, one truth is evident: the journey does not end at death. But how that journey unfolds is seen through different lenses, shaped by faith, experience, and the longing of the soul."

He let his words settle before continuing.

## Heaven and Hell: Realms of Reward and Reckoning

"In Christianity and Islam, the afterlife is often viewed as a moral reckoning—a destination shaped by the choices one makes in life.

In the Bible, Jesus speaks of heaven as the 'Kingdom of God,' a place of divine communion where the righteous find eternal joy. He also warns of hell—a state of separation from God, where the soul faces the consequence of its misdeeds.

Likewise, in Islam, the Quran describes Jannah (Paradise) as a garden of bliss, where souls are rewarded for their faith and good deeds. But there is also Jahannam (Hell), a place of purification for those who stray from righteousness. Yet, even in Islamic thought, divine mercy is paramount—some souls may find redemption even after judgment."

Guruji's voice softened, his words carrying the weight of deep reflection.

**Cycles of Rebirth: The Eternal Journey of the Soul**

"In contrast, Hinduism and Buddhism do not view the afterlife as a fixed destination but rather as an ever-turning wheel—the cycle of samsara.

In Hinduism, the soul (Atman) is eternal, bound by karma.

*'As a man sows, so shall he reap. Bound by karma, the soul takes birth again and again until it attains liberation.'*

Here, heaven and hell are not eternal but temporary states—places where the soul experiences the fruits of its deeds before returning to another life. True liberation (moksha) is not about reaching heaven but about breaking free from this cycle entirely, merging with the divine like a drop returning to the ocean."

He paused, letting the imagery settle in.

"In Buddhism, a different understanding emerges. There is no eternal soul, only a stream of consciousness shaped by karma. The six realms of existence—from heavenly to hellish states—are seen as manifestations of one's karma. But none of them are permanent. The ultimate goal is nirvana—not a place, but a state beyond suffering, beyond illusion, beyond even the idea of self."

## Mystical Visions: The Beyond as an Inner Experience

"But there are also those," Guruji continued, "who see heaven and hell not as places out there but as states of being within. The Sufi mystics describe paradise as the beloved's embrace, a nearness to the Divine that transcends form. The poet Rumi wrote:

*'Do not seek heaven and hell in the future. Both are now present. The first is found in love, the second in ego.'*

In the end, whether one envisions golden gates, a cycle of rebirth, or a journey beyond form, the message is the same—how we live shapes where we go."

## The Question That Remains

Guruji's gaze swept across the room. "So, the question remains—not just what happens after death, but how does that knowledge change how we live? Do we live in fear, or do we walk in love? Do we seek rewards, or do we strive for truth?

Each tradition offers a map, but the journey is ours to take."

He smiled, his voice gentle but profound. "And in walking that path with sincerity, perhaps we will find that heaven is not a distant promise, nor is liberation an abstract goal. Perhaps they are simply realised in the way we live, love, and awaken… here and now."

Guruji sat in silence for a long moment, his eyes half-closed, his presence as still as a mountain at dusk. Then, with slow, deliberate movements, he rose from his asana, his flowing robes whispering against the floor. The devotees, sensing the unspoken conclusion of the day's teachings, remained motionless for a breath longer before rising themselves. No words were needed—silence held them all in its embrace.

One by one, they stepped out of Buddha Hall, greeted by the cool night air. Above them, the vast sky stretched endlessly, scattered with shimmering stars. The moon, veiled in darkness, hid behind drifting clouds, leaving the world bathed in a soft, ethereal glow. The air was alive with the scent of wildflowers and the distant, rhythmic croaking of nocturnal creatures—a quiet symphony of nature's own retreat into the night.

As they made their way toward Annapoorneshwari, the ashram's food canteen, the aroma of spiced curries and steaming rice filled the air. The warmth of food after a long day of spiritual inquiry felt grounding, a gentle reminder of the body's needs amidst the soul's seeking. Some ate in silence, absorbing the weight of the day's wisdom; others engaged in hushed conversations, their minds still wrestling with the revelations from Guruji's discourse.

After dinner, the ashram came alive in its own quiet way. Some strolled through the gardens, listening to the rustling of leaves in the cold breeze. Others retired early, surrendering to sleep, letting their dreams weave together the lessons of the day.

But for a few seekers, the night was not yet over.

Akshay glanced at the group and spoke with quiet conviction. "Let's all meet at the fireplace after dinner."

Apeksha, Padma, and the others exchanged glances before nodding in agreement. Something in the air felt unfinished, a conversation waiting to be had, a thread of thought left unspun.

**Stories by Firelight**

An hour later, they gathered around a crackling fire. The flames danced, their golden tongues flickering against the cold night. Sparks rose and disappeared into the sky, merging with the constellations above, as if the fire itself were offering prayers to the heavens.

Kieron sighed, his voice filled with reflection. "Today's session was… sheerly thought-provoking."

Espen and Astyn nodded, still digesting the depth of what had been discussed.

Espen murmured, "So much to process… so many truths… some comforting, some unsettling."

Lalitha, warming her hands by the fire, smiled faintly. "I almost missed this retreat… if I had gone ahead with my leg surgery, I wouldn't be here. The Divine has a way of guiding us where we need to be. So many of my inner doubts feel… lighter now."

There was a moment of silence, heavy but not burdensome. Apeksha turned to Bhavya, her voice gentle.

"Bhavya, if you don't mind… would you share your story?"

The fire crackled, casting shifting shadows on Bhavya's face. She tilted her head back slightly, gazing up at the endless sky, where the stars blinked like ancient sentinels, witnessing the passage of time. The warmth of the fire on her skin contrasted with the chill of the night, a perfect mirror of the emotions stirring within her.

She exhaled, a breath carrying both hesitation and surrender.

*"Hmm… I don't know where to begin… but perhaps the beginning itself will guide me."*

She looked at them—her friends, her spiritual family—and began.

"I was born in a remote village, a place where the rivers embraced the land like a mother cradling her child. My grandparents ran a fishing business deeply connected to the rhythm of the waters. But my father, Rajaram, sought a different path—he studied hard and earned a respected government position. My mother, Kavitha, was the pillar of our home, her quiet strength shaping the very foundation of my childhood."

"I was born after many years of their marriage, and so, I was their world. They cared for me with a love so deep that I never knew loneliness. My father was my best friend. I told him everything. And then… there was my grandfather. He was my teacher, my storyteller, my guide. Every year, we returned to our village to celebrate the festivals, and those were the moments I cherished the most—when the entire community came together, when the air was thick with joy, when my grandfather and I would sit by the river, and he would answer all my endless questions with infinite patience."

Bhavya's voice softened, her gaze lost in the past.

"Then… when I was in the tenth grade, everything changed."

The warmth of the fire did nothing to shield her from the cold memory that surfaced.

"We received the news—my grandfather had died. A cardiac arrest, they said. Just like that, he was gone. We rushed to the village, but I… I couldn't understand it. How could someone just… not be there anymore? Why does someone have to die? Why is love given only to be taken away?"

She swallowed, her voice steady but weighed with remembrance.

"That night, after the rituals were completed, I couldn't sleep. Every time I came to the village, I would sit with my grandfather under the open sky, asking him questions, and he would always have an answer. That night, I stared at the stars, searching for him. And then I saw it—one star, brighter than all the others, burning with an intensity I had never noticed before."

"I asked aloud, 'Why is that star shining so bright?'"

"And then, as if he were still there, I heard his voice echo in my heart: 'Your great-grandfather is watching you.'"

Tears welled up in her eyes, but they did not fall.

"It was in that moment that I realised—my grandfather was gone. And yet, he wasn't. I had lost him, but I hadn't. My mind wrestled with the paradox, my heart a battlefield of longing and understanding. I kept asking myself—is he really gone, or is he still living somewhere? The loss felt unbearable, as if a part of me had been ripped away. My team had become smaller. The person who cared for me the most was now just… a memory."

She looked at the fire, watching the embers glow as if they, too, were remnants of something once whole.

*"Why do we have to lose the ones we love? Why must we say goodbye? What is the meaning of all this… coming and going?"*

A heavy silence settled over the group.

Then, Padma, placing a gentle hand on Bhavya's, whispered, "One day, we all must lose the most beloved people in our lives… but in that loss, we also find something else—a deeper understanding of love itself."

Bhavya nodded slowly.

The fire crackled once more, sending a flurry of sparks into the night.

Kiran sighed, glancing at the time. "It's late… we should rest before tomorrow's session."

One by one, they rose, making their way back to their shelter. But as Nita lay down that night, staring at the ceiling, she couldn't stop thinking about Bhavya's story. The questions stirred within her, unrelenting, weaving themselves into her dreams.

Somewhere in the distance, the wind whispered through the trees. Somewhere beyond the sky, a single star shone a little brighter.

# SECTION TWO

## Bridging Science and Spirituality

*"Science seeks to understand the mechanics of existence, while spirituality reveals its deeper meaning; together, they offer a holistic view of life's mysteries, where the seen and unseen are two sides of the same truth."*

- *Shree Shambav*

# CHAPTER IV

## Scientific Explorations of the Afterlife

*"In the pursuit of understanding the afterlife, science does not seek to dismiss the unknown but to explore it—offering a bridge between the tangible world and the mysteries that transcend it."*

*– Shree Shambav*

### Synopsis

*The chapter delves into modern scientific investigations into the afterlife, examining how emerging theories in quantum physics, energy fields, and consciousness challenge our traditional understanding of life and death. It explores quantum theories that suggest consciousness may exist beyond the physical brain, potentially providing a framework for understanding what happens after death. Additionally, the chapter looks at documented phenomena, such as near-death experiences (NDEs) and past-life recollections, seeking scientific explanations for these extraordinary occurrences. The chapter also highlights the contrasting perspectives between sceptics and proponents of the afterlife, showing how they interpret the same data in vastly different ways. Lastly, it addresses the challenges inherent in applying scientific methods to study metaphysical concepts like the afterlife, emphasising the limitations of empirical research when it comes to spiritual and consciousness-based phenomena. By blending science and spirituality, this chapter invites readers to reconsider what is possible beyond the material world.*

Nita awoke with a quiet thrill stirring in her heart, a sense of anticipation humming through her being. As she stepped out of her room, the ashram was already alive with the rhythm of the morning. The darkness of night was retreating, surrendering to the first golden fingers of dawn stretching across the sky. Birds, hidden in the canopies, had begun their melodic symphony, their songs weaving effortlessly with the low, resonant chants of "OM" drifting through the air. The sacred vibrations of bhajans reverberated through the ashram, their echoes lingering in the crisp morning stillness, filling every soul with an inexplicable sense of belonging.

Nita inhaled deeply, the scent of sandalwood incense and dewy earth filling her senses. She felt something shift within her—a profound stillness, a quiet ecstasy she could not name.

*"This place is peace,"* Sujitha murmured, standing beside her, her voice almost a whisper, as if speaking too

loudly would disturb the delicate harmony of the moment. *"So serene… so full of wisdom waiting to be absorbed."*

Just then, a fresh breeze stirred through the trees, caressing her face like an unseen hand, whispering untold truths. She closed her eyes as emotions surged within her, rising like waves upon an infinite ocean. Tears welled up, unbidden, flowing freely down her cheeks—not from sorrow, but from an overwhelming sense of awe. The world, for the first time, felt utterly complete. Goosebumps rose along her arms as she stared at the luminous horizon, where the sky blushed with hues of rose and amber.

*"Why am I so happy now? Why was I sad all these years? Which feeling is the true one?"* she wondered, her heart swelling with an unfamiliar lightness.

Soon, her friends gathered around her—Lalitha, Astyn, and Kieron—each of them drawn to the magnetic serenity of the moment. Akshaya joined them, carrying the warmth of quiet contemplation. Vasudeva, eyes gleaming with quiet determination, mentioned he was heading to the Zen meditation hall, and Rohith decided to join him.

As they walked towards the meditation hall, they saw Akshatha already seated in deep meditation, her form still as a statue, radiating an aura of inner peace. Around her, devotees engaged in pranayama, their breath synchronising with the rhythm of the universe, while others moved through the sacred motions of yoga. The entire space pulsed with a collective stillness, a silence so profound it felt as though time itself had slowed.

An hour passed in quiet introspection. When they finally emerged from meditation, their minds were as clear as the morning sky. They made their way to the Shambav Bhajan Hall, where Apeksha, Roopa, Akanksha, Akshaya, and Padma were already immersed in devotional singing. Their voices wove together in harmony, each note a thread in an unseen tapestry, lifting every heart towards something higher, something infinite.

As they wandered through the ashram, they encountered devotees engaged in their morning sadhana beneath ancient trees—some practising yogic postures with reverence, others seated in deep prayer. The entire ashram seemed to breathe as one, a living sanctuary where every blade of grass, every petal, every ripple in the pond carried the sacred essence of devotion.

They finally reached the Brindavan Garden, where the day was beginning to unfurl in all its splendour. The sun's rays filtered through the leaves, casting intricate golden patterns on the ground. Flowers swayed in the gentle breeze, their petals shimmering with the morning's first dewdrops. The air was thick with the intoxicating aroma of blossoms, a fragrance that seemed to whisper stories of ancient wisdom. Nearby, Astha and others tended to the garden with loving hands, their touch almost a prayer in itself.

*"This place is grand and rich,"* Abhilasha murmured, her voice carrying a deep reverence. *"It fills the heart and mind… making one feel whole."*

The Sofia and others nodded, their silence speaking louder than words.

The morning had unfolded like a sacred hymn, setting the perfect tone for what was to come. With hearts full and minds serene, they returned to their rooms to prepare for the revered morning session, each step lighter than before, as though they were walking towards something greater than themselves.

When they finally entered the hall, a hush fell over the gathering. Guruji sat before them, his presence alone commanding stillness. After a long, contemplative pause, he folded his hands and began his discourse with a heartfelt morning prayer.

The room grew heavy with an almost tangible energy—an anticipation so deep it felt like the very air was listening. Devotees closed their eyes, some in silent prayer, others merely soaking in the moment. Time itself seemed to bow in reverence.

## The Bridge Between Science and the Unknown

Guruji closed his eyes for a moment as if listening to the hum of the cosmos itself. Then, with a deep breath, he began, his voice carrying the weight of both ancient wisdom and modern inquiry.

"Akanksh, science, in its relentless pursuit of truth, has ventured into realms once thought to belong only to mystics and philosophers. Today, as the frontiers of physics, neuroscience, and consciousness studies expand, the question of life after death no longer belongs solely to faith—it now sits at the very crossroads of empirical discovery and human experience."

He looked around the gathering, his gaze filled with both reverence and curiosity.

## The Mind Beyond the Brain: Consciousness and Near-Death Experiences (NDEs)

"For centuries, the great debate has been: Is consciousness merely a byproduct of the brain, or does it exist beyond it?" Guruji paused, his words resonating through the silent hall.

"In the sterile corridors of hospitals, in moments where the brain should have ceased functioning, something inexplicable occurs. Patients declared clinically dead—no heartbeat, no brain activity—

return with stories. They speak of floating above their bodies, seeing doctors work to revive them. They describe tunnels of light, visions of deceased loved ones, and an overwhelming sense of peace.

Dr. Raymond Moody, a pioneer in near-death experience (NDE) research, collected thousands of such accounts. Astonishingly, these experiences share uncanny similarities across cultures, religions, and backgrounds. Blind people have described seeing for the first time. Patients have recalled verifiable details from operating rooms they should never have perceived. How does one explain this, if consciousness were only a flickering flame within the brain, snuffed out at death?"

**Quantum Physics: A Glimpse into the Afterlife?**

Guruji's eyes gleamed with the excitement of discovery. "If material science alone cannot fully explain these phenomena, then perhaps we must turn to the very fabric of reality itself—quantum physics."

*"Consider quantum entanglement—where two particles, separated by light-years, remain mysteriously connected, their states instantly influencing each other. If the universe itself defies the barriers of space and time, could consciousness, too, be something beyond the physical—something entangled with the infinite?"*

He let the thought linger before continuing.

*"Physicists like Roger Penrose and Stuart Hameroff propose that consciousness arises from quantum processes within the brain's microtubules—tiny structures within neurons. And what happens when the body dies? These quantum processes, they argue, do not disappear but return to the fundamental field of the universe itself, much like a drop dissolving back into the ocean. If true, this would mean that our awareness does not simply vanish; it transcends, merging with the cosmos in ways we are only beginning to comprehend."*

## Reincarnation and Past-Life Memories: Evidence Beyond Belief

*"If consciousness is not confined to the body, could it travel across lifetimes?"*

Guruji's voice softened as he spoke of children—young souls who, without any prompting, recalled lives they never lived.

*"Dr. Ian Stevenson, a psychiatrist, spent decades researching past-life memories of children. In thousands of cases, children spoke in unknown languages, identified past families, and recalled deaths with astonishing accuracy—many of which were later verified. Some bore birthmarks corresponding to wounds they claimed to have suffered in a past life. How can we dismiss this? Mere coincidence or evidence that consciousness endures beyond a single lifetime?"*

He let the question hang in the air, a whisper in the vast unknown.

## Energy Fields and the Persistence of Self

The statement **"Energy can neither be created nor destroyed"** reflects the **law of conservation of energy**, which asserts that the total energy within an isolated system remains constant over time. While energy cannot be created or eliminated, it can be transformed from one form to another.

*"Modern science also tells us something profound: Energy cannot be created or destroyed—it merely transforms. If we, too, are energy, what happens to the essence of our being when the body ceases?"*

He looked at the gathering with quiet intensity.

*"Is death truly an end, or merely a transition—like ice melting into water, water evaporating into mist? The form changes, but the essence remains."*

## The Mystery Remains, But So Does the Search

Guruji took a deep breath, his voice now filled with both wonder and humility.

*"Science may not yet hold all the answers, but it has begun to ask the right questions. It has glimpsed what the mystics have long known—that life is more than mere biology, and death is not the extinguishing of light but the passing of it into another form."*

He smiled gently. "Perhaps the truth lies not in proving what comes after but in understanding that the journey itself is sacred. And in living with that awareness, we prepare for whatever lies beyond—not with fear, but with awe."

*Vasudeva asked, "Guruji, how do quantum theories and energy fields contribute to our understanding of the afterlife?"*

"Vasudeva," he began, "the universe is not what it seems. Our ancestors, the rishis and sages of old, spoke of an unseen fabric that binds all existence—a web of energy, consciousness, and vibration. Today, physicists speak of a similar reality hidden beneath what we call 'matter.' The bridge between science and spirituality has always existed; we are only now beginning to see its form."

He paused for a moment, allowing the depth of his words to settle, then continued, his voice imbued with quiet reverence.

"Consider the paradox of light. It behaves both as a particle and a wave—two forms, yet one essence. Quantum mechanics tells us that reality itself is shaped not by absolutes but by probabilities, by the very act of observation. The famous double-slit experiment shows that particles change their behaviour simply by being watched. What does this mean? That consciousness is not separate from reality—it *interacts* with it, shapes it, perhaps even *creates* it."

He leaned forward slightly, his eyes scanning the room, ensuring that each soul present was following him on this profound journey.

"If the physical world itself is fluid, governed by invisible forces and unseen energies, then why should death be a rigid boundary? Could it not be, instead, a transition—much like a wave dissolving into the ocean, yet never truly ceasing to exist?"

A gentle breeze stirred through the hall as if the universe itself had chosen this moment to whisper its secrets.

"Roger Penrose and Stuart Hameroff," Guruji continued, "suggest that consciousness is not merely a byproduct of brain activity, but something much deeper—something woven into the very structure of reality. Their *Orchestrated Objective Reduction* (Orch-OR) theory proposes that consciousness arises from quantum processes inside the microtubules of brain cells. These microtubules, infinitesimal in size, are connected to the quantum field, the fundamental fabric of the universe itself. And when the body dies,"—he lifted his hand gently, as though releasing something invisible into the ether—"these quantum processes do not simply vanish. They *return*—like a raindrop merging back into the vast ocean."

"But this idea is not new," Guruji continued. "The Upanishads spoke of a reality beyond form, beyond name—an eternal, boundless field of pure awareness. What modern physicists call the 'zero-point energy field' bears striking resemblance to what ancient seers called Brahman—the unchanging, infinite source from which all things arise and to which all things return."

He closed his eyes for a brief moment, as if listening to something beyond this realm, then spoke again, his voice softer now, filled with almost reverent awe.

"And then there is the phenomenon of entanglement. Two particles, separated by vast distances, remain *connected*—instantaneously responding to each other, as if no space existed between them. Einstein himself called this 'spooky action at a distance.' But tell me, Vasudeva, if two mere particles can transcend space and time, why not consciousness itself? If our awareness is not merely a function of the brain but a field extending beyond the body, then death is not an ending—it is simply a shift, a return to the interconnected whole."

A deep hush settled over the gathering. Some sat with their eyes closed, lost in reflection; others stared at Guruji as if seeing the universe anew.

"And so," he said, his voice now almost a whisper, "perhaps we do not truly die at all. Perhaps we, like photons of light, merely change form. Like a river merging into the vastness of the sea, we dissolve—but we are not lost. We become the ocean itself."

*Vidyarthi asked, "Guruji, what scientific evidence supports the phenomenon of near-death experiences (NDEs) and past-life recollections?"*

Guruji closed his eyes for a moment, as if reaching into the vast expanse of the unknown. The devotees sat in rapt attention, their breath slowed, their hearts open, waiting for the revelation that would follow.

"Vidyarthi," he began, his voice rich with both gravity and wonder, "science and spirituality, once seen as opposing forces, now find themselves converging at the frontier of consciousness. What was once dismissed as mere myth or illusion is now being explored through the lens of empirical study. And among the most compelling mysteries that bridge this divide are *near-death experiences* (NDEs) and *past-life recollections*."

He paused, letting the weight of his words settle into the still air before continuing.

"Consider the countless accounts of those who have been declared clinically dead—no heartbeat, no brain activity—yet upon their return, they speak of journeys beyond the body. They describe travelling through tunnels of light, encountering luminous beings, and feeling a love so profound that words fail to capture its depth. Many speak of watching their lifeless forms from above, perceiving doctors and family members with perfect clarity. Some even recount conversations that were later verified, despite their physical senses having ceased to function. How can this be explained?"

He gestured towards the devotees with open palms, as if inviting them to step beyond the limits of their own understanding.

"Dr. Raymond Moody, in his pioneering work *Life After Life*, documented thousands of cases of NDEs, revealing remarkable consistencies across cultures, ages, and beliefs. Dr. Bruce Greyson, a psychiatrist, dedicated decades of research to this phenomenon, finding that those who experience NDEs undergo profound transformations—becoming more compassionate, less materialistic, and deeply connected to a greater sense of purpose. If these visions were merely hallucinations, why do they inspire such radical and lasting change?"

A hush settled over the hall. The devotees listened, their minds stretching into the unknown, grappling with the implications of what they had just heard.

"But there is more," Guruji continued, his voice now tinged with a quiet intensity. "The University of

Virginia's Division of Perceptual Studies, led by Dr. Ian Stevenson and later Dr. Jim Tucker, has spent over half a century investigating *past-life memories in children.* They found thousands of cases where young children, often as early as two or three years old, recall vivid details of lives they could not possibly have known. They remember names, places, and even the manner in which they died. Many of these accounts have been verified with astonishing accuracy."

**James Leininger – The WWII Fighter Pilot**

In the quiet town of Lafayette, Louisiana, a young boy named James Leininger began having intense nightmares at just two years old. He would wake up screaming, "Plane on fire! Little man can't get out!" His parents, Andrea and Bruce Leininger, initially dismissed these episodes as typical childhood dreams—until James began sharing disturbingly specific details.

James spoke of flying a Corsair fighter plane off a ship named the Natoma Bay. He recalled the name Jack Larsen as a fellow pilot and insisted he had been shot down over Iwo Jima. His parents, both sceptical, decided to investigate. To their astonishment, they discovered that a WWII pilot named James Huston Jr. had flown off the USS Natoma Bay and was killed in action near Iwo Jima in 1945. Furthermore, Jack Larsen was a real person—another pilot from the same squadron, still alive.

When James was shown a photograph of his supposed past-life self and his squadron, he pointed at one of the men and said, "That's me." When asked how he had died, he described being hit in the engine and crashing into the sea—a detail that matched historical records exactly.

James's story was later investigated by Dr. Jim Tucker and became the subject of the book "Soul Survivor", written by his parents. Even as he grew older, James retained memories of his past life, though they gradually faded.

## Shanti Devi – The Girl Who Remembered Her Past Life in Mathura

In the early 1930s, a little girl named Shanti Devi, born in Delhi, India, began speaking about her previous life in a town called Mathura, nearly 140 kilometres away. At the age of four, she startled her parents by insisting that she had a husband and a son in Mathura. She claimed her name had been Ludgi Devi, and she had died shortly after childbirth.

Her parents were bewildered, but Shanti's conviction never wavered. She spoke of her past husband, Kedar Nath, and described their home, specific details about her life, and even a hidden money stash. When news of her case reached Mahatma Gandhi, he ordered an investigation.

A group of researchers accompanied Shanti to Mathura, where she recognised Kedar Nath instantly and provided intimate details about their life together. She also recognised her former son, now older, and broke down in tears upon seeing him. When taken to her previous home, she identified rooms and items without hesitation, including the hidden money that only Kedar Nath had known about.

Her case was thoroughly documented by Indian scholars and remains one of the most famous past-life recollection cases in history.

### The Case of P.M. – The Burmese Boy Who Remembered Being a Japanese Soldier

Dr. Ian Stevenson, a pioneering researcher in past-life studies, documented the case of a Burmese boy who claimed to have been a Japanese soldier during World War II. From an early age, he displayed an unexplained fascination with Japanese culture, language, and military life—despite never having any exposure to them.

He repeatedly told his parents that he had been a Japanese soldier stationed in Burma and described how he had died—shot in the chest while trying to flee from enemies. The boy had an unusual birthmark on his chest, precisely where he claimed to have been shot.

When taken to a village where Japanese soldiers had been stationed decades earlier, he recognised the area, identified locations he had never seen before, and even used Japanese words fluently, though he had never learned the language. Witnesses from the village confirmed that a Japanese soldier had indeed been shot and killed in that exact spot during the war.

Dr. Stevenson meticulously investigated this case, documenting how the boy's behaviors, memories, and birthmarks aligned with his past-life claims.

***Reference:***

- *Stevenson, Ian. Twenty Cases Suggestive of Reincarnation.*
- *Stevenson, Ian. Children Who Remember Previous Lives: A Question of Reincarnation.*

## Final Thoughts

Each of these cases presents compelling evidence that challenges conventional understanding of consciousness and identity. Whether one believes in reincarnation or not, the detailed, verifiable recollections of these children continue to intrigue researchers, opening doors to deeper discussions about the nature of life, death, and the possibility of an existence beyond the physical.

**Echoes Across Lifetimes**

Guruji's voice softened as he concluded the story. "These are not isolated incidents. They are not fairy tales spun from the minds of children. They are echoes—fragments of a deeper truth, whispering through the veil of time.

If consciousness were merely the byproduct of a fleeting existence, how could these memories remain? If life were but a single chapter, why do some remember stories from a book already closed?"

He folded his hands, looking into the eyes of his devotees, his gaze filled with both wonder and reverence.

"The river may forget the path it carved through the mountains, but the ocean remembers every drop of water that returns to it. So too does the soul remember—flowing from one life to another, carrying the stories of who we once were and who we are yet to become."

"What does this tell us, Vidyarthi?" he asked gently. "That consciousness is not bound by the body. That memory is not merely a function of the brain. If our awareness were merely the result of neurons firing, then how could such memories persist beyond death?

And why do they emerge with such clarity in young children before they have been shaped by culture or conditioning?"

He turned his palms upward, his voice now carrying the weight of both science and spirit.

"Is it not like the river meeting the ocean, yet still carrying the memory of its path? Is it not like the wind, unseen yet felt, moving through time, whispering its truth to those who dare to listen?"

A single tear escaped from the corner of a devotee's eye. It was not sadness but an overwhelming sense of awe. The mystery of existence, once a distant thought, now felt like something real, something present—something waiting to be remembered.

*Aastha asked, "Guruji, how do sceptics and scientists interpret the same data differently when exploring the afterlife?"*

## The Lens of Belief and Doubt: Science, Scepticism, and the Afterlife

Aastha's question lingered in the air like the soft echo of a temple bell. Guruji spoke with a voice that carried both the weight of centuries and the lightness of a drifting cloud.

*"The afterlife is a river, and those who study it stand on opposite banks. On one side, the believers see its current stretching endlessly into the horizon, an unbroken flow of existence. On the other side, the sceptics see only what is measurable—the ripples on the surface, the reflections of light. But whether one sees an infinite river or only a fleeting stream depends on the eyes with which one looks."*

He paused, letting the metaphor settle, before continuing.

**The Sceptic's Lens: The Mind as a Machine**

"Sceptics and materialist scientists see the human mind as a biological machine, a marvel of neurons and synapses, but nothing beyond. For them, consciousness is not a soul but a byproduct of brain activity. When the brain dies, like a candle extinguished in the wind, the light of consciousness is gone.

They argue that **near-death experiences (NDEs)**—the tunnels of light, the floating above the body, the visions of departed loved ones—are merely neurological hallucinations. The dying brain, they say, releases a surge of endorphins, floods with DMT, and struggles against oxygen deprivation, crafting an illusion of an afterlife to comfort itself in its final moments.

Past-life memories? Perhaps they are **cryptomnesia**, a trick of the mind where forgotten information resurfaces in dreams or childhood imagination. Or perhaps cultural conditioning leads children to unknowingly absorb and later express these narratives as their own.

Their stance is grounded in logic, in empirical evidence, and the language of reason. 'Show us the proof,' they say. 'Where is the soul? Where is the ghost in the machine?'"

**The Seeker's Lens: Consciousness Beyond the Body**

Guruji's voice softened as though shifting into another realm.

"But on the other side of the river, the seekers stand with open hearts. To them, consciousness is not confined to the body, just as the moon's reflection is not confined to the lake that holds it.

Dr. Ian Stevenson, Dr. Jim Tucker, and many researchers have documented cases of children who remember past lives—cases so specific, so detailed, that chance or coincidence alone cannot explain them. These seekers point to people who have died, been declared clinically gone, and yet returned with stories of **a world beyond—a world of love, light, and unity.**

Quantum physics itself hints at a reality beyond the visible. If particles can be entangled across vast distances, responding to each other instantaneously, why should consciousness be any different? If an electron exists in multiple states at once, could the soul not transcend the physical form?

To them, the sceptics are like a man examining a butterfly's cocoon and declaring there is no butterfly—only a husk, only decaying matter. But the seeker knows that the cocoon is not the end; it is a transition."

**Bridging the Divide: The Dance Between Science and Spirit**

Aastha listened intently, her mind swimming in the depths of Guruji's words. She spoke hesitantly, "But Guruji, can these two views ever meet?"

Guruji smiled.

"Science is like a child who has just begun to learn the vastness of the ocean. It measures the waves and maps the currents, but it has yet to fathom the depths. Spiritual wisdom, on the other hand, is like an ancient mariner who has sailed across endless waters guided by the stars.

The two do not contradict each other—they complete each other. Science gives us tools, but spirit gives us meaning. The sceptic asks 'How?' but the seeker asks 'Why?'

The truth, my dear one, is neither on one shore nor the other but in the river itself. And all of us—believers, sceptics, seekers, and doubters—are simply travellers upon it."

Aastha felt a strange peace settle in her heart. The debate was not about proving or disproving but about seeing with **both eyes**—the eye of reason and the eye of the soul. And in that balance, perhaps, lay the true understanding of life beyond life.

*Abhirami asked, "Guruji, what challenges exist in using scientific methods to study metaphysical concepts like life after death?"*

*Bridging the Seen and the Unseen: The Challenge of Studying Life After Death*

Abhirami's voice carried a quiet urgency as if she were asking not just for knowledge but for a truth that could soothe the deepest questions of the soul. The air in the hall was still as though nature itself had paused to listen. Guruji's eyes, deep pools of wisdom, reflected the weight of the inquiry.

He inhaled slowly, the soft scent of sandalwood and jasmine lingering in the morning air. Then, in a voice both gentle and profound, he began.

"Imagine a fisherman who has spent his entire life at sea. His only tool is a net woven with fine threads, perfect for catching fish. One day, he is told that there exist creatures so small they pass through his net unseen and others so vast that no net could ever contain them. He scoffs. 'If my net cannot catch them,' he says, 'they do not exist.'"

He paused, letting the story settle in their hearts.

*"This," he continued, "is the challenge of using science—a net designed to measure the physical—to capture the metaphysical."*

**The Limits of Empirical Measurement**

"In the world of science, something is considered 'real' only if it can be measured, tested, and repeated. We can study the weight of a stone, the speed of light, the structure of a cell—but how do we measure a soul? How do we quantify the experience of a consciousness leaving the body?

Near-death experiences (NDEs), past-life recollections, and moments of transcendence—**these are deeply personal, subjective phenomena.** Science relies on external observation, but what if the answers lie within? What if reality is not only what we see and touch but also what we feel and know in the deepest corners of our being?"

He looked at the seekers before him, their eyes filled with silent contemplation.

*"It is like trying to measure the wind with a ruler or capturing love in a beaker. The very nature of the inquiry defies the tools we have."*

## The Problem of Subjectivity

*"Another challenge," Guruji continued, "is that experiences of the afterlife are deeply personal and unique to each individual. One person sees a tunnel of light; another meets long-lost loved ones; yet another experiences nothing at all. How can science create a universal law from experiences so varied?*

This is why sceptics say NDEs are nothing more than chemical reactions in the brain, illusions crafted by a mind struggling against death. Yet, how do we explain cases where the clinically dead recall details they could not have known—conversations in distant hospital rooms, visions of events later verified? How do we explain children who recall past lives with such accuracy that their previous families recognise them?"

He leaned forward slightly.

"If a blind man tells you the sun does not exist because he has never seen it, does that mean the sun is not there?"

## The Quantum Enigma: Science on the Edge of the Unknown

"But," Guruji's voice softened, carrying the weight of centuries of wisdom, "even science itself is beginning to whisper of deeper mysteries."

"In the world of quantum mechanics, reality behaves in ways that defy logic. A particle can exist in two places at once. An electron can disappear and reappear without travelling the space in between. Two entangled particles can communicate across vast distances instantly, as though distance does not exist at all.

*What does this tell us? That reality is not as solid, not as material, as we once believed. If the very fabric of existence is fluid, interconnected, and beyond time and space, could consciousness not also be?"*

The seekers in the hall listened in rapt silence.

## Bridging Science and Spirituality: The Path Forward

*"So," Guruji said, turning back to Abhirami, "the challenge is not that science cannot study the afterlife—it is that our tools are not yet refined enough to grasp it. Just as the ancient sages explored consciousness through deep meditation, we must explore beyond the material world in ways science has yet to comprehend."*

He folded his hands in a quiet gesture of reverence.

"Science and spirituality are not enemies, but travellers on the same road. One walks with the lamp of reason, the other with the torch of intuition. And if they walk together, perhaps—just perhaps—the unseen will one day become seen."

A deep silence filled the hall—not an emptiness, but a space brimming with wonder. The net may not yet be strong enough to catch the infinite—but the ocean still exists.

Guruji remained still for a long moment, his eyes half-closed as if listening to something beyond the realm of words. The silence in the Buddha Hall was profound, heavy with contemplation. Then, with a quiet nod, he signalled for the midday break.

The devotees slowly stirred, rising from their seats like waves retreating from the shore. Some walked toward Annapoorneshwari, where the air was rich with the comforting aroma of freshly cooked meals. Others wandered into the gardens, seeking solitude among the swaying trees. A few returned to their rooms, their minds still absorbed in the depths of the discourse.

Beneath the great Banyan Tree, where Akshaya's group often gathered, Vasudeva, Nita, Lalitha, Rohith, and Sujitha sat in quiet reflection. The tree's ancient roots stretched deep into the earth, a silent witness to the stories and discussions that unfolded under its vast canopy.

A gentle breeze rustled through the leaves, carrying whispers of the past. Soon, Espen, Astyn, and Kieron joined them, their faces calm yet expectant. From a distance, Padma and the others approached, their figures bathed in the golden warmth of the afternoon sun.

For a while, no one spoke.

Then, in the hush of the moment, Nita turned toward Bhavya and said softly, "Bhavya, why not continue from where we left off yesterday?"

Apeksha and Roopa nodded, their eyes filled with quiet anticipation.

Bhavya met their gaze, then exhaled slowly, nodding. The weight of memory settled over her like a familiar cloak.

"We left the village with heavy hearts," Bhavya began, her voice carrying the weight of years gone by. "Before we left, we pleaded with my grandmother to come with us, but she refused. I think, deep down, we knew she wouldn't leave. Her roots ran deeper than we could ever understand."

She paused, staring at the ground as if the past was etched into the earth beneath her.

"For a few days, she tried to adjust to city life. But the air felt different to her. The streets were too crowded, the sky too far away. She couldn't bear the sound of traffic replacing the song of the river, nor the absence of familiar faces who knew her without words. And so, she went back."

A breeze stirred through the Banyan leaves, carrying the scent of earth and distant water.

"We started visiting the village more often after that. My grandmother lived with my aunt and cousin, and each time we went, it felt as though we were trying to hold onto something slipping through our fingers. The village had changed. My grandfather was gone, and the warmth of our home felt incomplete. But we still belonged there, or so we thought."

Bhavya's voice grew quieter.

"Then, when I was in my twelfth grade, we received a call from the village."

The words alone sent a ripple of unease through the group.

"The river had risen. The flood had come."

For a moment, there was only the sound of the wind whispering through the ancient tree.

"When we reached the village, the destruction was unlike anything I had ever seen. Whole houses—homes that had stood for generations—had been carried away as if they were nothing more than paper boats. Trees had been uprooted. The river had taken what it wanted, leaving behind only the shattered remains of what once was."

She swallowed, her fingers gripping the edge of her shawl.

"Our house stood, but barely. Water had filled its insides, leaving mud and ruin in its wake. But we were lucky. Many weren't."

A murmur of emotion passed through the listeners.

"My father, shaken by the devastation, told my grandmother it was time to leave. He pleaded with her, saying it was no longer safe, that we couldn't risk another flood."

Bhavya's voice trembled slightly as she repeated her grandmother's words as if they were still echoing in her ears.

*"She stood at the threshold of our broken home and said, 'Your great-grandparents lived here, your grandfather lived here, your father was born here. Every stone, every tree, every grain of soil*

*carries their memories. The river has taken much, but it has also given us life. You ask me to leave? This is not just a place—it is a part of me. How can I abandon it?'"*

The group listened in silence, their hearts caught in the depth of her words.

"My father tried. He tried so hard. But my grandmother wouldn't move. To her, the village wasn't just a location. It was her history. Her identity. Her promise to those who had come before her. And so, in the end, we cleaned what we could, salvaged what remained, and left her there—where she wanted to be."

**The Unfinished Story**

For a while, no one spoke. The sunlight filtered through the banyan leaves, dappling the ground with shifting patterns of gold and shadow.

Then, Bhavya continued, her voice distant.

"Years passed. I completed my engineering and got placed in a good organisation. Life moved forward, as it always does. My father retired, finding peace in small routines. But part of him never left the village. He visited my grandmother often, spending days with her, as if trying to make up for lost time."

A sad smile flickered across her lips.

"Then, after two years, we decided to go back to the village festival. We hadn't returned for a long time, and something in my heart told me it was time. Maybe it was longing, and maybe it was destiny. But I knew we had to go."

She fell silent, gazing at the ground as if the rest of the story lay buried beneath it.

Before she could continue, Kiran sighed, checking the time.

"It's late. The next session will begin soon."

A quiet murmur of agreement passed through the group.

As they stood up, stretching their limbs, a strange stillness settled over them. Bhavya's story was unfinished, lingering in the air like an unspoken prayer.

They began walking toward the Buddha Hall, their footsteps slow and thoughtful. The sky stretched vast and endless above them, the afternoon sun beginning its slow descent. The wind carried the scent of wildflowers, and in the distance, the echoes of unseen waters whispered through the trees.

And somewhere, in the depths of the village Bhavya had left behind, the river continued to flow, carrying with it both loss and memory.

# CHAPTER V

## The Role of Karma and Conscious Evolution

*"Conscious evolution is the soul's journey toward greater awareness, where every thought, every deed, shapes not just our future, but the very essence of who we are becoming."*

*– Shree Shambav*

### Synopsis

*The chapter explores the integral roles that karma and conscious evolution play on the soul's journey after death. It begins by examining how various spiritual traditions define karma—understood as the law of cause and effect that governs actions, thoughts, and their consequences. Karma shapes the soul's path and influences its journey after death, creating opportunities for learning and growth in future lives. The chapter also delves into the concept of conscious evolution, which proposes that the soul's evolution occurs through awareness, learning, and spiritual growth across lifetimes. By investigating how different spiritual traditions, especially Eastern and Western views, interpret karma and conscious evolution, the chapter offers a comparative understanding of these concepts. Furthermore, it explores the idea that the soul evolves not just through external experiences but through conscious efforts to align more deeply with higher spiritual truths. The chapter also discusses the evidence—both anecdotal and scientific—that supports the theory of reincarnation, suggesting that the soul continues its journey of learning across different lifetimes.*

## The Weaving of Destiny: Karma and the Soul's Eternal Journey

"Guruji," Padma asked, "how does karma shape the journey of the soul? And how does consciousness evolve across lifetimes?"

Guruji closed his eyes for a moment as if listening to a melody only he could hear. When he spoke, his voice was like the river—gentle, flowing, yet carrying depths unknown.

## The Loom of Karma: Threads Woven Across Time

"Imagine a grand loom," Guruji said, his fingers tracing the air. "Each action you take is a thread woven into the fabric of your soul's existence. Some threads are golden, shimmering with kindness, love, and wisdom. Others are dark and heavy with pain, ignorance, and selfishness. But all are necessary, for they make the tapestry complete."

He looked at Akshaya, his gaze filled with knowing. "Karma is not punishment, nor is it reward. It is merely the echo of your own actions, rippling across lifetimes."

He paused, allowing the weight of his words to settle. "You do not plant a mango seed and expect a rose to bloom. You do not send forth anger and expect peace in return. The universe is precise; it gives back what you put forth in ways both seen and unseen."

Akshaya nodded slowly. "So, does that mean our future is set in stone?"

Guruji smiled. "Not at all. While karma shapes the path, it does not chain you to it. Each moment is a choice, an opportunity to weave a new thread into your story. Even the darkest patterns can be rewritten with the light of wisdom."

**The Evolution of Consciousness: Lessons Across Lifetimes**

He then picked up a nearby lamp, its flame steady and unwavering. "Consciousness is like this flame, passing from one candle to another. Life after life it carries forward the essence of what was learned, leaving behind the wax of past identities."

*"Think of a child who is drawn to music as if the notes live within her. Or a young boy who, without ever being taught, speaks with the wisdom of an old sage. These are not accidents.*

*They are echoes of past lives, and wisdom carried forward like a river that never forgets its source."*

He continued, his voice now weaving a story.

"Imagine a warrior, hardened by battle in one life. He believes strength is found only in steel and blood. But in his next life, he is born as a healer, his hands now learning to mend what they once destroyed. The soul does not seek revenge—it seeks balance, understanding, and growth."

Akshaya's eyes widened. "So, each life is a lesson?"

Guruji nodded. "Yes. Every joy and every sorrow, every bond and every loss—it all serves a purpose: to refine the soul, to lift it higher, to dissolve ignorance and reveal truth."

## The Journey Towards Liberation: From Karma to Moksha

"But Guruji," Padma asked, "does this cycle go on forever?"

He smiled, the light in his eyes deep as the ocean. "No, Padma. Just as a student does not remain in school forever, the soul does not wander endlessly."

"When all lessons are learned, when every attachment has been understood and released, the soul no longer needs to return. It merges with the infinite, like a drop dissolving into the ocean. This is Moksha—liberation from the cycle of birth and death. It is not an escape but a return. A return to that which we have always been but had forgotten."

**The Choice of the Soul: A Path of Awakening**

The hall was silent now, and the seekers were lost in the vastness of Guruji's words. The lamp flickered as if bowing in reverence to the truth that had been spoken.

Guruji folded his hands. "So, Padma, the question is not just 'What karma have I brought from the past?' but also, 'What karma am I creating now?' For your choices today, shape the tapestry of your tomorrows."

He looked at the gathering before him. "Live with awareness. Act with love. Seek wisdom over ignorance. And the threads you weave shall not bind you—they shall set you free."

**The Invisible Threads: Karma and the Soul's Eternal Journey**

*Bhavya, her voice steady yet filled with wonder, asked, "Guruji, how do different spiritual traditions define karma, and how does it influence the journey of the soul after death?"*

Guruji closed his eyes for a brief moment as if listening to the whispers of eternity. When he spoke, his words carried the depth of the ages.

## Karma: The Unseen Architect of Destiny

"Karma is the great law of cause and effect," he began. "It is neither punishment nor reward. It is simply the echo of our own actions, rippling through time, shaping the path ahead."

Guruji, after a pause, said, "A farmer sows a seed and reaps a harvest—not by luck, not by chance, but by the nature of the seed itself. In the same way, our thoughts, words, and deeds plant the seeds of our future experiences. Each action, no matter how small, leaves an imprint upon the soul, carrying forward into this life and beyond."

Bhavya's eyes reflected a quiet contemplation. "So, karma is like destiny?"

Guruji smiled. "Destiny is not something imposed upon us by an external force. It is simply the unfolding of our own past actions. Karma is not fate—it is choice, woven across lifetimes. A bird does not blame the wind for the direction it flies; it spreads its wings and chooses its path."

## The Soul's Journey Through the Lens of Karma

Guruji's voice deepened with emotion as he continued.

"Imagine a traveller," he said. "Life after life, they walk a vast and endless road. With each step, they collect memories, burdens, joys, and sorrows. The weight they carry determines how easily they move forward. Some walk lightly, unburdened by regret, guided by wisdom. Others stumble beneath the weight of past choices, learning through struggle."

He paused, letting the imagery sink in. "Karma is the unseen luggage we carry from one life to the next. It shapes the body we are born into, the experiences we face, the lessons we must learn. But the beauty of karma is that it is never fixed—it evolves as we do."

## Hinduism: Karma and the Liberation of the Soul

Looking at Bhavya, Guruji continued, "In Hinduism, karma is deeply linked to samsara—the cycle of birth, death, and rebirth. As the Bhagavad Gita Chater 2 Verses 22 says:

*"As a man discards worn-out clothes and puts on new ones, so does the soul discard an old body and take on a new one."*

"The soul is eternal, but it takes birth again and again, shaped by the karma it has accumulated. A life of virtue, truth, and dharma (righteous action) lightens the soul's burden, leading it toward moksha—liberation from this cycle."

He gestured to the vast sky. "Moksha is not an end, but a return—to the infinite, the formless, the divine. When a drop merges into the ocean, does it lose itself? No, it becomes the ocean itself."

**Buddhism: Karma as the Momentum of Existence**

"Buddhism," he continued, "offers a different perspective. Here, there is no unchanging soul, but rather a stream of consciousness that flows from one existence to the next, carried by karma like a river shaping the land it touches."

"Imagine a candle," he said, pointing to a small flame flickering in the breeze. "One candle lights another. The flame is not the same, yet it continues. So, too, our thoughts, intentions, and actions pass forward, creating the conditions for the next life. The goal is nirvana—the extinguishing of craving, of illusion, of suffering."

His voice softened. "A flame does not go anywhere when it is blown out. It simply ceases to burn. And yet, in that cessation, there is peace."

## Christianity and Islam: Karma as Divine Justice

Guruji then turned his gaze toward the gathering. "In Christianity and Islam, karma is understood in the form of divine justice. 'As you sow, so shall you reap.' Both traditions teach that after death, the soul faces judgment, its deeds weighed, its intentions measured."

He looked at Bhavya and smiled. "Yet at the heart of these faiths lies grace—an understanding that redemption, forgiveness, and transformation are always possible."

## The Power of Choice: Karma in Every Moment

Guruji then pointed to a single leaf falling from a tree, twirling gently before landing on the earth.

"In this moment," he said, "you are planting seeds. The way you speak, the way you act, even the thoughts you hold in your heart—each one shapes the life ahead."

"If you carry anger, you will walk in a world that mirrors it back to you. If you carry love, life will reflect it in return. Karma is not a force outside you. It is within you, responding, shifting, evolving as you do."

He leaned forward, his gaze deep and unwavering. "So, Bhavya, the question is not merely 'What karma have I inherited?' but 'What karma am I creating at this very moment?'"

## The River of Light: Conscious Evolution and the Soul's Journey Across Lifetimes

Aarna, her eyes filled with quiet curiosity, leaned forward slightly and asked, "Guruji, what role does conscious evolution play in the idea of spiritual growth across lifetimes?"

Guruji smiled—a smile that carried the softness of compassion and the sharpness of knowing. He picked up a small pebble, rolling it gently between his fingers before speaking.

## The Seed and the Sun: An Analogy of Growth

*"Imagine," he began, his voice as calm as a still lake, "a seed buried deep within the earth. In darkness, it sleeps—unaware of the vast sky above, unaware even of its own potential. But something within it stirs an ancient memory, a whisper from the sun it has never seen. Slowly, it begins to push through the soil, drawn by an invisible longing. First a fragile sprout, then a tender shoot, until one day, it breaks free into the light."*

He paused, letting the image bloom in the minds of his listeners.

*"This seed," he continued, "is the soul. The sun is the ultimate truth, the divine source. And the journey from darkness into light—that is conscious evolution."*

## The Soul's Long Pilgrimage

Guruji's gaze grew distant, as if he were seeing not just the faces before him but countless lives woven together in an endless tapestry.

"The soul is timeless," he said softly. "It wears many bodies, speaks many names, loves many hearts. But beneath all these forms, it carries a single purpose: to awaken. Each lifetime is a classroom, each experience a lesson written in joy or sorrow, gain or loss. Sometimes, we are kings; sometimes, we are beggars. Sometimes, we build; sometimes, we destroy. But through it all, we are learning—not with the mind, but with the heart, the spirit."

Aarna listened intently, her breath quiet, as if afraid to disturb the sacred unfolding of truth.

## Consciousness: The Flame That Grows Brighter

Guruji picked up a small oil lamp, its flame flickering gently. "Look at this flame," he said. "It is small, but it gives light. Now imagine feeding it with more oil and more air. It grows stronger, brighter, and warmer. This is consciousness. In our earliest lives, the flame flickers dimly, consumed by survival, by fear, by instinct. But as we move through lifetimes, we begin to question, to seek. Who am I? Why am I here? What is beyond this life?"

He looked at Aarna with eyes that seemed to hold galaxies. "The moment we ask these questions, we step onto the path of conscious evolution. We are no longer just existing—we are awakening."

### The Spiral of Growth: Not Linear, but Expansive

"Many think spiritual growth is a straight path," Guruji continued, drawing a spiral in the dust with his finger. "But it is more like this—a spiral. We revisit the same lessons and the same patterns, but each time from a higher perspective. Perhaps in one life, we learn about love through heartbreak. In another, through devotion. In yet another, through loss. The lesson is the same, but our understanding deepens."

He gently blew on the spiral of dust, and it scattered into the breeze. **"Nothing is wasted,"** he whispered. **"Every tear, every smile, every mistake—they are the threads of the soul's evolution."**

### The Role of Suffering and Joy in Evolution

Aarna's brow furrowed slightly. "But Guruji, why must there be suffering? Why can't the soul grow through joy alone?"

Guruji's face softened with compassion. "Ah, Aarna," he said gently, "imagine a river. If the water flows smoothly, it reflects only the surface—trees, sky, and clouds. But when the river meets rocks, when it tumbles and crashes, what happens? The water stirs from its depths. Hidden stones are revealed. In the same way, suffering stirs the soul from its depths, uncovering layers of strength, wisdom, and compassion we never knew were there."

"Joy is the sunlight that helps us bloom," he added, "but suffering is the rain that nourishes our roots."

**The Choice to Awaken**

Guruji leaned forward slightly, his voice becoming more intimate.

"Here is the secret," he said softly. "Conscious evolution is not automatic. Many live countless lives asleep, driven by desire, fear, and habit. But the moment you choose to awaken, to live with awareness, to seek truth—that is when evolution accelerates. You begin to live not as a victim of karma but as a conscious co-creator of your destiny."

He tapped his heart gently. "Awakening is not about becoming something new. It's about remembering who you have always been—a spark of the infinite."

**Awakening Across Lifetimes**

Guruji's eyes grew distant again as if reaching into the archives of time.

"Let me tell you a story," he said. "Long ago, there was a warrior named Rian. Fierce and proud, he lived by the sword, conquering lands driven by ambition. Lifetime after lifetime, he was reborn as a man of power—king, general, and ruler. But with each life, something felt empty, a hunger that no victory could satisfy."

"One day, as an old man sitting alone in a palace filled with gold, Rian looked at a simple flower growing through a crack in the stone floor. For the first time, he saw—not with his eyes, but with his soul. He realised that all his conquests were meaningless compared to the quiet beauty of that single bloom."

Guruji's voice softened like a breeze brushing the soul. "In that moment, something shifted. In his next life, he was not born a king but a poet. No longer obsessed with conquering the world, he sought to understand it. And through his words, he awakened others. That is conscious evolution—not a change of fate, but a transformation of perception."

## The Final Truth

Guruji's gaze settled back on Aarna. "So, you see," he said gently, "the soul is not climbing a ladder—it is unfolding like a lotus rising from the mud toward the light. Each life is a petal. Each experience, whether joyful or painful, is a stroke of colour on the canvas of eternity."

The sky above grew darker, but the hearts around Guruji glowed brighter. Aarna felt a warmth bloom within her chest—not the answer to a question, but the birth of a deeper question, the kind that would guide her for lifetimes to come.

"Conscious evolution," Guruji whispered, "is the art of remembering that you are the river, the flame, the seed, the sun—and the boundless sky in which it all unfolds."

**Threads of Destiny: The Diverging Rivers of Karma in Eastern and Western Spiritual Traditions**

A gentle breeze carried the faint scent of jasmine, mingling with the soft rustle of robes and hushed voices.

*Dev, his eyes alight with both reverence and curiosity, leaned forward and asked, "Guruji, how do concepts of karma differ between Eastern and Western spiritual traditions?"*

Guruji closed his eyes for a brief moment, as if listening to the echoes of ancient wisdom carried by the wind. When he opened them, his gaze held the stillness of mountains and the depth of oceans.

**The Loom of Life:**

"Imagine," Guruji began softly, "a vast loom stretching across the universe. Each life is a thread, and every thought, word, and action is a stitch woven into the fabric of existence. The design is not random—it unfolds with a hidden symmetry, shaped by the choices we make."

He traced invisible patterns in the air with his fingers. "But here's the paradox: while the loom is universal, the way we interpret its patterns differs from culture to culture, tradition to tradition. This is the story of karma."

**Karma in the Eastern Tapestry: The Law of Cause and Effect**

Guruji's voice deepened, carrying the weight of timeless truths.

"In Eastern spiritual traditions—Hinduism, Buddhism, Jainism—karma is not punishment or reward. It is simply a natural law, like gravity. It means 'action,' and every action has a consequence. Not because a deity sits in judgment, but because the universe is an intricate web of cause and effect."

He picked up a small stone and tossed it gently into a nearby pond. Ripples spread outward in perfect circles.

"See how the ripples move? They don't stop until they've touched the entire surface. Your actions are like this stone—what you do, say, and even think sends ripples through the fabric of existence. Some ripples return quickly within the same life. Others may take lifetimes to circle back."

Guruji paused, his eyes reflecting the rippling water. "In this view, karma is also about learning. It's not about being 'good' to avoid punishment—it's about evolving. If you sow seeds of anger, you experience the fruits of anger until you understand its nature and choose differently. Life itself becomes the teacher."

**The Cycle of Samsara: Karma Across Lifetimes**

Guruji said, "Eastern traditions see life as cyclical—birth, death, rebirth—samsara. Karma is the force that propels the soul through these cycles. But the goal is liberation, moksha, or nirvana: to step off the wheel by transcending karma, realising the true Self beyond cause and effect."

A hush fell over the group, the weight of eternity pressing gently against their hearts.

**Karma in the Western Mind: Morality and Divine Judgment**

Guruji's tone shifted, tender yet thoughtful.

"Now, in many Western spiritual traditions, especially those rooted in Abrahamic faiths—Christianity, Judaism, Islam—the focus is more linear. Life is seen as a single journey, from birth to death, followed by an eternal afterlife. Actions in this life determine your fate in the next: heaven, hell, or divine judgment."

He paused, letting the words settle.

"Here, karma takes on the form of moral law—sin and virtue, right and wrong, judged by an external God. The emphasis is on obedience, faith, and divine grace. Suffering is often seen as a test of faith or part of a divine plan rather than the direct consequence of past actions."

Guruji smiled gently. "It's like comparing two kinds of gardens. In the Eastern Garden, every plant grows from seeds you've sown, tended by your own hands across many seasons. In the Western Garden, the gardener is often seen as separate—a divine being who rewards or prunes based on how well you followed the rules."

**Bridging the Divide: The Underlying Unity**

Dev's brow furrowed slightly. "But Guruji, which one is true?"

Guruji chuckled softly, his laughter like the rustling of leaves—light yet profound.

"Ah, Dev, truth is not a coin with only two sides. It's more like a diamond—each facet reflecting a part of the whole. Eastern and Western views of karma are not opposites; they are different languages describing the same mystery."

He leaned forward, his voice a whisper woven with wonder. "What if both are true, depending on how you look at life? Perhaps karma is both impersonal law and divine grace. Perhaps we are both sowers of seeds and beloved children of the universe. One path teaches us responsibility for our actions; the other teaches us the power of surrender. Together, they form a bridge between doing and being, effort and acceptance."

**A Story from the Heart**

Guruji's eyes grew distant as if reaching into the vault of time.

"Let me tell you a story," he said. "Long ago, there was a man named Elias. He lived in a small village, deeply religious, believing in a God who judged every deed. He tried to be perfect, fearing divine punishment for any mistake. But his heart grew heavy, burdened by guilt and fear."

"One day, Elias met an old traveller—a wandering sage from the East. They shared a meal under the stars. Elias confessed his fears, expecting the sage to lecture him on sin and virtue. But the sage simply smiled and said, 'Life is not a courtroom, my friend. It's a school. You are not here to be judged—you are here to learn.'"

Guruji's voice softened as if speaking directly to the heart. "Those words lit a spark in Elias. He realised he wasn't condemned by his flaws; he was shaped by them like a sculptor chisel stone to reveal the hidden beauty within."

"From that day, Elias still prayed, but not from fear. He prayed to listen, to grow, to love. He discovered that the divine wasn't just above him—it was within him, woven into the very fabric of his being. He became a bridge between two worlds, where karma was not punishment or reward, but the sacred dance of cause, consequence, and consciousness."

## The Final Whisper of Truth

Guruji's gaze returned to Dev, filled with both gravity and warmth.

"So, you see," he said gently, "whether you believe karma is the ripple of your own actions or the judgment of a divine being, the essence remains the same: every choice matters. Every act carries energy that shapes not just your fate but your soul. Life isn't about avoiding mistakes—it's about learning from them, growing through them, and, ultimately, awakening to the truth that you are both the weaver and the thread, the ripple and the ocean."

## Echoes Across Lifetimes: The Evidence of the Soul's Journey Through Reincarnation

John leaned forward, his voice carrying the weight of inquiry that spanned centuries of human wonder.

*"Guruji," he asked, "what evidence, if any, supports the theory of souls learning and evolving through reincarnation?"*

Guruji closed his eyes briefly. When he opened them, it was as if he gazed not just at John, but through him—into the depths of countless lives lived and lessons learned.

**The River and the Raindrop:**

"John," Guruji began, his voice as calm as the twilight sky, "imagine a single raindrop falling into a vast river. It merges and loses its shape, yet it continues—flowing, moving, changing. Though it no longer looks like a drop, its essence travels within the river, sometimes becoming mist, sometimes snow, and sometimes rain again. That is the soul."

He let the words hang in the air, like ripples expanding outward from an invisible centre.

"The soul does not disappear with death. It transforms, evolves, and carries the imprint of experiences across lifetimes. And while much of this journey remains hidden, like the river beneath the thick mist, there are moments—fleeting, profound—where the echoes of past lives emerge."

## The Children Who Remember: Cases of Past-Life Recall

Guruji's eyes grew distant as if sifting through the sands of time before he spoke again.

"Consider the remarkable cases studied by Dr. Ian Stevenson, a psychiatrist from the University of Virginia. He dedicated over four decades of his life to researching young children who spontaneously recalled detailed memories of past lives—often between the ages of two and five before cultural conditioning could shape such narratives."

He paused, letting the gravity of his words settle.

### The Case of Shanti Devi (India):

"In the 1930s, a young girl named Shanti Devi in Delhi began speaking of a past life in Mathura, over 100 miles away. She recalled specific details—her former husband's name, the colour of her house, and even personal family dynamics. Sceptics and officials investigated, expecting to disprove her. But when taken to Mathura, she recognised streets, people, and belongings with uncanny accuracy, even identifying her former husband, who confirmed her memories."

Guruji's voice softened, carrying the weight of awe. "How could a child with no exposure to these places or people possess such knowledge? It's as if the soul's memory, usually veiled, found a crack through which to shine."

**The Case of James Leininger (USA):**

"Half a world away, in modern America, a boy named James Leininger began having vivid nightmares at the age of two—screaming about plane crashes, explosions, and being trapped in a cockpit. He described intricate details of a World War II fighter plane, including its model and the name of an aircraft carrier. His family, initially sceptical, researched and discovered a striking resemblance to the life of a real pilot, James Huston Jr., who had died in combat decades before. James recognised fellow pilots from photographs, identified locations he had never visited, and recounted technical details beyond a child's comprehension."

Guruji's gaze held John's, as if bridging the gap between doubt and wonder.

"This wasn't a story learned from books—it was as if the soul had carried the echoes of battle, woven into the fabric of his being."

**The Case of Barbro Karlén (Sweden):**

"In Sweden, a young girl named Barbro Karlén insisted she was not Barbro but 'Anne Frank.' She described details of Anne Frank's life, unpublished diary entries, and locations she had never visited—until, as a teenager, she stood before the Anne Frank House in Amsterdam, recognising it instantly. Her parents were stunned, for Barbro had never been told about Anne Frank before."

Guruji's voice grew quiet, almost reverent. "Barbro's memories were not mere fantasies; they carried an emotional weight—a lived experience, raw and undeniable."

**The Soul's Fingerprint: Beyond Mere Stories**

John's scepticism lingered in his eyes, but curiosity had crept in like dawn's first light.

Guruji continued gently, "Sceptics argue these could be coincidences, fabricated memories, or subconscious absorption. And yet, how do we explain cases where children recall obscure historical facts, personal relationships, or languages they've never been exposed to? Not just memories, but emotional imprints—fears, talents, and even physical birthmarks corresponding to injuries from past lives."

He traced a circle in the air. "The soul carries more than memory—it carries patterns. A child prodigy who plays the piano with no training, a fear of water despite never having a traumatic experience or a deep connection to a culture they've never known—these are the fingerprints of the soul's journey."

## The Garden of Growth: The Purpose of Reincarnation

Guruji's eyes softened with compassion. "But John, the real evidence isn't just in extraordinary cases. It's in the quiet unfolding of your own life. Have you ever met someone and felt an instant connection, as if your souls recognised each other? Or faced struggles that felt disproportionately heavy, as if rooted in something deeper than this life's story?"

He leaned forward slightly, his voice a tender whisper. "Reincarnation is not about the spectacle of past-life memories. It's about the evolution of consciousness. Just as a student progresses through grades, learning different lessons, the soul moves through lives, each one offering new experiences to foster growth, compassion, and wisdom."

"Let me tell you a tale," Guruji said, his voice weaving through the gathering like a sacred thread.

"There was once a sculptor named Arjun who worked tirelessly on a statue of a divine figure. Each day, he chipped away, frustrated by imperfections. One day, in despair, he struck the statue too hard, and a large piece broke off. He wept, believing he had ruined it. But as he looked closer, he saw that beneath the rough exterior, a beautiful form had been hidden all along. The flaw had revealed the masterpiece."

Guruji smiled softly.

"The soul is like that statue. Each life is a chisel stroke. We may not remember every strike, but the soul remembers the shape it's becoming. Our mistakes, our triumphs, our heartbreaks—they're all part of uncovering the divine within."

"So, John, the evidence of reincarnation isn't confined to stories or scientific studies. It's etched in the heart's longings, the soul's patterns, and the inexplicable wisdom we carry. The real question isn't whether reincarnation exists—but whether we are awake enough to recognise the lessons we've carried across lifetimes."

### Reflections in the Evening Glow

As Guruji concluded the session, a deep silence settled over the gathering, like the hush before the first drop of rain. The devotees slowly rose, their hearts heavy with contemplation. The words spoken in the Buddha

Hall had stirred something deep within them—unspoken truths, forgotten pains, and the eternal search for meaning.

They drifted toward the beverage counter, where the aroma of freshly brewed tea and spiced coffee mingled with the cool evening breeze. The sun had begun its slow descent beyond the horizon, bathing the ashram in a golden hue. Shadows stretched long across the stone pathways and the murmur of quiet conversations blended with the occasional rustling of leaves.

As the minutes passed, darkness embraced the space gently, as if nature itself understood the depth of the devotees' thoughts. Stars began to awaken in the vast sky, their soft glow mirrored in the flickering lamps that lined the pathways. The world seemed to exhale, slowing down as devotees finished their drinks. Some chose to take slow, mindful strolls, allowing the session's wisdom to settle within them, while others engaged in quiet discussions, dissecting Guruji's words with reverence.

But one figure stood apart.

Under the old mango tree, Dev stood in solitude, his arms crossed, his gaze distant. The soft glow of lanterns cast long shadows around him, but within his eyes, a different storm raged—a storm of emotions, of memories, of questions too vast for words.

From a distance, Akshaya, Vasudeva, and Padma noticed him standing alone, unmoving, lost in thought. Exchanging glances, they walked toward him. Vasudeva was the first to place a gentle hand on his shoulder.

"Dev, why are you standing here alone?" Akshaya asked, her voice gentle."

At first, Dev did not respond. His lips parted, but no words came. Then, slowly, his eyes shimmered with unshed tears.

"A lot of things are flooding my mind," he finally whispered. His voice trembled, and for a moment, he struggled to hold back the emotion swelling within him.

Vasudeva smiled—a knowing, understanding smile that only those who had walked the path of inner transformation could offer.

"Dev," he said softly, "Guruji has touched many souls, and we—each one of us—are becoming part of that greater soul. We are not just students. We are fragments of something larger, something eternal."

Dev looked at him as if trying to grasp the depth of his words.

Akshaya, standing beside them, spoke next, his voice carrying the weight of wisdom that time had gifted him.

*"Life is not something we can pause, rewind, or recreate. Every moment, every joy, every suffering—it happens only once. It will never repeat itself in the same way. It is a one-time opportunity to learn, to grow, to embrace what is given to us."*

A silence followed. A silence not of emptiness but of understanding.

Then, Padma stepped forward, her voice as steady as the flowing river.

*"Imagine yourself sailing a boat. Along the way, you will face many hurdles—strong winds, unexpected storms, and waves that shake your very core. But do you jump off the boat to escape them? No. You hold on. You learn. You grow stronger. The hurdles don't disappear, but you become someone who knows how to sail despite them."*

Her words settled in the air like sacred chants, filling the space with profound stillness.

Dev inhaled deeply, allowing their words to wash over him like a healing balm. The storm within him did not vanish, but suddenly, it felt like a river rather than a flood, flowing rather than overwhelming. He looked at them, a small but genuine smile forming on his lips—a smile of gratitude, of understanding, of quiet acceptance.

Before anyone could speak further, Kiran appeared from a distance, lifting his hand in a familiar gesture.

*"Time for the session,"* he called out.

The four of them exchanged one last glance before turning toward the Buddha Hall. As they walked, the night deepened around them. The fragrance of wildflowers drifted through the air, and in the distance, the soft hum of temple bells echoed in the silence.

And though nothing had visibly changed, something within Dev had shifted.

Perhaps, for the first time, he understood—that life was not about escaping pain but about embracing its lessons.

# CHAPTER VI

## Deathbed Visions and Mystical Encounters

*"In the final moments of life, the veil between worlds thins, and deathbed visions become a doorway—offering glimpses of those we have loved and those who guide us to the next realm."*

*– Shree Shambav*

### Synopsis

*The chapter explores the profound phenomenon of deathbed visions and mystical encounters, where individuals nearing the end of life report seeing deceased loved ones or spiritual beings or experiencing otherworldly events. These visions are often described as comforting and reassuring, guiding the soul as it transitions from life to death. The chapter examines common themes that emerge across cultures and traditions, such as the presence of angels, family members, or divine beings, all offering a sense of peace and connection. Through these accounts, we begin to explore what these experiences might reveal about the nature of the soul's journey and the transition between the physical and spiritual realms. The chapter also delves into both scientific and spiritual interpretations of these mystical encounters, considering whether they are purely psychological phenomena or glimpses into a higher reality. Finally, it addresses how personal beliefs and cultural contexts shape the way these experiences are perceived and understood. By examining deathbed visions, this chapter invites readers to reflect on the nature of life, death, and the mysteries that lie beyond.*

## Whispers Beyond the Veil: Deathbed Visions and Mystical Encounters

Among the circle of seekers was Vasudeva, a man whose heart bore both curiosity and the silent ache of loss. His eyes held questions that words could barely contain, but eventually, his voice rose softly above the quiet hum of the evening.

*"Guruji," he asked with trembling sincerity, "what do deathbed visions and mystical encounters reveal about the transition between life and death?"*

Guruji closed his eyes for a brief moment as if listening to a silent song only his soul could hear. When he spoke, his voice was like the first light of dawn—gentle yet illuminating.

## The Flickering Lamp

"Vasudeva," Guruji began, "imagine a lamp burning steadily through the night. As dawn approaches, the flame begins to flicker—not because it is dying, but because the light of the sun is rising. The flame trembles, sensing that a greater illumination is near. Death is like that flickering—an awareness that what we've known as life is giving way to something vaster, more radiant."

He paused, his words sinking deep into the hearts gathered around him.

"And in those final moments, when the soul stands on the threshold between worlds, many witness visions not visible to ordinary eyes. These are not hallucinations born of fear or fading consciousness—they are glimpses of the eternal light just beyond the veil."

## Stories Etched in the Soul's Memory

Guruji's gaze drifted into the distance as if peering into the unseen realms he spoke of.

### The Vision of Sir William Barrett's Wife (England):

"Consider the story of Sir William Barrett, a respected physicist and professor. His wife, Florence, a fellow scientist and sceptic of spiritual matters, lay on her deathbed. As her breathing grew shallow, she suddenly opened her eyes wide, filled with wonder. She whispered, 'Oh, William, William… I see them, and they're so beautiful!' She described seeing long-departed loved ones standing in radiant light, waiting for her. Then, with a peaceful smile, she passed away."

Guruji's voice softened.

"William Barrett, the scientist, was so moved by this experience that he devoted the rest of his life to studying deathbed visions, seeking to understand what science could not explain."

**The Child Who Saw Angels (India):**

"In a small village in India, a young boy named Aarav lay dying from a severe illness. His family, heartbroken, sat vigil by his side. But Aarav, with a radiant smile, whispered, 'Don't cry, Amma. They've come for me.' When his mother asked who, he pointed upward, his eyes filled with awe. 'Angels,' he said softly, 'beautiful beings of light.' His face was peaceful, free from fear, as he took his final breath."

Guruji paused, letting the sacredness of the story linger.

"How does a child, untouched by complex religious ideas, describe such vivid visions with absolute serenity? It's as if the soul remembers what the mind has forgotten."

**The Nurse's Witness (Across Cultures):**

"Many hospice nurses across the world, regardless of cultural or religious background, report strikingly similar accounts. Patients often speak of deceased loved ones standing at the foot of their bed, smiling, sometimes calling them by name. Some describe crossing beautiful landscapes, radiant fields, or bridges of light. Even those who were unconscious for days suddenly awaken, lucid and filled with joy, as if reunited with someone dearly missed."

Guruji's eyes met Vasudeva's. "Can all these accounts, across different times, cultures, and belief systems, be mere coincidence? Or are they threads woven into the same universal tapestry?"

**The Soul's Transition: A Door, Not an End**

Guruji's voice grew quieter as if he spoke from the depths of another realm.

*"Death is not a full stop, Vasudeva. It's a comma in the long sentence of the soul's journey."*

Guruji said, "When a caterpillar enters its cocoon, it might seem like the end. But within that stillness, transformation is happening. The caterpillar does not die—it becomes the butterfly. The cocoon was never a tomb; it was a sacred passage."

He looked back at Vasudeva with gentle eyes. "In the same way, the body is but a cocoon. When it falls away, the soul spreads its wings."

## The Mystery of the Unseen: Not Just Hallucinations

Vasudeva's brow furrowed slightly, his heart wrestling with both belief and doubt. "But Guruji, could these be just the mind's last illusions—hallucinations caused by the brain shutting down?"

Guruji nodded thoughtfully. "A fair question, Vasudeva. But consider this—hallucinations are chaotic and disjointed, often causing confusion or fear. Yet, deathbed visions are remarkably consistent, peaceful, and filled with profound clarity. Even those who were deeply sceptical in life often speak of these encounters with awe and joy. And what's more intriguing? Many patients report seeing loved ones they didn't know had already passed—only for the family to later confirm their death."

He leaned in slightly, his eyes filled with warmth. "Isn't it curious how the mind, in its most fragile state, creates not fear but profound peace? Perhaps it's because it's not the mind creating it at all—it's the soul remembering."

Guruji grew quiet for a moment, his eyes reflecting a tender memory.

*"I once sat with a dear disciple as he took his final breath. In his last moments, he squeezed my hand weakly, his eyes suddenly clear after days of unconsciousness. He whispered, 'Guruji… the light… it's everywhere. I hear music, but not of this world.' And then, with a smile that outshone even the sun, he left."*

Guruji's voice trembled slightly, but his smile remained serene.
*"I did not feel grief at that moment. I felt in awe. For I had witnessed not an ending, but a homecoming."*

*"Vasudeva, deathbed visions are like the final strokes of a great masterpiece—revealing that life's canvas was always painted with invisible colours. They remind us that we are more than flesh and bone. We are stardust and spirit, echoes of the eternal."*

Guruji, after a pause, said, "The next time you fear death, remember this—it is not a journey into darkness, but a return to the light."

Vasudeva sat in silence, tears glistening in his eyes—not from sorrow, but from the profound beauty of realising that love, like the soul, never truly dies.

### The Universal Language of the Soul: Common Themes in Deathbed Visions Across Cultures

The evening breeze whispered through the ancient trees of the ashram, carrying with it the scent of sandalwood and jasmine. With a voice filled with both reverence and curiosity, *Espen asked, "Guruji, what common themes emerge from accounts of deathbed visions across cultures?"*

Guruji's gaze softened as if he were looking not at Espen but through him—into the very heart of the question, where words dissolve, and only truth remains. He closed his eyes briefly, gathering the silent echoes of countless souls who had danced at the threshold of life and death.

**The River That Runs Through All Lands**

"Espen," Guruji began, his voice gentle yet resonant, "imagine a great river that flows across many lands. In each place, it might be given a different name, its waters coloured by the soil it touches, yet the essence of the river remains the same—fluid, life-giving, eternal."

He paused, letting the image ripple through the minds of his listeners.

"Deathbed visions are like that river. They emerge from hearts shaped by different languages, beliefs, and cultures, yet their essence flows with striking similarities, as if the soul speaks a universal language when it stands at the threshold of eternity."

Guruji leaned forward slightly, his eyes reflecting the dimming light of dusk yet glowing with the inner flame of timeless wisdom.

1. **The Presence of Deceased Loved Ones: The Call of Familiar Shores**

"Across the world," Guruji said softly, "one of the most common themes is the presence of departed loved ones who appear at the bedside of the dying. It is as if the soul, nearing the vast ocean of the beyond, hears familiar voices calling from the shore."

**The Story of Anaya – Varanasi, India**

"Let me share the story about Anaya," Guruji began, "his gaze distant as if seeing her final moments etched upon the canvas of his memory."

Anaya was an 84-year-old woman from Varanasi, the ancient city where the Ganges flows like a river of time, carrying countless souls toward liberation. She had lived a simple life filled with small joys, deep faith, and the rhythms of devotion.

In her final days, Anaya's body grew frail, but her spirit seemed to grow brighter. On the evening she was to leave this world, her daughter, Meera, sat by her side, holding her fragile hand. The room was filled with the soft murmur of prayers, incense weaving delicate trails in the dim light.

Suddenly, Anaya's closed eyes fluttered open. She stared beyond the room's walls, her gaze fixed on something—or someone—unseen by the living. A radiant smile lit her face, washing away the shadows of pain and age. Her thin arms reached out, trembling with a mixture of longing and joy. She whispered softly, *"Papa... Ma... you've come for me."*

Meera, overwhelmed, watched tears stream down her mother's face—not of fear, but of reunion as if she was meeting beloved companions after a long journey. Anaya's face glowed, serene, and peaceful as she exhaled her final breath—a breath that felt more like a gentle sigh of homecoming.

Guruji paused, his eyes reflecting the flickering flame. "This was not just a death," he said softly. "It was a return—a reunion with love that transcends lifetimes."

**The Light on the Fjords – Norway**

Guruji's gaze shifted as if his mind sailed from the sacred banks of the Ganges to the snow-clad fjords of Norway.

"Now, let me take you to a distant land where the icy winds whisper through the mountains, but the warmth of the soul knows no cold."

In a small coastal town, an elderly man named **Einar** lay on his deathbed. A stoic fisherman all his life, Einar was not known for sentimentality. His family gathered around him, expecting his final hours to be met with the same quiet resilience he'd shown through storms and hardships.

But something remarkable happened. Einar, whose eyes had grown dim with age, suddenly stared at the corner of the room, his expression softening into wonder.
He whispered in Norwegian, *"Mamma… Far… dere er her." ("Mother… Father… you are here.")*

His face, weathered by years at sea, glowed with an inner light, a warmth that seemed to defy the chill outside. He smiled, tears rolling down his rugged cheeks, as if he was seeing not death but a homecoming on the horizon—a harbour beyond this life's turbulent waters.

His family, deeply moved, described how the room itself felt different—filled with an inexplicable peace, as if the veil between worlds had thinned for just a moment.

**The Ancestors' Call – Ghana, West Africa**

Guruji's voice grew richer, coloured with reverence as he spoke of the Akan people of Ghana, where death is not seen as an end but a sacred transition into the realm of the ancestors.

"In many African cultures, the dying does not fear the crossing. They prepare for it as one would prepare to meet honoured guests."

Guruji recounted the story of Kwame, an elder of his village. As Kwame lay on his woven mat, surrounded by family, he began to speak—not to the living, but to those unseen.

His family reported hearing him say, *"Nana… Esi… I see you standing there."* He described vivid images of his ancestors—dressed in traditional attire, radiant and strong, waiting to guide him across the threshold.

There was no fear in his voice, only a steady, peaceful acceptance as if he had been expected, and now his time had come.

After he passed, the village held a celebration—not of death, but of his return to the ancestral fold, where he would continue to watch over the living.

## The Hospital Room Filled with Light – Chicago, USA

Guruji's words then shifted to a modern setting, far from sacred rivers or ancient rituals—a sterile hospital room in Chicago.

"Even in places where the mystery of death is often hidden behind machines and medical charts, the soul's journey reveals itself."

A nurse named Linda, who had worked in palliative care for over two decades, shared her profound experiences. She had seen many passes from this life, but one story stood out.

An elderly woman named Margaret was in her final hours, unresponsive for days. Suddenly, Margaret's eyes flew open wide with astonishment. She smiled and whispered, *"Oh, there you are… I've missed you so much."*

Linda described how the entire room seemed to shift. "It was as if the air grew lighter, filled with warmth and an unexplainable presence," she recalled.

Margaret reached out with trembling hands as if embracing someone invisible to everyone else. Moments later, she passed peacefully, her face serene, as though she had stepped into the arms of someone she had longed for.

**The Universal Thread: Love Beyond Borders**

Guruji's voice softened, blending with the stillness of the night.

*"Do you see, my dear ones?"* he asked gently, his eyes moving from face to face, "whether in Varanasi or

Norway, Ghana or Chicago, the song is the same. Death is not a lonely descent into darkness. It is a sacred passage—guided by love, lit by light, embraced by those who await us beyond the veil."

He leaned back, his expression serene, as if he too had seen that light many times—not with his eyes, but with his soul.

"These stories are not mere coincidences," Guruji whispered. "They are echoes of a truth that the heart has always known: We do not walk this path alone."

His voice grew softer.

"The message is clear—the soul does not cross alone. Love transcends the boundaries of life and death."

## 2. The Journey Through Light: The Bridge of Radiance

Guruji closed his eyes, his voice becoming a melodic thread woven into the fabric of the night.

"Another common thread is the vision of a brilliant light—a light unlike any seen in this world. Some describe it as a tunnel, others as a radiant field, but always, it is filled with warmth, peace, and an overwhelming sense of unconditional love."

**The Story of Yuki – Japan**

"Let me tell you about Yuki," Guruji began, his gaze soft, reflecting both the mystery and the clarity of what he was about to share.

Yuki was an ordinary man from Kyoto, a city where ancient temples coexist with bustling streets. A software engineer by profession, Yuki had never given much thought to spirituality. His life revolved around work deadlines, morning commutes, and quiet evenings spent with his family.

But everything changed one winter evening when Yuki suffered a sudden cardiac arrest. Paramedics arrived swiftly, and though his body was lifeless for several minutes, what Yuki experienced during that time could not be measured by any machine.

"I floated above my body," Yuki recalled later, his voice trembling—not with fear, but with awe. "I saw the paramedics working frantically, my wife crying beside me, yet I felt none of their panic. I was calm, observing it all from above as if the body lying there wasn't really 'me.'"

Then, Yuki described being drawn toward a radiant, golden light. It wasn't blinding but warm—soothing, like an embrace made of pure love.

"I felt an overwhelming peace, a sense of belonging as if I were returning to a place more familiar than home.

It wasn't just light. It was... everything—comfort, love, understanding—all at once."

But it wasn't Yuki's time. He felt a gentle pull, and with it, he awoke back in his fragile body, gasping for breath. Though he survived, Yuki's life was never the same.
He no longer feared death. *"I know now,"* he often said, *"that life doesn't end. It just... changes form."*

**The 'Heavenly Glow' – A Christian Near-Death Experience (USA)**

Guruji's voice grew softer, carrying the story across oceans to a hospital in Texas, where a woman named Sarah experienced something eerily similar, though shaped by her own faith.

Sarah was a devout Christian, a Sunday school teacher who had always believed in heaven but never imagined she'd get a glimpse of it herself. After complications from surgery led to her heart stopping, doctors worked tirelessly to revive her.

During those critical minutes, Sarah later described being surrounded by what she called a *"heavenly glow."* She saw a brilliant light, softer than the sun yet brighter than anything earthly. In that light stood figures she recognised—her grandmother, her best friend who had passed years earlier—all radiant, smiling, and filled with love.

She heard no spoken words, yet felt messages in her heart: *"You are loved. You are safe. But it's not your time."*

When Sarah was revived, tears streamed down her face—not from fear, but from the bittersweet ache of leaving that light behind.

*"It wasn't a dream," she insisted. "It was more real than anything I've ever known."*

## The 'Clear Light' – Tibetan Buddhist Teachings (Tibet)

Guruji's eyes gleamed as he shifted to the mystical landscapes of Tibet, where the "Bardo Thödol"—the Tibetan Book of the Dead—describes the after-death experience in vivid detail.

Tenzin, a Tibetan monk, once shared his own near-death experience after a severe fall during a pilgrimage. While unconscious, Tenzin reported encountering the "clear light"—a phenomenon deeply rooted in Tibetan Buddhist teachings.

"It wasn't just light," Tenzin explained. "It was clarity itself. There was no sense of 'me' or 'I,' only boundless awareness, like merging into the vastness of the sky."

In Tibetan tradition, this **"clear light"** is considered the purest state of consciousness—a luminous awareness that every soul encounters after death. The teachings emphasise recognising this light as the true nature of the mind, a gateway to liberation. Tenzin's experience transformed his practice. "Before, I recited prayers. After that day, I lived them."

### The 'Brilliant Gate' – Islamic Tradition (Egypt)

Guruji then spoke of Amir, a man from Cairo, Egypt, whose story echoed these same universal themes. After a car accident left Amir clinically dead for several minutes, he described an extraordinary vision.

Amir found himself standing before what he called a **"brilliant gate of light,"** beyond which he sensed an overwhelming presence—merciful, vast, and filled with love.
Though raised in the Islamic faith, Amir admitted that he'd always feared death. *"But in that moment," he shared, "I felt no fear. Only peace. A serenity so profound that words cannot capture it."*

He heard no human voices, yet the silence spoke volumes—of forgiveness, understanding, and an eternal connection to something greater than himself. When he returned to life, Amir's faith deepened, not out of obligation but from an unshakable sense of divine presence.

*"I don't just believe in the afterlife now," he would say. "I have touched its edges."*

## The Common Thread: A Light That Transcends Boundaries

Guruji's voice grew quieter, not from hesitation but from reverence.

"Do you see the pattern?" he asked gently, his gaze sweeping across the attentive faces. "Yuki saw the golden light in Japan. Sarah felt the heavenly glow in America. Tenzin merged with the clear light in Tibet. Amir stood before the brilliant gate in Egypt. Different cultures. Different faiths. Yet the same light."

He paused, allowing the weight of his words to settle in the hearts of his listeners. "This light is not confined to any one religion, any one land. It is the soul's compass, pointing us home. Whether we call it heaven, nirvana, Jannah, or simply peace, the soul recognises it instinctively—as if it has always known its way."

"Death," Guruji whispered finally, "is not the end of the story. It is just the turning of a page."

## 3. The Life Review: The Mirror of the Soul

Guruji's voice took on a deeper, reflective tone.

"Many describe a profound review of their lives, not with judgment but with understanding. It's as if the soul watches a sacred film—not of achievements or failures, but of moments when love was given or withheld."

**The Story of David – Ireland**

"Let me tell you about David," Guruji began, his eyes reflecting both the sorrow and the grace woven into the tale.

David O'Connell was an ordinary man from Galway, Ireland—a schoolteacher, father, and husband. He was the kind of man who believed in what he could see, touch, and explain. Faith, spirituality, and the afterlife were, to him, comforting stories for others but not something he truly embraced.

That belief shattered one quiet autumn evening when David suffered a massive heart attack while walking his dog along the misty shores of Galway Bay. Paramedics arrived swiftly, but David's heart had already stopped. For seven long minutes, he was clinically dead—no pulse, no breath, just silence.

But David was far from gone.

When he was later revived, pale and trembling in the sterile lights of the hospital, he spoke of something extraordinary. *"I didn't just 'see' my life flash before my eyes,"* he recounted, his voice quivering not with fear but with awe. *"I relived it—every moment, every detail, but not just from my own perspective. I felt it all through the hearts of others."*

David described how, in what felt like both an instant and an eternity, he experienced a **"life review."** He wasn't merely observing his past like scenes in a film; he was **inside** each moment, feeling the ripple effects of his actions on others.

- He felt the **pure joy** of a classmate from childhood when he shared his lunch without thinking twice.
- He felt the **sting of humiliation** in a boy he'd teased during his teenage years, a moment David had long forgotten—but the boy hadn't.
- He felt the **comfort and warmth** his late-night talks had given his lonely mother, and the **silent sadness** in his wife's heart during arguments he thought had been trivial.

David was overwhelmed—not with guilt or pride, but with a profound understanding of how interconnected we all are.

"But here's the miracle," Guruji's voice softened, "there was no judgment. No divine figure wagging a finger. No voice condemning or praising. Just… presence. A boundless, compassionate presence that held every part of him in unconditional love."

David described it as standing before a "mirror made of light," not to punish him but to help him see clearly—to learn, to grow.

*"It wasn't about what I did 'wrong,'" David said later. "It was about what I could understand differently, how I could love better. The universe wasn't a courtroom—it was a classroom."*

**Echoes Across Cultures: Similar Life Reviews**

Guruji's words lingered in the hush that followed. Then he continued, his voice weaving David's story into a larger tapestry of human experience. "David's experience is not unique to him, nor to Ireland. Across time, across cultures, souls describe the same phenomenon—the life review. It's as if the universe speaks one language when it comes to the soul's growth."

**The Case of Dannion Brinkley – USA**

Guruji spoke of Dannion Brinkley, an American man struck by lightning in 1975. Pronounced dead for nearly 28 minutes, Dannion reported a similar life review.

*"I saw my life, but I felt it from everyone's perspective I'd ever met,"* Dannion recalled. Like David, he wasn't judged by an external deity. The pain he caused others hurt him in the review, not out of punishment, but to teach him empathy.

## The Story of Anita Moorjani – Hong Kong

Then there was Anita Moorjani, who slipped into a coma after battling cancer. During her near-death experience, she encountered not judgment but limitless love. She reviewed her life not with shame but with clarity, realising how often she had lived in fear instead of embracing her own worth. When she returned to her body, Anita's cancer miraculously healed, but more profoundly, her heart had healed.

## The Lesson of the Life Review

Guruji's gaze softened, his eyes shimmering with emotion as he addressed the silent listeners. "Do you see the thread?" he asked gently. "The life review is not about condemnation. It's about connection. It's not heaven's court; it's the soul's classroom."

He paused, letting the truth settle like sacred ash on the hearts before him.

"The universe does not keep score like an accountant tallying sins and virtues. It is more like a teacher who shows you your work—not to shame you, but to help you learn. Because in the end, the question isn't, 'Were you perfect?' The question is, 'Did you learn how to love?'"

## 4. The Sense of 'Going Home': The Return to the Source

Guruji's voice softened into a near whisper. "Perhaps the most beautiful common thread is the overwhelming sense that death is not an end, but a return—a going home. People from all walks of life, whether raised in religious faiths or none at all, often describe this feeling with startling clarity."

He paused as if listening to an ancient echo before continuing.

### The Story of Fatima – Morocco

"Let me narrate the story of Fatima," Guruji said, "Fatima was an elderly woman from a small village near Marrakesh, Morocco—a life woven with the rich tapestry of family, faith, and the rhythm of desert winds. She had lived through love, loss, seasons of abundance, and times of hardship, her days marked by the simple beauty of prayer mats, olive trees, and the call to prayer echoing across golden sands."

In her final days, weakened by illness, Fatima lay on a humble woven mat, surrounded by her children and grandchildren. The room was quiet except for the soft murmur of Quranic verses recited by her son. Her breathing grew shallow, yet her face bore no trace of fear—only a serene calm as if she were listening to a song only she could hear.

Then, with her last breath, she **smiled**—not a faint, fading smile, but one radiant with peace, her eyes shimmering with an inner light. She whispered softly in Arabic, *"I am going home."*

Her family wept, not out of despair, but from witnessing something sacred—a departure wrapped in grace, like a leaf carried gently by the wind, not lost but guided.

### Echoes Across the World: Different Voices, Same Song

Guruji's voice grew quieter, yet each word carried the weight of countless souls' final whispers. "Fatima's words are not hers alone. Across continents, languages, and beliefs, people nearing the threshold of life often speak of 'going home.' It is a feeling, a recognition—not taught, not learned, but remembered."

### The Story of George – England

In London, an elderly man named George, a lifelong atheist faced his final hours in a hospice bed. His family expected fear or regret, given his firm disbelief in any afterlife. But instead, George's face softened, his eyes fixed on a distant point beyond the room. *"It's all right now,"* he whispered, smiling faintly. *"I'm going home."*

His daughter, holding his hand, later said, "It felt like he'd arrived somewhere peaceful long before his body stopped."

**The Experience of Kavi – India**

In Varanasi, where the sacred Ganges River cradles the hopes of countless souls, there was Kavi, an old boatman who had ferried pilgrims his entire life. On his deathbed, as the sounds of temple bells mingled with the river's whispers, he murmured, *"The river flows back to the ocean. So do I."* And with that, he exhaled his last breath as if it were not an end but a continuation—a current merging with a greater tide.

**The Case of Betty Eadie – USA**

Guruji also mentioned Betty Eadie, an American woman who underwent a near-death experience after surgery. She described leaving her body and being enveloped by an indescribable love, a sense of familiarity so profound that she thought, *"I'm home. I've always been here. I just forgot."*

**The Deeper Meaning: What Is 'Home'?**

Guruji's hand remained over his heart as he spoke, his voice carrying the tenderness of a lullaby.

*"But what is this 'home' they speak of? It's not a place on a map—not a city, not a country. It's a space within the soul. A*

*memory—not of something new, but something eternal we've always known."*

He leaned slightly forward, his gaze meeting the wide, wondering eyes of his listeners.

"Imagine a wave in the ocean. For a while, the wave believes it is separate—unique, rising high, crashing down. But when its time comes, it returns to the sea, not as a loss, but as a reunion. It was never separate to begin with. It just forgot."

**A Sacred Memory**

Guruji's words wove a bridge between life and death, not of fear but of remembrance.

"Whether whispered in Arabic, English, Hindi, or the silent language of the heart, the message is the same: We are not going somewhere unknown. We are going home—to a love that never left us, to a light that has always been within us."

A gentle silence settled over the gathering, filled not with emptiness but with a quiet, sacred fullness—like the pause between heartbeats, where eternity resides.

### 5. The Transformation of the Living: Echoes That Heal

Guruji's voice grew quiet, filled with reverence. "And here's something often overlooked—the transformative impact these visions have on the living. Families who witness a loved one's peaceful passing often find their own fears of death softened. Grief, though natural, is wrapped in a strange comfort, as if they've glimpsed a sacred truth beyond their understanding."

He smiled gently at Espen.

"Isn't it curious? Death, the thing we fear most, often leaves behind not just sorrow, but awe."

## The Final Reflection: A Thread That Binds All Hearts

Guruji's voice became a tender echo in the vastness of the night. "Espen, the common themes of deathbed visions are like notes in a universal song—a melody sung not with words but with the soul's deepest knowing. Across continents, across languages, the song is the same: You are not alone. You are loved beyond measure. Death is not the darkness you fear; it is the light you've forgotten."

He looked around at his disciples, his gaze finally resting on Espen, whose eyes glistened with quiet tears—not of sadness, but of a heart touched by something greater than itself.

"When the final breath comes," Guruji whispered, "it is not the end of your story. It is the turning of the page."

It was Padma, her voice trembling with both wonder and uncertainty, who broke the sacred silence.

*"Guruji," she asked softly, "how might deathbed visions provide insights into the transition between life and death?"*

Guruji closed his eyes briefly as if listening to an ancient memory, then opened them with a gaze filled with deep knowing.

"Ah, Padma," he began, his voice as gentle as the breeze, "deathbed visions are not mere hallucinations or fading illusions of a mind in decline. They are like windows—brief openings—between this world and the next. Through them, we glimpse not just the mystery of death but the eternal nature of life itself."

### 1. The Story of Amina – The Veil Growing Thin

"Let me tell you about Amina," he said, his tone dipping into a deeper well of emotion.

Amina was an elderly woman from Cairo, Egypt, whose life had been filled with love, laughter, and the quiet prayers whispered at dawn. As her health declined, her family gathered around her—sons, daughters, and grandchildren—all holding her fragile hands, afraid of the inevitable.

In her final hours, Amina's eyes, once clouded with the weight of years, suddenly cleared. She stared at a corner of the room, her face illuminated by an invisible light. She smiled—softly, serenely—and whispered,

*"Mama… Baba… you've come."*

Her family saw nothing, but Amina's gaze was unwavering, filled with recognition and joy. She began speaking to them, nodding, laughing faintly, even reaching out as if to hold invisible hands. Then, with a sigh so peaceful it felt like a breeze settling after a storm, she whispered her final words: *"I'm ready now."*

Guruji's voice softened, his eyes distant as if he, too, could see beyond the veil.

"Padma, in that sacred moment, Amina was standing on the threshold—not alone, but greeted by loved ones who had crossed before her. It's as if the soul, when freed from the body's constraints, becomes capable of seeing dimensions that were always there but hidden from view."

## 2. The Pattern Across Cultures: A Universal Language

Guruji's voice, gentle but resonant, carried the weight of countless stories passed through time, culture, and human hearts.

"This is not unique to Amina," he began, his eyes glinting with both wisdom and wonder.

"It happens everywhere, to everyone—across borders, beyond beliefs. It's as if, at the edge of life, the soul speaks a universal language."

He paused, allowing the silence to cradle his words, then continued.

"Let me tell you some stories—whispers from the threshold between this world and the next."

### In Rural Ireland: The Ancestors by the Hearth

Guruji's eyes softened as he spoke of a small village in County Clare, Ireland, where mist often clung to the emerald hills like a memory refusing to fade.

"There was a man named Seamus," Guruji recounted, "a simple farmer, rugged from years of toil, his hands etched with the lines of the earth he'd tended."

When Seamus fell gravely ill, his family gathered around his modest cottage, the air thick with the scent of peat from the hearth. In his final hours, Seamus's gaze drifted—not towards the living, but beyond them, to a space no one else could see.

With tears streaming down his weathered face, he whispered,
*'Da… is that you? And Ma… by the fire?'*

His daughter, Moira, later described how her father's face transformed—no longer twisted in pain but glowing with recognition, warmth, even laughter. He reached out, fingers trembling as if to touch hands only he could feel. Moments later, Seamus passed, his expression serene, a man who had gone home.

Guruji's voice lingered in the hush, heavy with meaning.
"In Irish folklore, the hearth is not just a place of warmth—it's the heart of the home, the sacred space where stories are shared and ancestors remembered. Seamus's vision wasn't a hallucination; it was his soul recognising familiar faces, waiting by the hearth that had always been his spiritual anchor."

## Among Native American Tribes: Spirit Guides Under Sacred Trees

Guruji shifted slightly, "Now, travel with me to the lands of the Lakota Sioux," he whispered, "where the sky stretches endlessly, and the earth holds the footprints of countless ancestors."

He spoke of White Feather, an elderly and respected shaman who had spent his life teaching the sacred ways of his people. As White Feather approached his final days, his tribe gathered in a circle, offering prayers, songs, and the burning of sweetgrass to guide his spirit.

In his final hours, White Feather's breath grew shallow, but his eyes widened with awe. He spoke softly in his native tongue:

*'I see the Great Tree. The roots touch the earth, but the branches hold the stars. And there… my spirit guide waits.'*

White Feather described an eagle soaring above the tree, and beneath it, shadowy figures—ancestors and spirits—welcoming him without fear, only love. With one last breath, he smiled as if carried on invisible wings.

Guruji's voice grew tender, almost reverent. "In Lakota tradition, the sacred tree symbolises life's connection between the earthly and the divine. White Feather's vision wasn't just comfort—it was a map, a guidepost written in the language of his soul."

**In Tibetan Monasteries: The Clear Light of Death**

The room grew quieter as if even the air itself listened more intently. Guruji's gaze drifted eastward in his mind.

"And high in the Himalayan monasteries of Tibet," he

continued, "the monks speak not of figures or faces but of light—pure, radiant, beyond description."

Guruji recounted the story of Lama Tenzin, a revered monk who had meditated in solitude for years, preparing for the great transition he called the 'Bardo'—the intermediate state between life and rebirth. When Lama Tenzin fell ill, his fellow monks gathered around him, chanting softly, guiding his consciousness with sacred mantras.

As his breathing slowed, Lama Tenzin suddenly opened his eyes, wide and filled with an indescribable brilliance. In his final words, he whispered,

*'Ah… the Clear Light. It is everything and nothing. I am home.'*

After his passing, the monks noted that his body remained unusually serene, untouched by the typical signs of death for days—a phenomenon not uncommon in Tibetan Buddhist accounts.

Guruji's voice grew hushed, filled with awe. "In the Tibetan Book of the Dead, the 'Clear Light' represents the true nature of the mind—pure, boundless consciousness. Lama Tenzin didn't just see it; he became it. Death, to him, was not an end but a return to what had always been."

### The Thread That Binds Them All

Guruji's eyes slowly returned to the faces around him, some wet with tears, others wide with wonder. His voice softened, now more like a heartbeat than a sound.

"What connects Seamus, White Feather, and Lama Tenzin?" he asked gently.

"Different lands. Different beliefs. Yet the same experience—of being welcomed, guided, and embraced by something greater than themselves. Whether it's ancestors by a hearth, spirit guides under sacred trees, or the formless Clear Light, the message is the same: Death is not abandonment. It is a reunion."

He placed his hand over his heart, his fingers pressing softly as if touching an invisible thread.

"These visions are not fantasies born of fear. They are echoes of a truth we've always known but forgotten—until the moment we stand at that sacred threshold."

"Death," Guruji whispered, "is not the closing of a door. It's the opening of the one we've been walking toward all along."

He paused, allowing the weight of his words to sink in. "What do these shared visions tell us? That perhaps death is not a lonely descent into darkness but a sacred return—a reunion with those we've loved and the essence we've always belonged to."

### 3. The Bridge Between Worlds: Not a Hallucination, but a Revelation

*Padma's eyes glistened with unshed tears. "But Guruji, couldn't these be just the brain's last flickering moments? A trick of chemicals and fear?"*

Guruji smiled gently, his gaze warm and patient. "A valid question. But consider this: Why are these visions often filled with peace, clarity, and even new knowledge? Why do people on the brink of death see loved ones they didn't even know had passed—only for their families to confirm it later?"

He leaned closer, his voice a soft thread woven with ancient wisdom.

"If you were standing at the shore, watching someone sail away, you might say, 'They are gone.' But on the other side of the ocean, another voice exclaims, 'They have arrived.' Deathbed visions are the echoes of those voices—heard from both shores at once."

### 4. The Story of Ravi – A Glimpse Beyond the Horizon

Guruji's eyes darkened with memory as he shared another story.

"There was a boy named Ravi," he whispered, "only ten years old, fragile from an illness that even the best doctors could not cure."

As Ravi's time drew near, his mother sat by his side, tears streaming down her face. But suddenly, Ravi's expression changed. His eyes, once dull with sickness, sparkled with awe.

*'Mama,' he said softly, 'why are you crying? Don't you see the beautiful people? They're everywhere. They're smiling at me.'*

Then, after a pause, he added with absolute certainty, 'They say I'll be okay. They say it's not goodbye.'

With that, he closed his eyes, his little face serene, as if he'd simply drifted into another room.

Guruji asked, "What did Ravi see? A hallucination? Or did the innocence of his soul allow him to glimpse a reality our fearful minds cannot comprehend?"

## 5. The Analogy: The Caterpillar and the Butterfly

Guruji took a deep breath, allowing the sacred silence to settle once more before speaking again.

"Think of a caterpillar," he said, "who has spent its life crawling upon the earth. One day, it feels an irresistible pull to stop, to surrender, and enters the cocoon. To the caterpillar, this might feel like the end—darkness, stillness, dissolution."

His eyes sparkled with quiet wonder.

"But is it the end? No. It is a transformation. On the other side of that darkness, the caterpillar emerges—not as it was, but as a butterfly with wings that were always destined to be. Deathbed visions are like the first cracks of light seeping into that cocoon. They are reminders that we were never meant to crawl forever."

### 6. A Classroom, Not a Curtain

Guruji placed his hand gently over his heart, his voice now a soft prayer.

"Padma, death is not a wall but a doorway. The visions people experience as they approach it are not mere dreams but sacred glimpses of the greater reality that lies beyond."

He looked around at the faces filled with both tears and wonder.

"The universe is not cruel enough to let us be born, love, suffer, and grow, only to vanish into nothingness. Life is not a sentence—it's a story. And death… death is simply the next chapter."

The wind carried his words into the vastness of the evening, mingling with the stars as they began to pierce the darkening sky—tiny lights, reminding everyone that even the deepest night is filled with countless unseen suns.

**Between Worlds: The Science and Spirit of Deathbed Visions**

The air inside the ashram was still, thick with the quiet hum of contemplation. The golden glow of the evening lamps cast long shadows on the walls, flickering like unseen whispers. Guruji sat in the centre, his presence radiating both warmth and an unshakable depth as if he carried within him the wisdom of many lifetimes.

Roopa's voice, gentle yet filled with curiosity, broke the silence.

*"Guruji, what scientific and spiritual interpretations exist for visions of deceased loved ones or spiritual beings at the end of life?"*

A knowing smile played upon Guruji's lips. He closed his eyes for a moment as if listening to something beyond the realm of sound. Then, with a deep breath, he began.

"Ah, Roopa," he murmured, "your question is like asking why the ocean sings when it touches the shore.

Is it the science of waves or the poetry of the sea? Perhaps both."

He leaned forward slightly, his hands resting like gentle anchors on his knees.

"Let me tell you a story."

**The Story of Elena: A Bridge Between Worlds**

Guruji's voice softened, woven with both tenderness and awe.

"There was a woman named Elena, a nurse from Florence, Italy. She had spent her life beside the dying—holding hands, whispering comfort, watching countless final breaths. But when her own time came, the mystery unfolded not beside her, but within her."

Elena had been diagnosed with terminal cancer. In her final weeks, drifting in and out of consciousness, she often spoke softly to people no one else could see. One night, she startled awake, her frail face lit with a radiant smile.

'Mama?' she whispered into the dim light, tears of joy slipping down her cheeks. *'Oh, you've come to walk me home.'*

Her daughter, Anna, sitting by her bedside, wept—not from fear, but from witnessing something sacred.

Moments later, Elena passed, her face serene, as if carried by unseen hands.

Guruji paused, letting the weight of the story settle. "Now, was that just the mind's final flicker? Or was it the soul's first glimpse of something eternal?"

He leaned back, his gaze sweeping the silent circle.

"Let's explore both paths—the scientific and the spiritual—not as contradictions, but as two rivers meeting the same sea."

### The Scientific Lens: Mapping the Mind's Final Frontier

Neurochemical Changes:

"As the brain begins to shut down," Guruji explained, "there's often a surge of neurochemicals—endorphins, dopamine—that can create vivid experiences. The brain, facing hypoxia (lack of oxygen), may produce hallucinations, much like in dreams or near-death experiences."

He likened it to the way the sky blazes with colour at sunset: "The colours are real, but they happen because of how light bends. Perhaps the mind, in its final moments, bends reality to reveal something beautiful."

Memory and Emotional Processing:

"The brain might replay deep emotional memories as a coping mechanism," Guruji continued.

He shared the case of Dr. Christopher Kerr, a hospice physician who documented thousands of end-of-life visions. "His patients consistently reported seeing deceased loved ones—sometimes people they hadn't thought of in decades. Not random memories, but meaningful ones, full of love and closure."

The Brain as a 'Filter,' Not a 'Factory':

Guruji's eyes twinkled. "Here's an interesting idea, even from some neuroscientists: What if the brain isn't creating consciousness but filtering it? Like a radio tuning into specific frequencies. When the body begins to die, the filter weakens—and perhaps, just perhaps, we start to receive 'signals' from beyond."

The group sat in thoughtful silence. The scientific explanations provided structure, but the heart sensed there was more—something just beyond the edges of logic.

## The Spiritual Perspective: The Call from Beyond

Guruji's expression softened as if he were now stepping into the realm of the unseen.

"While science examines the mechanics, spirituality asks the greater question: What if these visions are real?"

He told them of a case in Los Angeles, where a young woman named Emily, dying of a terminal illness, suddenly reached out into empty space, her face alight with joy.

*'Mom? Dad?' she whispered. 'You've come?'*

Her family stood around her, stunned—her parents had passed away decades before. Yet Emily spoke to them as if they were right there in the room, smiling, waiting. Moments later, she was gone, a peaceful smile still lingering on her lips.

**Guruji said, "Now let's step beyond the map of the brain and into the landscape of the soul."**

The Veil Grows Thin:

"Many spiritual traditions believe the boundary between the living and the departed is not a wall, but a veil—a thin, delicate curtain that becomes translucent at the moment of death."

He spoke of the ancient Celts, who called this space 'the thin places,' where the sacred and the ordinary touch. "At the edge of life, that veil lifts, and we glimpse what's always been there."

Guides for the Journey:

Guruji shared the Tibetan Buddhist belief in the 'Bardo'—the transitional state after death. "Tibetan monks prepare for this all their lives, believing that enlightened beings or loved ones come to guide the soul through the passage, like lantern-bearers in the dark."

**Universal Patterns Across Cultures:**

"Isn't it fascinating," he mused, "that people from vastly different cultures—whether in India, Africa, Europe, or the Americas—describe the same experiences? Seeing deceased relatives, feeling overwhelming love, encountering beings of light. How could that be mere coincidence?"

Guruji paused, his eyes reflecting both the depth of the question and the humility of not claiming all the answers.

"Perhaps these visions aren't hallucinations but homecomings. Not fabrications of the mind, but invitations from the heart of the universe itself."

**The Bridge Between Science and Spirit: A Doorway, Not an End**

Guruji smiled, sensing the shift in the room. He continued, his voice carrying both certainty and wonder.

"Perhaps the mistake is thinking that science and spirituality must be in opposition. What if they are two eyes seeing the same reality from different perspectives?"

He turned to Roopa and said, "Science explains the mechanics—the changes in the brain, the surge of neurochemicals. But it cannot explain the meaning. It cannot tell us why these visions bring comfort or why they carry the same themes across cultures and centuries. That belongs to the realm of the soul."

He placed a hand on his heart. "A candle, when it burns out, does not destroy the flame—it merely allows it to rise. So, too, with life. When the body fades, the light of consciousness is not extinguished. It returns to the Source."

A deep hush fell over the gathering as if they, too, had glimpsed something beyond the physical.

Guruji gently picked up a small wildflower from a nearby vase, holding it delicately between his fingers.

"Think of this flower," he said softly. "Science can tell us everything about it—its biology, its structure, the way sunlight nourishes it. But science can't fully explain why its beauty moves us, why its fragrance stirs something deep within."

He looked around, his voice a tender whisper. "Deathbed visions are like that. Science can describe the 'how,' but the 'why'—ah, the why belongs to the soul."

**The Final Invitation: What Do We Choose to See?**

Guruji's eyes sparkled as he asked, "So when the time comes, what will we see?"

He leaned in, almost whispering, "Will we see only the workings of a fading mind? Or will we recognise the hands reaching for us, the faces we have longed for, the light we have always known?"

A tear slipped down Roopa's cheek.

"Guruji," she whispered, "perhaps we do not have to wait for death to know the answer. Perhaps, if we quiet our minds, if we open our hearts, we can sense it even now."

Guruji smiled, his silence saying, Yes, Roopa. Yes.

Guruji leaned back, letting the stillness return. "Roopa, in the end, perhaps the miracle isn't in choosing between science or spirit. The miracle is that both point to the same mystery—that love does not end with breath, that consciousness might be more than neurons firing, that when we die, we may not be going into darkness but into light."

After a long pause, Guruji smiled gently. "And maybe, just maybe… the ones we thought we lost were never gone. They've just been waiting for us to see."

*Martina asked, "Guruji, how do personal beliefs and cultural contexts shape the interpretation of mystical encounters near death?"*

Guruji's eyes softened. Then, with a quiet breath, he said, "Martina, imagine a river flowing through many lands. In each region, it takes on a different name—the Ganges in India, the Nile in Egypt, and the Amazon in South America. Yet, it is the same water, the same current, simply seen through different eyes. Our mystical encounters near death are much like that river. The experiences are universal, but the names, the interpretations, are coloured by the soil of our personal beliefs and cultural landscapes."

He paused, letting his words settle like falling leaves.

**The River of Light**

In a quiet village perched on the cliffs of the Aegean Sea, an elderly woman named Sofia lay on her simple bed, the faint scent of olive oil and saltwater lingering in the air. As her breath grew shallow and her family gathered, she suddenly opened her eyes, once dim with age, now alight with an otherworldly glow. A soft smile curved her lips as she reached out with trembling hands, her gaze fixed on something unseen.

*"The Angel of Light,"* she whispered, her voice fragile yet filled with awe. *"Archangel Michael… you've come for me."*

Her daughter wept softly, not from sorrow but from the overwhelming peace radiating from Sofia's face, as if the room itself had been touched by the divine.

Far across the world, high in the mist-veiled mountains of Bhutan, an elderly monk named Tenzin sat in meditation, his final moments unfolding like the last petal of a lotus. His breath slowed, yet his mind remained clear. With closed eyes, he described a radiant brilliance emerging from the vastness within—a luminous presence without form, guiding him gently toward what he called the *Clear Light of the Dharmakaya.* There was no fear, no clinging—only an expansive peace, as if he were dissolving into the very fabric of existence, the light both around him and within him.

Meanwhile, in the warm, earthy heart of a Nigerian village, an elder named Olufemi rested beneath the shade of an ancient baobab tree. His family surrounded him, whispering prayers, their voices mingling with the rustle of the wind. As the boundary between worlds grew thin, Olufemi's face lit up. He spoke of seeing his ancestors—tall, majestic figures adorned in radiant garments, their eyes filled with wisdom from beyond the veil. They stood at a threshold invisible to all but him, calling him home, their voices a harmonious echo woven into the pulse of the earth.

*Different lands. Different languages. Different symbols.*

Yet beneath it all, the same profound encounter—a radiant presence, a beckoning light, a familiar warmth that transcended the barriers of culture and creed. Some called it an angel, others the clear light of truth, others still the spirits of beloved ancestors. But the essence remained unchanged, like a single river flowing through many landscapes, known by different names, yet always water—pure, eternal, and life-giving.

Perhaps the greatest mystery was not in the forms these visions took but in the universal thread, they wove through the heart of humanity. It was as if, in the sacred threshold between life and death, the soul remembered something deeper than language, something older than belief—a silent knowing that beyond all divisions, we are all part of the same endless light, returning home.

Guruji leaned forward slightly, his voice lowering into a tender, reverent tone.

"You see, Martina, our beliefs act like stained glass windows. The divine light shines the same for everyone, but as it passes through the glass, it takes on different colours and patterns. A Christian might see saints or angels, a Hindu may see Krishna or Shiva, and an atheist might simply feel an overwhelming presence of love and peace without form or face. The experience is shaped, not by the light itself, but by the lens of our hearts."

He touched his chest lightly as if feeling the echoes of countless souls.

"This is not to say one is right and the other wrong. The river is not lesser because it's called by different names. The heart of the experience—the connection, the peace, the sense of returning home—is the same. It speaks to something deeper than dogma, something universal, woven into the very fabric of our being.

Perhaps the greatest mystery isn't what we see in these moments, but what it reveals about us—that no matter how far apart our lands, our languages, or our lives, we are all sipping from the same sacred current."

The room fell into a hushed stillness, as if the very air was holding its breath, honouring the invisible threads that connect every soul across time, space, and belief.

As Guruji slowly rose from his asana, a deep silence filled the Buddha Hall—the kind of silence that followed profound realisation. His presence, like the final note of a sacred chant, lingered even as he began to move away, signalling the end of the day's session.

One by one, the devotees followed, stepping into the night's embrace. The sky above stretched vast and endless, glittering with stars, their light flickering through the swiftly moving clouds. The moon, partially hidden, cast a soft glow upon the ashram, blending with the illumination from the temple lamps.

A Night of Reflections

After dinner, some devotees chose to stroll through the ashram gardens, their thoughts still marinating in the wisdom shared during the session. Others sought the solitude of their rooms, reflecting in silence. But for Akshaya and the others, the night was not yet over.

The fireplace, nestled in a quiet corner of the ashram, had become their sacred space—a place where conversations were raw, where truths were spoken without hesitation, and where they could be vulnerable. The flames flickered, casting dancing shadows upon their faces, as they gathered, wrapped in warm shawls against the chilly night breeze.

Nita was the first to speak, her voice thoughtful.

"Today's session was very deep… a lot of learning, and with such clarity."

Padma and the others nodded, their expressions solemn. The weight of Guruji's words still rested heavily on their minds.

From the other side of the circle, Abhirami's voice broke through the quiet murmurs.

"Some stories today… they were truly touching."

Her words seemed to echo into the stillness of the night.

Across from her, Sam sat motionless, his head lowered, silent tears escaping down his cheeks.

Without hesitation, Alice placed a comforting hand on his shoulder. She said nothing—she didn't need to. Sometimes, presence was enough.

A few moments passed before Aarna turned to Bhavya and gently asked, "What happened next?"

Bhavya exhaled slowly. She glanced at the fire, watching as the flames twisted and curled toward the sky, mirroring the storm that once tore through her life.

"We travelled to the village as planned. The festival was beautiful… but the memory of my grandfather never left me. Everywhere I turned, I saw him. I remembered how we would light crackers together, how he would hold my hand as we walked through the festival, buying me toys and sweets… It felt as though his laughter still lingered in the air, but when I turned, he was not there."

Her voice wavered, but she continued.

"The next day, the village's fate changed."

A hush fell over the group.

"The weather turned rough. A red alert was issued—there was no time to prepare. The sky darkened, the clouds grew heavier, and then the rains came. But this wasn't unusual. Our village was used to floods. People had learned to prepare for the worst. It was almost a ritual: houses would be damaged, some would be washed away, but life would go on."

She swallowed, her hands tightening into fists.

"But that night… it was different."

"At midnight, we heard an unearthly roar. Before we could even grasp what was happening, the water came like an unstoppable force, swallowing everything in its path. It was not a flood—it was a beast. I heard cries, desperate shouts, and then—nothing."

Her eyes glistened as she stared at the fire. The embers crackled, mirroring the storm inside her.

"Water filled our home within seconds. I remember seeing my grandfather… he was leading me somewhere, trying to get me to safety. And then… darkness."

A deep breath. A pause.

When I woke up… two days had passed. I was pulled from the debris, weak, injured, alone. The first words that left my lips were—

She clenched her jaw, trying to steady her breath.

"Where is my father? Where is my grandfather?"

Silence.

"No one answered me. No one could answer me."

She looked up at the sky as if searching for something.

"I was surrounded by strangers. My home, my village… gone. My family… gone."

Padma gasped softly, pressing her hand to her mouth.

Akshatha's eyes brimmed with tears.

"It was only later that I realised… my father, my grandfather, my entire family—wiped away by the flood."

A heavy silence engulfed the group. Even the fire seemed to burn quieter.

Bhavya closed her eyes as if reliving the emptiness of those days.

"When I recovered enough to travel, I returned to the city. But home… home was no longer home."

She took a shaky breath, her voice now a whisper.

"The house was silent. No laughter, no voices calling my name, no footsteps echoing through the corridors. It was like living in an empty shell—a space where memories haunted every corner, but the people who created them were gone."

A single tear escaped down her cheek.

"I began to feel like a burden. A weight I couldn't carry. I grew angry—angry at nature, at fate, at life itself. I blamed my grandmother—why did she refuse to leave the village? If she had, would things have been different? I blamed the river, the very waters that once gave us life but had now stolen everything from me. But mostly… I blamed myself."

She looked around at the faces of her friends, her voice breaking.

*"I could not understand—why do the people who love us have to die? Why do we have to lose those who mean the most? This*

*question destroyed me. It tossed me into an ocean of confusion, where there were no answers… only suffering."*

A long silence followed. The only sound was the distant chirping of crickets, the crackling of the fire, and the occasional whisper of the night wind.

Kiran, standing at the edge of the gathering, finally spoke, his voice gentle.

"It's very late… we should rest for tomorrow's session."

One by one, the group slowly dispersed. But the weight of Bhavya's words did not leave them.

As Nita walked back to her shelter, she felt the story settling deep in her heart. The pain, the questions, the silence—it all echoed within her.

*Tonight, sleep would not come easily.*

# SECTION THREE

## Life Beyond the Physical Realm

*"Life beyond the physical realm is not a distant place, but a state of being—where the soul sheds the limitations of the body and expands into the boundless truths of existence."*

*-Shree Shambav*

# CHAPTER VII

## What Happens Immediately After Death?

*"Death is not an end but a threshold—a passage where the soul is gently guided toward its next stage of awakening, embraced by light, love, and a timeless wisdom."*

*– Shree Shambav*

### Synopsis

*In this chapter, we explore various spiritual teachings and firsthand accounts to uncover what happens to the soul immediately after physical death. Central to many near-death experiences (NDEs) is the vision of a "tunnel of light" that many describe as a comforting, transformative passage leading the soul away from the body. We discuss the significance of this experience and its interpretation in different spiritual contexts. The role of spirit guides is also examined—how these benevolent beings are believed to assist the soul in navigating the transition from life to death, offering guidance and protection along the way. The concept of a "life review" is explored in depth, where the soul revisits its past life to gain a clearer understanding of its actions, choices, and lessons learned. This review is seen as a powerful tool for personal growth and spiritual evolution. Additionally, we delve into how various spiritual traditions and personal accounts portray the immediate aftermath of death, noting the similarities and differences in these interpretations. Through these accounts, the chapter provides profound insights into the soul's journey after death, inviting reflection on the process of release, learning, and transition.*

## The Sacred Dawn in Kanchipuram

The early morning in Kanchipuram was bathed in a soft drizzle, the raindrops gently kissing the earth, leaving behind a fragrance that blended with the lingering scent of jasmine, sandalwood, and damp soil. A mystical haze wrapped itself around the ancient town, as if the heavens were whispering secrets to the waking world.

Akshaya, along with the other devotees, walked silently through the temple pathways, their footsteps merging with the rhythmic sound of nature—the chirping of birds, the rustling of leaves, and the occasional chime of temple bells in the distance. The breeze, cool and crisp, carried the aroma of blooming lilies from the temple pond, mingling with the sacred scent of incense that drifted from the sanctum.

As they walked, the Bhajan Hall came alive with soul-stirring melodies. From one corner, the deep, resonant sound of "Om" chanting rose, filling the air with an almost celestial vibration. The very air seemed to thrum with energy, as though the universe itself had paused to listen. From another end, the sweet voices of devotees sang hymns, their devotion pouring through each syllable, merging like streams into an ocean of divine presence.

The towering trees lining the temple corridors swayed gently, their branches dancing in the rhythm of the wind. Leaves, kissed by the morning drizzle, floated gracefully down, surrendering to the breeze like tiny messengers of impermanence. The first rays of sunlight, still shy, peeked from the horizon, slowly attempting to penetrate the mist, casting an ethereal glow over the sacred land.

The village beyond the ashram was also awakening. From a distance, they could see lamps flickering in doorways and women drawing intricate kolams at their thresholds, marking the beginning of another blessed day. The air carried the faint sound of temple bells and conch shells, signalling the first morning prayers. The whole scene felt less like the mere beginning of a day and more like a sacred preparation—a celebration of life itself.

A Morning Ritual of Reflection

After some time, as the drizzle faded into a soft mist, Akshaya and the others made their way to the coffee counter, a simple wooden stall nestled under a large peepul tree. The rich aroma of freshly brewed filter coffee filled the air, mingling with the scent of damp earth.

The warmth of the coffee cups in their hands felt comforting against the morning chill. The golden-brown froth danced as they gently swirled their cups, taking slow sips, allowing the bitterness and sweetness to merge seamlessly on their tongues—just like the dualities of life itself.

A few moments passed in silence, each person lost in their own reflections.

"Yesterday's session… it was profound," Akshaya finally said, setting her cup down.

The others nodded, their expressions thoughtful. The previous day's discourse had left them with unanswered questions and lingering thoughts that needed clarity.

They moved toward the Brindavan Garden, a serene space within the ashram where blooming flowers and the whispering breeze made it a perfect sanctuary for contemplation. Here, amidst the vibrant greens and fragrant blossoms, they sat in a circle, discussing, questioning, and deepening their understanding of Guruji's teachings.

The conversation flowed effortlessly—insights were exchanged, doubts were clarified, and moments of realisation dawned like the morning sun.

As the discussions drew to a close, the devotees slowly dispersed, returning to their shelter spaces to prepare for the day's session.

### The Journey Beyond the Veil

*Akanksh asked, "Guruji, What Happens Immediately After Death?"*

Guruji sat quietly for a moment, his eyes reflecting the golden hues of the setting sun. The question hung in the still air like a sacred whisper. Then, with a gentle breath, he began to speak, "What happens immediately after death?" he repeated, his gaze distant, as though peering into a realm just beyond sight. "This question is as old as humanity itself, woven into the fabric of every spiritual tradition, whispered through sacred texts, and carried in the fragile hearts of those left behind."

He picked up a small stone, rolling it thoughtfully between his fingers. "Imagine life as a river," he said, "flowing tirelessly toward the vast ocean. Death is not the end of the river but the moment it merges with the infinite sea. The form changes, but the essence remains."

**From the Bhagavad Gita (Hinduism):**

Guruji's voice deepened, imbued with a quiet reverence as he recited the timeless verse from the Bhagavad Gita Chapter 2, Verse 22:

*"Just as a man discards worn-out clothes and puts on new ones, so does the soul discard a worn-out body and take on a new one."*

"In Hindu thought," he began gently, "the soul, or Atman, is eternal—unchanging, indestructible, beyond birth and death. The body is but a garment, temporary and fragile, while the soul is the essence, the eternal spark of divine consciousness."

He paused, picking up a dried leaf from the ground, brittle and faded. "This leaf once danced in the wind, vibrant and green. Now, it has withered, but the tree—the source—remains untouched, giving life to new leaves. In the same way, the soul moves from body to body, untouched by the decay of the physical form."

Guruji leaned slightly forward, his voice lowering, drawing his listeners into the sacred mystery. "The Upanishads, the very heart of Vedic wisdom, describe the soul's journey after death. The Brihadaranyaka Upanishad speaks of the 'silver cord'—a luminous thread connecting the soul to the body. This cord is delicate, almost invisible to the physical eye, but it holds the soul tethered to life. When death comes, the cord is severed, and the soul is released, like a bird slipping from an open cage."

He closed his eyes briefly as if seeing that very moment of transition. "Some souls, especially those who have lived with awareness, are met by beings of light—guides, ancestors, or divine presences—who assist them in navigating the realms beyond. This isn't just mythology. Even modern near-death experiences echo these descriptions. People speak of being greeted by luminous figures, feeling an overwhelming sense of peace, love, and belonging."

Guruji's voice grew softer yet more profound. "But not every soul recognises this light immediately. In the Garuda Purana, it is said that the soul carries the impressions of its actions—its karma—which shape its experiences after death. Some souls move effortlessly toward higher realms, while others, bound by attachments, linger in confusion, caught between worlds."

He picked up a small lamp from beside him, its flame flickering gently. "Imagine this flame," he said, "as the soul. The lamp may break, but the flame can be transferred, undiminished, to another vessel. Death is not the extinguishing of the flame; it is simply the changing of the lamp."

Guruji looked around, his eyes filled with a gentle, timeless knowing. "This journey is not one to fear. For beneath the layers of existence, beyond the cycles of birth and death, the soul remains untouched—eternal, radiant, one with the infinite."

**Christianity:**

Guruji paused, allowing the weight of his words to settle like the hush that follows a sacred hymn. His gaze softened, reflecting both wisdom and compassion, as he continued, his voice imbued with quiet reverence.

"In Christian traditions," he said gently, "there are countless accounts from those who have stood on the threshold between life and death, describing a phenomenon often referred to as the 'tunnel of light.' This is not just poetic imagery—it's a recurring experience across cultures and ages, where individuals speak of being drawn toward an all-encompassing, radiant light. But this light is not just brightness; it is infused with a profound, unconditional love, a warmth beyond earthly comparison. It pulls the soul gently, not with force, but with an irresistible sense of belonging—as if the soul is returning to a home, it never knew it had forgotten."

He paused again, his fingers lightly tracing the rim of his prayer beads, then continued,

*"In the Gospel of Luke, as Jesus hung upon the cross, he turned to the repentant thief beside him and said, 'Truly I tell you, today you will be with me in paradise.' (Luke 23:43) This powerful promise suggests an immediate passage after death, not delayed, not distant—an instant crossing into the embrace of divine grace. It's as if, at the moment of death, the soul steps through a veil thinner than a breath, guided not by fear, but by love."*

Guruji leaned forward slightly, his voice softening to a near whisper, drawing his listeners closer in spirit. "And then comes the life review—an experience spoken of in both ancient scriptures and modern near-death testimonies. But here's the profound truth: it's not a courtroom where the soul stands trial before a judge. There is no gavel, no stern verdict. Instead, it is like standing before a mirror that reflects not the face but the heart. The soul relives every act of kindness, every word spoken in love—but also feels the ripples of its harsh words, the pain it may have unknowingly caused. Yet even in facing these shadows, there is no condemnation—only an overwhelming presence of compassion, as if the light itself whispers, 'See, learn, grow.'"

His voice grew tender, his eyes shimmering with the depth of unspoken understanding. "Imagine standing under the warm sun after a long, cold night. The sun does not punish the frost; it simply melts it away. The soul's life review is like this—the light reveals all, but not to shame. It reveals to heal, to awaken, to guide the soul's evolution."

He fell silent then, the sacred stillness of the space holding his words like a fragile, beautiful flame.

**Buddhism (Tibetan Book of the Dead):**

"In Buddhist teachings," he began gently, "particularly within the Tibetan tradition, there is a profound text known as the Bardo Thödol, or The Tibetan Book of the Dead. This sacred scripture serves as both a guide for the dying and a map for the living, illuminating the journey the soul undertakes in the space between death and rebirth—a realm known as the Bardo."

He paused, letting the name linger in the air like the soft chime of a distant bell, then continued, "The Bardo is not just a place; it is a state of consciousness—a luminous, shifting landscape shaped by the mind itself. Imagine standing between two worlds, where the familiar boundaries of time, body, and identity dissolve. In this space, the soul encounters vivid visions—dazzling lights, peaceful deities radiating serene compassion, and even wrathful, fearsome forms. But here lies the profound teaching: these are not external beings in the way we might imagine. They are mirrors, reflections of our own consciousness, the raw projections of our deepest fears, desires, wisdom, and ignorance."

Guruji's hands moved gently as if tracing invisible currents in the air. "For the enlightened—those who have cultivated awareness and insight during life—these visions are recognised for what they truly are: illusions, like clouds passing before the vast, unchanging sky of the mind. They see through the dazzling lights, the comforting figures, and the terrifying shapes, understanding that none of these appearances hold ultimate reality. With this recognition comes liberation—freedom from the cycle of birth and death, known as samsara."

His gaze grew tender, filled with both compassion and gravity. "But for those still bound by attachment, fear, or ignorance, the journey through the Bardo can be bewildering. Instead of recognising the visions as fleeting projections, they cling to them—reaching for what seems familiar, fleeing from what appears frightening. This clinging creates momentum, drawing the soul toward another birth, another life, shaped by the karmic imprints carried forward."

He paused, his words resting gently in the hush that followed, then added softly, "Think of it like a dream. If, while dreaming, you realise it's a dream, you're free. You can observe without fear, knowing nothing can truly harm you. But if you forget, the dream feels real. You run from monsters, ache for lost love, and feel trapped in what is only an illusion. The Bardo is the ultimate dream—a dream between lives. The awakened see through it. The unawakened get lost within it."

Guruji's voice grew quieter as if sharing a sacred secret, "This is why Tibetan Buddhists prepare for death not with fear, but with mindfulness. They meditate on impermanence, on the nature of mind, on compassion—so that when the great transition comes, they will not be strangers to the journey. They will recognise the Bardo as a mirror and, with wisdom as their guide, step through the illusions into the boundless light of liberation."

The silence that followed was not empty. It was full—full of wonder, reflection, and the quiet stirring of souls contemplating the great mystery of what lies beyond.

**Sufism (Islamic Mysticism):**

Guruji's voice softened, taking on a lyrical, almost musical quality as if the very air around him carried the rhythm of ancient poetry. "In Sufi mysticism," he began, his words flowing like a gentle stream, "death is not seen as an end, but as the return—a sacred homecoming to the Beloved, the divine source from which we all emerge. It is not a farewell but a reunion."

He paused, then recited softly, the words rolling off his tongue like sacred silk:

*'Don't grieve. Anything you lose comes around in another form.' "These are the words of Jalaluddin Rumi, the great Sufi poet whose verses are like lanterns guiding souls through the darkness of the unknown. For the Sufi, the soul is not a separate, isolated entity but a drop of water longing to merge back into the boundless ocean of divine love."*

Guruji's gaze drifted to the horizon as if seeing beyond what the eyes could hold. "Let me narrate a story," he continued, "of a dervish named Zayd, known for his simple life and boundless love for God. When Zayd was on his deathbed, his disciples gathered around him, weeping silently. But Zayd was radiant, his face glowing with an inner light. He looked at them with gentle amusement and whispered, 'Why do you cry? I am not leaving—I am arriving.'"

"In his final moments, Zayd's breathing grew shallow, but his eyes shone brighter than ever. His lips moved in silent prayer, and then, with a soft sigh, he passed. Later, one of his closest disciples shared a dream: in it, Zayd was standing in a vast, luminous garden unlike anything found on Earth. Flowers glowed with colours beyond imagination, and the air vibrated with a piece of music not heard with ears but felt with the soul. Zayd was surrounded by radiant beings—perhaps angels, perhaps other awakened souls—yet his eyes were fixed on a single point of dazzling light. At that moment, all separation dissolved. There was no Zayd, no garden, no dream—only the pure, boundless presence of the Beloved."

Guruji's voice grew even softer as if speaking directly to the heart.

"This is what the Sufis call the unveiling—the haqq, the ultimate truth. In life, we wear countless veils of identity, fear, desire, and illusion. Death, to the Sufi, is the gentle removal of these veils, one by one until nothing remains but the raw, infinite light of divine presence. Some describe meeting radiant beings or finding themselves in gardens beyond imagination, as described in the Qur'an. But beyond these images lies something deeper: not a place, but a state of being where all illusions dissolve, and only love remains."

He placed his hand over his heart, his eyes shimmering with emotion.

"In the end," he whispered, "death is not a shadow to fear but a threshold to cross. Not a goodbye but a return to the home we never truly left. The soul does not disappear—it unfolds, like a wave merging back into the ocean from which it was born."

**Taoism:**

Guruji's smile deepened, gentle and serene. "In Taoist wisdom," he began, his voice as fluid as a quiet stream, "death is not a tragedy, not an end, but a simple transformation—like the shift from day to night, from winter to spring."

The Tao Te Ching whispers to us:

*'When you realise where you come from, you naturally become tolerant, disinterested, amused, kind-hearted as a grandmother.'*

*"What is this place we come from? It is not a physical location. It is the Tao—the nameless, formless source of all things, the great flow of life that moves through the universe, through rivers and stones, through trees and stars, through you and me."*

He paused as if allowing the words to ripple across the stillness of the gathering. Then, with a quiet breath, he began a story.

"Long ago, in ancient China, there lived a humble farmer named Wei. Wei's life was simple: tending to his rice fields, caring for his old ox, and watching the seasons paint the world in ever-changing colours. One day, his beloved son fell from a horse and died. The villagers gathered, offering their tears and condolences, expecting Wei to be broken with grief. But Wei sat quietly under a peach tree, his face calm, his hands resting on his knees."

"A neighbour finally asked, 'Wei, why are you not weeping? Has sorrow not touched your heart?'"

Wei looked up, his gaze as steady as the earth itself, and replied, "Who can say what is truly good or bad?

My son has simply returned to the Tao, as the leaf returns to the soil. Just as spring does not mourn the passing of winter, I do not mourn the passing of my son. He was never truly mine to keep."

Guruji let the story linger, like the echo of wind in the leaves, then continued softly, "This is not indifference. This is in deep harmony with the nature of existence. In Taoism, life and death are not opposites—they are partners in the dance of transformation. Just as the river does not fear becoming the sea, the soul does not fear death because it is only flowing back to where it has always belonged."

"The Tao is like the great sky. Clouds come and go, but the sky remains untouched. We are the clouds—ever-changing, beautiful in form, but temporary. The Tao is the sky—vast, eternal, and unbound."

Guruji placed his hand gently over his heart, his eyes reflecting a tender wisdom.

"So, when the time comes, do not fear the letting go. Like Wei under the peach tree, know that nothing is truly lost. The soul does not vanish—it transforms, it shifts, it flows. It returns, not as a stranger, but as water returning to the ocean, as breath returning to the wind, as light returning to the source from which it was born."

The silence that followed wasn't empty. It was full—full of meaning, full of peace, like the stillness of a mountain after the wind had passed, leaving only the quiet hum of the eternal.

**Jainism:**

Guruji's voice grew soft. His eyes, filled with quiet contemplation, swept across the gathering as if to touch each soul with the gravity of his words.

"Jainism," he began, his tone reverent, "teaches that the soul—pure, radiant, yet bound by the invisible threads of karma—never pauses, never lingers. The moment the body breathes its last, the soul moves on, like a traveller stepping from one doorway into the next. There is no waiting room between lives, no hesitation, only the inevitable current of continuity."

He paused, then leaned in slightly as though about to share a sacred secret.

"Imagine a seed carried by the wind," he said gently. "Wherever it lands, it cannot choose the soil, the sun, or the rain. Yet it carries within it everything it needs to grow—a memory of what it has been and the potential of what it can become. The soul is like that seed. The karmas we accumulate in life—our actions, thoughts, and intentions—are etched into the very essence of our being. When the soul departs, it carries these karmic imprints, and wherever it is reborn, those seeds will sprout, whether as fragrant flowers or thorny brambles."

He let the image settle, like ripples on a pond, then continued with a story that seemed woven from the very fabric of time.

Guruji, after a pause, said, "Let me narrate a story: In the ancient city of Pataliputra, there lived a wealthy merchant named Surya Dutt. His life was marked by grandeur—opulent homes, lavish feasts, and endless riches. But his heart was a fortress of pride, sealed by greed and indifference to the suffering of others. When he died, his family erected monuments, engraved with his name, believing his legacy would endure. Yet Surya Dutt's soul, stripped of all material wealth, was carried swiftly into another life—not as a prince or a merchant, but as a poor, blind beggar in the dusty streets of a distant village."

"He could not remember his past life, but within him, the seeds of arrogance and selfishness remained. However, life as a beggar softened those seeds. He experienced hunger, dependence, and humility. And in this new life, despite his blindness, he learned to see with his heart. He shared what little he had with other beggars, spoke gently to children, and found peace not in gold but in kindness. When he died once more, the karmic seeds he had carried had blossomed into compassion, and his soul rose to a higher state of existence."

Guruji's gaze grew distant as if looking beyond the veil of the physical world.

"This is the profound lesson Jainism offers," he continued softly. "Our actions are not fleeting. They are threads woven into the eternal tapestry of our soul's journey. The ultimate goal is to purify the soul, to burn away the dense layers of karma through the triad of right conduct, right knowledge, and right faith. When the soul is free from all karmic bonds, it ascends to Siddhashila—a state of eternal bliss, beyond the cycles of birth and death, beyond suffering, beyond time."

He placed his hands gently together, fingers forming a simple mudra of balance.

"In that state," he whispered, "the soul shines in its original, unblemished form—pure as a diamond, infinite as the sky, weightless as the wind. No longer a seed carried by the wind, but the wind itself—free, boundless, eternal."

**A Universal Thread:**

Guruji drew in a quiet breath, letting the sacred stillness settle before his voice rose, gentle yet profound.

“Across deserts and mountains, in bustling cities and quiet villages, under star-strewn skies and temple domes, the stories echo,” he began, his gaze sweeping across the wide-eyed faces before him. “Different languages, different rituals, but listen closely—and you’ll hear the same thread woven through them all. A light. A guide. A review of life. A feeling of going home.”

He paused, letting the words ripple like a stone cast into still water.

“Let me tell you a story,” he said softly. “In the sun-baked hills of Mexico, there lived a young boy named Diego. At the tender age of seven, he fell gravely ill. His small body lay motionless, yet Diego later described an experience that no child could have imagined. He spoke of floating above his fragile form, of seeing his mother weeping beside his bed, her tears falling like silent prayers. But then—he saw a tunnel, filled with a radiant light, warmer than the sun, yet softer than a mother’s embrace. Standing in that light was his grandfather, who had passed away years before. He reached out, smiling, not with words but with a feeling—a pull, a call toward something vast and loving.”

Guruji’s fingers traced the air gently as if sketching the scene.

"Now, thousands of miles away, in the snow-laden landscapes of Finland, an elderly woman named Leena suffered a heart attack. She, too, spoke of a tunnel of light unlike any earthly glow, and there in that brilliance stood her sister, who had died decades earlier. Leena felt no fear, only an overwhelming peace, a sense of returning to a place more familiar than any home she'd ever known."

He leaned forward slightly, his voice a tender whisper.

"And then, in the sacred temples of Varanasi, an old priest named Hariram breathed his last. But in his final moments, his lips curled into a serene smile. Witnesses said he whispered of crossing a river, guided by beings of light, toward a realm where the soul rests in eternal grace."

Guruji's gaze drifted upward as if peering beyond the veil that separates the seen from the unseen.

"Different cultures. Different faiths. Yet the stories… remarkably the same. Some call it heaven. Others call it Moksha, Nirvana, the Clear Light of the Dharmakaya. In Sufi poetry, it's the Beloved's embrace. In Taoist thought, it's the return to the eternal flow."

He paused again, his voice softening like a sacred hymn carried on the wind.

"But perhaps," he continued gently, "what matters is not the name we give it, but the experience itself—the profound realisation that we are not our bodies, not even our names. We are timeless travellers on an endless journey. Drops returning to the ocean, sparks reuniting with the flame, rivers flowing back to the sea from which they came."

Silence followed, deep and sacred. It wasn't an absence of sound—it was a space filled with something vast and eternal, as if the universe itself had paused to listen.

Guruji finally placed his hand over his heart, his voice barely a whisper now. "We fear death because we believe it's an end. But what if it's not an end at all? What if it's simply the next chapter in a story that never truly began… because it was always there, unfolding, like the sky beyond the clouds?"

He placed the small stone gently back. "And when the journey continues beyond this life, it's not an end, but a return—a remembering of who we've always been."

*Abhilasha asked, "Guruji, what do spiritual teachings and firsthand accounts reveal about the 'tunnel of light' experience?"*

Guruji sat quietly for a moment. Then, with a serene breath, he began to speak. "The 'tunnel of light'…" he murmured, as if tasting the words. "It is one of the most profound and universal experiences shared by those who have danced on the thin line between life and death. Across continents, across centuries, people speak of it with the same awe—as if it's a memory etched into the very fabric of the soul."

He leaned forward slightly, his gaze distant, as though he was seeing beyond the physical world into realms unseen.

"Let me tell you a story," he said softly. "In a small village nestled within the snow-clad valleys of the Alps, there was a woman named Elena. She was a schoolteacher, an ordinary woman with no great interest in spiritual matters. One winter, after a tragic car accident, Elena's heart stopped for several minutes before she was revived. But in those few minutes, she described an experience more vivid than anything she had known in life."

"She spoke of leaving her body, floating above the wreckage, watching the scene with a strange, peaceful detachment. Then she felt herself being pulled—gently, irresistibly—into what she described as a tunnel. It wasn't dark but filled with a soft, radiant glow that seemed to come from everywhere and nowhere at once. As she moved through it, she felt an overwhelming sense of peace, warmth, and love—deeper than anything she had ever known. At the tunnel's end was a light so brilliant, yet it didn't hurt her eyes. She felt as though the light wasn't just around her, but within her, as if she was becoming part of it."

Guruji's voice grew softer, imbued with reverence.

"Elena wasn't religious, yet she spoke of this light as if it knew her completely—her joys, her sorrows, her flaws—and loved her unconditionally. She described a life review not as judgment but as understanding. She felt the ripple effects of her actions, both the kindness she'd offered and the pain she'd caused, not from a place of guilt but from a place of deep compassion. Then she was told, wordlessly, that it wasn't her time. And she woke up."

Guruji paused, letting the story settle in the hearts around him.

"Now, what's remarkable," he continued, "is that Elena's story is not unique. In the ancient texts of Tibetan Buddhism, the Bardo Thödol, or the Tibetan Book of the Dead, speaks of the 'clear light' encountered after death—a luminous presence that reveals the true nature of the mind. In Christianity, many near-death experiences describe this light as the presence of Christ or divine angels, welcoming souls home. Islamic traditions refer to the Barzakh, a barrier where souls await, often bathed in divine light. Even in the ancient Egyptian Book of the Dead, there are descriptions of the soul's journey through portals of light toward the afterlife."

His eyes softened, glimmering like the surface of a calm lake.

"But what is this tunnel? What is this light?" he asked gently, more to stir reflection than to demand answers. "Some scientists suggest it's the brain's response to trauma—a flood of chemicals creating vivid hallucinations. Perhaps that's partly true. But can chemicals explain the profound transformation many feel afterwards? People like Elena return changed—less afraid of death, more loving, more present."

Guruji said, "I believe the tunnel is not just a passage through space, but through consciousness itself. Imagine the soul as a drop of water, separated for a time from the vast ocean. At the moment of death, the tunnel is the stream guiding that drop back to the ocean of existence. The light is not outside us; it is what we've always been—a reflection of our true, boundless nature. The tunnel is the birth canal of the soul, not into life as we know it, but into life beyond form."

He smiled softly, his words landing like gentle feathers.

"So, Abhilasha," he said, "whether we call it a tunnel, a path, or a bridge, it seems to be a universal invitation. A reminder that when the time comes, we are not falling into darkness—we are returning to the light we never truly left."

*Apeksha asked, "Guruji, how do spirit guides play a role in assisting the soul immediately after death?"*

Guruji sat quietly for a moment, and then he spoke, "Apeksha," he began softly, "imagine a child lost in a dense forest. The towering trees, the unfamiliar sounds, the vastness of it all can stir fear. But then—a hand appears. Gentle, warm, familiar. A guide—not to carry the child, but to remind them of the path home. This is the role of spirit guides after death."

His eyes, filled with a quiet knowing, swept across the attentive faces gathered before him.

"In the immediate moments after the soul leaves the body," he continued, "there can be confusion. Imagine waking from a vivid dream, not quite sure where you are, lingering between two realities. The soul feels light, unbound, yet disoriented. This is where spirit guides appear—not as strangers, but as beings whose essence feels like home, like a melody the heart has always known."

Guruji leaned in slightly. "Let me narrate a story," he said, "of a young boy named Karim from the Middle East. He was only eight when he fell gravely ill. As he drifted between life and death, he described seeing a radiant figure standing at the foot of his bed. The figure was neither male nor female but radiated a warmth that filled Karim with peace. The guide spoke without words, communicating through feelings—assurance, love, and a gentle invitation. Karim later recovered, and when he awoke, he told his mother, 'I met someone who knew me before I was born."

"Across cultures and traditions, these guides appear in forms shaped by our beliefs and hearts," he explained. "In Tibetan Buddhism, they speak of the 'dakinis'—feminine energy beings who assist souls through the bardo, the intermediate state between lives. In Christian accounts, people describe angels bathed in light, their presence filled with an unconditional love that words fail to capture. Indigenous tribes often speak of ancestors—wise spirits of the lineage—who come to greet and guide the soul across the great river separating the worlds."

"But here's the deeper truth," Guruji said, "spirit guides are not just external beings. They are reflections of the soul's own higher wisdom. Like the moon reflecting sunlight on a dark night, they illuminate what's already within us. Some souls see guides in the form of ancestors, saints, or luminous beings because that's how their heart recognises divine presence. Others feel it as an overwhelming sense of peace like being wrapped in the arms of love itself."

He smiled gently, his eyes glistening with unspoken tenderness. "There is a beautiful passage from the Bhagavad Gita Chapter 15, Verse 15:

*sarvasya chaaham hridi sannivishto*
*mattah smritir jnaanam apohanam cha*
*vedaish cha sarvair aham eva vedyo*
*vedaanta-krid veda-vid eva chaaham*

Meaning: "I am seated in the hearts of all living beings. From Me come memory, knowledge, and forgetfulness. I am to be known through all the Vedas; indeed, I am the compiler of the Vedanta, and I am the knower of the Vedas."

This verse beautifully reflects the idea that the divine presence resides within every heart, manifesting as inner wisdom, guidance, and the silent witness to all of life's experiences.

Guruji's voice grew softer as if speaking directly to the heart.

And what do these guides do? They don't judge. They don't command. They remind. They show the soul glimpses of its journey—sometimes through a life review, where the soul feels the echoes of its actions, both gentle and harsh. But this review isn't about punishment. It's about understanding. The guide stands beside the soul, not as a judge but as a compassionate witness, saying, 'See? This was your journey. This was your growth.'

He paused, then added quietly,

"For some, the guide leads them toward the light. For others, toward another life, another chapter. But in every case, their presence whispers the same truth: *You are not alone. You have never been alone.*"

"So, Apeksha," Guruji said gently, "when the time comes for each of us to cross that threshold, we need not fear. There will be a guide—whether in the form of an angel, an ancestor or simply a feeling of profound love—waiting to take our hand and remind us of the way home."

The silence that followed wasn't empty. It was filled—with something eternal, something known yet long forgotten.

*Akanksh asked, "Guruji, what is the purpose of the life review, and how does it influence the soul's understanding of its past life?"*

Guruji began, his voice a gentle thread weaving through the hearts gathered before him: "Imagine standing at the edge of a vast, serene lake. You pick up a pebble—small, insignificant—and toss it into the water. You watch as ripples spread, expanding far beyond where the stone sank, touching shores you cannot even see. The life review is much like witnessing those ripples—not just the stone's fall, but the unseen waves it created in the vast ocean of existence."

Guruji paused, his gaze distant, as though peering through the veil of time itself.

"King Janaka, the 'King of Wisdom,' was no ordinary ruler. His kingdom flourished, but it was said his greatest empire was not the land he governed but the vastness of his consciousness. He was a seeker, a philosopher-king whose dialogues with sages like Ashtavakra are etched in the Upanishads, exploring the depths of self-realisation and the nature of the soul."

Guruji paused, letting the silence cradle his words before continuing.

"It is said that upon his death, Janaka's soul crossed the threshold between the worlds, entering not into judgment but into revelation. He found himself in a realm without time, where past, present, and future unfolded like an eternal tapestry. There, he was not King Janaka, the ruler draped in silks and adorned with jewels. No throne, no crown, no subjects. He was simply a soul—bare, luminous, and infinitely vulnerable."

Guruji's fingers gently traced the edge of his shawl, as if feeling the delicate threads of destiny woven within it.

"In this realm, his life unfolded before him—not as a distant memory, but as living moments. But here was the profound mystery: he experienced each event not just through his own eyes but through the hearts of those he had touched. When he gave alms to the poor, he felt not only the pride of a generous king but the tears of gratitude from the beggar whose life was changed. When he spoke harshly in anger, he felt not only the fire of his own wrath but the sting of humiliation in the heart of the one he had scorned."

Guruji's voice softened, rich with emotion.

"There was no divine figure standing in judgment. No celestial scales weighing sins against virtues. The universe did not need a judge because the soul, in its purest form, is its own mirror—reflecting truth without distortion. The soul itself was both witness and learner. It saw the interconnectedness of every action, every word, every fleeting thought. The ripples of his choices had touched countless shores, far beyond what he had known in his earthly life."

He looked around, his gaze tender and knowing.

"This is the sacred life review that many spiritual traditions speak of—not as punishment, but as awakening. The Upanishads tell us,

'As you think, so you become; as you sow, so shall you reap.'

But this is not about external rewards or punishments. It is about understanding. The soul grows not through fear of judgment, but through the light of awareness."

Guruji leaned forward slightly, his voice dropping to a near whisper.

"Imagine holding a fragile glass bowl filled with water. If you move it carelessly, the ripples disturb the clarity. But if you hold it with stillness and reverence, you see your reflection clearly. Life is like that. In the realm beyond, we do not face a deity's wrath—we face the undistorted reflection of our own hearts."

Guruji leaned slightly forward, his voice dropping to a reverent hush.

"This is the essence of the life review. It is not a courtroom where sins are tallied and virtues weighed. It is a sacred classroom. The purpose is reflection, not punishment. The soul sees how its choices wove the intricate fabric of interconnected lives. It experiences the echoes of its deeds—not to condemn, but to understand."

Guruji picked up a simple leaf, holding it delicately between his fingers.

"Consider this leaf. It did not choose where to fall, yet its landing nourishes the earth, feeds the soil, and becomes part of something greater. Our actions are like that—falling into the world, their impact spreading silently, often beyond our knowing. The life review allows the soul to see how even the smallest acts—a smile, a word, a gesture—held the power to heal or to harm."

Guruji's voice grew even softer, filled with tender wisdom.

"In many near-death experiences, people speak of this life review with profound emotion. There's the story of Annie Kagan, who wrote about her brother's afterlife journey in The Afterlife of Billy Fingers. Billy described watching his life like a panoramic movie, feeling the ripple of every joy and pain he'd caused—not with shame, but with clarity and compassion. There was no voice shouting 'right' or 'wrong.' Just an overwhelming understanding of how deeply connected we all are."

He placed the leaf gently back as if honouring its small place in the universe.

"The true purpose of the life review is growth. It is the soul's mirror, reflecting not just who we are but who we are capable of becoming. And in that sacred space, the soul doesn't carry guilt—it carries wisdom. It learns, evolves, and prepares for the next journey, wiser and more luminous than before."

The hall remained still, the only sound was the faint rustle of the wind—a soft, invisible witness to the echoes of lives long lived and lessons eternally learned.

*Akshatha asked, "Guruji, how do accounts of the immediate aftermath of death vary across spiritual traditions and personal experiences?"*

**Guruji's gaze softened, his voice carrying the weight of centuries of wisdom as he began to speak.**

"Akshatha," he said gently, "death is not a single door but a vast corridor with many thresholds. Different souls walk through it in different ways, guided by their beliefs, consciousness, and the echoes of the lives they've lived."

He paused, then continued with a story woven from the threads of diverse spiritual traditions.

"Imagine a great river," he said, "flowing endlessly, with countless streams feeding into it. Each stream is like a spiritual tradition, its waters shaped by the landscape it travels—mountains, forests, deserts—but in the end, all streams meet the same vast ocean."

**The Journey in Hinduism:**

Guruji's voice grew tender as if each word carried the weight of timeless wisdom.

"In the Bhagavad Gita (Chapter 2, Verse 20), Krishna tells Arjuna: '

*na jaayate mriyate va kadaachin*
*naayam bhutvaa bhavita va na bhuyah*
*ajo nityah shaashvato 'yam purano*
*na hanyate hanyamaane sharire*

Meaning: 'For the soul, there is neither birth nor death at any time. It is unborn, eternal, ever-existing, undying, and primaeval. It is not slain when the body is slain.'"

He paused, letting the profound truth sink in.

"This verse reveals the essence of Hindu philosophy—that the soul, or Atman, is beyond the confines of time, untouched by the cycles of birth and death. The body is like a garment, temporary and perishable, but the soul is the eternal wearer, discarding the old only to take on the new when the time comes."

Guruji's gaze softened, and he continued with gentle clarity:

"Upon death, many Hindus believe that the soul slips from the body as effortlessly as a bird leaving its nest. Some scriptures, like the Garuda Purana, describe the soul's journey after death in vivid detail. It speaks of Yama, the god of death, whose messengers—Yamadutas—guide the soul toward its next destination. But these are not grim or fearsome beings in essence; they are facilitators of transition, much like cosmic ushers."

He leaned in slightly, his hands gracefully illustrating the flow of his words.

"In some traditions, the soul is said to cross a symbolic bridge or river—a metaphor found in many cultures. In Hindu texts, there's the 'Vaitarani River,' described as a boundary between the earthly realm and the afterlife. For the righteous, it's as gentle as a calm stream, but for those burdened with negative karma, it's a turbulent crossing. This imagery reflects a deeper truth: our experiences after death mirror the seeds we've sown in life."

Guruji's voice grew softer, filled with a quiet reverence.

"Karma," he said, "is like the wind carrying seeds. Some seeds land in fertile soil, others on barren ground. But every action, thought, and intention leaves an imprint. After death, these karmic imprints guide the soul—not as punishment or reward, but as natural consequences, like ripples following a stone cast into the water."

He smiled gently as if seeing beyond the veil of life and death itself.

"So, the journey of the soul isn't random. It's a continuation, a flow, much like a river that remembers every bend and stone along its path. Death is not the end; it's simply the next chapter, written by the ink of our deeds and the parchment of eternity."

**The Christian Passage:**

"In Christian accounts," he began, "there is a recurring and profound imagery—the 'tunnel of light.' This isn't just a poetic metaphor, but a description echoed by countless people who've had near-death experiences across different times and cultures."

He paused as if to allow the sacredness of the words to settle.

"Many describe the sensation of moving through a long, dark passage, a tunnel, toward a radiant light unlike anything in this world. But this light is not blinding; it is warm, tender, and filled with an indescribable sense of peace and belonging. People often say that within this light, they feel completely known—every flaw, every mistake laid bare—yet embraced with unconditional love."

Guruji's gaze grew thoughtful as he quoted from the Scriptures, his voice carrying the echo of ancient wisdom:

"In the Gospel of John Chapter 14.2, Jesus offers a comforting promise:

*'In my Father's house are many rooms; if it were not so, would I have told you that I go to prepare a place for you?'.*

This speaks not just of a physical place, but of a spiritual reality—a realm of belonging, uniquely prepared for each soul."

Guruji, after a pause, said, "Let me narrate a story: There's an account of a woman named Betty Eadie, who had a near-death experience after surgery. She described being enveloped in darkness at first, then seeing a pinpoint of light in the distance. As she moved toward it, the light grew larger and warmer until she found herself standing in the presence of an overwhelming radiance. She felt as though she was returning home—not to a house or a city, but to a love she had always known, yet somehow forgotten."

Guruji's voice grew softer, more reflective.

"For some, this place is described as paradise—a garden of unimaginable beauty, much like the 'heavenly realms' in the Book of Revelation. Others recount sacred reunions with departed loved ones, encounters with angelic beings, or even Christ Himself. Yet, beyond the details—the landscapes, the figures, the symbols—the common thread is always the same: an encounter with pure, unconditional love."

He folded his hands gently as if cradling an invisible truth.

"And this love," he whispered, "asks no questions, demands no proof. It does not weigh our worth on scales of judgment. It simply embraces. It is as if the soul, stripped of all earthly identities, remembers what it truly is—light returning to light, love returning to love."

**Buddhist Teachings:**

Guruji's voice softened, carrying the weight of ancient wisdom, his words flowing like a gentle stream through the hearts of those gathered.

"In Buddhism, particularly within Tibetan teachings," he began, "the soul's journey after death is not seen as an abrupt end, but as a transition—a passage through what is known as the Bardo, an intermediate state that bridges the gap between death and rebirth."

He paused for a moment as if inviting everyone to step into that sacred space with him.

"The Tibetan Book of the Dead, or Bardo Thodol, serves as a guide for the soul during this journey. It describes the Bardo as a realm not bound by time as we know it, where the mind encounters vivid, dream-like visions—brilliant lights, majestic deities, and even terrifying forms that seem both real and surreal. But here's the key—the deities, whether peaceful or wrathful, are not external beings. They are not 'others' waiting to judge or punish. They are reflections, projections of the soul's own consciousness."

Guruji's eyes glimmered as if seeing beyond the present moment.

"Imagine holding a mirror—not one that reflects your face, but one that reveals the deepest layers of your mind. In the Bardo, every thought, emotion, fear, and wisdom comes alive, manifesting as radiant lights or shadowy figures. The enlightened recognise these as illusions, like mist rising from a lake at dawn. They understand that these visions hold no power over them, and with that realisation, they move beyond—into liberation, into the freedom from the cycle of birth and death."

He leaned forward slightly, his voice a tender whisper, sharing a story as ancient as the mountains.

"There is a tale of a monk named Karma Yeshe, a disciple deeply versed in Tibetan teachings. When he felt his life nearing its end, he told his students not to weep. He said, 'I will meet my mind face-to-face.' After his passing, his body remained in tukdam—a meditative state—where signs of decomposition were absent for days. It's said that during this period, his consciousness was navigating the Bardo, recognising each vision as his own creation, dissolving fear with wisdom."

Guruji's gaze swept across the silent faces before him.

"But not all souls carry such clarity. For many, attachments to life—desires, regrets, fears—cling like shadows. They see the radiant lights and are either drawn to them with craving or recoil in fear. Some souls grasp for familiar forms, unable to let go, and this very clinging pulls them back into the cycle of samsara—the wheel of birth, death, and rebirth."

He gently clasped his hands, his voice like a soft breeze.

"The Bardo is not just a place we pass through after death. It is here, too—in every transition, in every moment, we face change or uncertainty. Life itself is a series of Bardos, and each one is an opportunity to meet our mind with clarity, to dissolve fear with wisdom, and to awaken."

**The Sufi Homecoming:**

Guruji's voice grew softer, woven with the fragrance of ancient wisdom. "In Sufi mysticism," he began, his eyes reflecting an inner horizon, "death is not an end but a return—a homecoming to the Beloved. It is the soul's most intimate reunion, shedding the illusion of separation to dissolve into the boundless ocean of divine love."

He paused as though listening to an echo from centuries past, then continued,

"Jalaluddin Rumi, the great Sufi poet, captured this truth beautifully when he said,

*'Don't grieve. Anything you lose comes around in another form.'*

In these simple words lies the profound understanding that nothing is ever truly lost. The form changes, but the essence remains eternal, flowing from one vessel to another like water poured from cup to cup or like a melody shifting from one instrument to the next."

Guruji's gaze softened, and he began to tell a story—a story that seemed to rise not from memory but from the very soil of the earth.

"There was once a Sufi dervish named Zayd, who spent his life wandering the deserts of Persia, singing poems to the sky, searching not for riches but for the Beloved—the Divine Presence hidden behind all things. As Zayd grew old, his body weakened, but his heart burned brighter with an inner flame. On his final day, as he lay beneath the open sky, his disciples gathered around him, weeping softly, afraid to lose their beloved teacher."

Guruji's voice dipped into a tender whisper as if he were there beside Zayd himself.

"Zayd smiled faintly and said, 'Why do you grieve? The river does not mourn when it meets the ocean.' His breath grew shallow, yet his eyes shone with a light that seemed too vast for this world. Just before his final breath, he whispered, *'I see Him. The Friend has come.'*"

Guruji paused, letting the sacredness of the moment linger, then spoke again.

"After his passing, his disciples reported that the air around them felt different—charged with an invisible presence. Some described the scent of roses, though no flowers were near. Others felt an overwhelming peace, as if they were standing in the very heart of love itself. They understood then that Zayd had not gone anywhere. He had simply returned—like a drop merging back into the vast, infinite ocean."

His eyes shimmered with quiet knowing.

"In Sufi teachings, this return is known as 'fana'—the dissolution of the self, not into nothingness, but into everything. It is the unveiling of the haqq—the ultimate truth, where all veils of illusion fall away. Some souls, as they cross this threshold, describe seeing radiant beings, gardens of unimaginable beauty, or rivers of light. But beyond these visions lies something even greater: the realisation that the Beloved was never separate. The soul awakens to the truth that it has always been held, always been home."

Guruji closed his eyes for a brief moment, as if offering a silent prayer.

"Rumi once wrote,

*'When the soul lies down in that grass, the world is too full to talk about.'*

That's the mystery of death in Sufi mysticism—not an end, not even a beginning, but a silent, sacred merging where words fall away, and only love remains."

**Indigenous Wisdom:**

"Among Indigenous cultures—whether the Native American tribes, the Aborigines of Australia, or the tribes of Africa—death is seen as a passage, not an end. Many describe crossing rivers, walking spirit paths, or being met by ancestors. In these traditions, there's an intimate connection between the living and the dead. The ancestors are not distant memories—they are present guides, walking alongside us, whispering through dreams and the rustle of leaves."

Guruji paused, letting the depth of his words settle like a mist over still water.

"And yet, Akshatha," he said softly, "for all these varied stories, there is a universal thread—a sense of movement, of transition, of being met with something or someone familiar. Whether it's a light, a guide, an ancestor, or the divine itself, the soul does not journey alone. The fear we hold about death often comes from the illusion of separation, but these accounts, across time and culture, reveal the opposite. We are never truly alone."

He leaned forward slightly, his eyes reflecting both mystery and warmth.

"Think of it like this," he whispered. "When the sun sets, it disappears from one horizon only to rise on another. Death, too, is just a sunrise we cannot see from this shore."

The silence that followed was not empty but filled with the quiet hum of realisation, like the space between heartbeats—a reminder that life, in all its forms, never truly ends.

## The Sacred Interlude

After a long, reflective pause, Guruji gently signalled for a short break. The devotees slowly dispersed—some taking a quiet stroll under the ancient banyan tree, their minds still echoing with the depth of his teachings, while others gravitated toward the beverage counter, where the rich aroma of freshly brewed coffee and herbal tea wafted through the air.

The air was thick with contemplation, as if the collective energy of the devotees' thoughts had created an invisible current of stillness and reflection. Some sat in silence, staring into the horizon, while others murmured in hushed voices, discussing the revelations that had unravelled in the session.

Seated on a stone bench under the peepal tree, Astyn, eyes filled with wonder, whispered, "I can't believe I am here…"

There was a tremor in her voice—an awe that comes when one stands at the edge of something profound, something life-altering.

Kieron, leaning against the wooden railing, let out a deep breath before saying, "The session… it was revealing. So many things we have spent our lives fearing—things that kept us awake at night, things that felt so heavy on our chests—now, they don't seem as terrifying."

His words hung in the air like the last notes of a distant temple bell, resonating in the hearts of those around him.

After a long silence, Sujitha spoke, her voice barely above a whisper yet filled with an ache so deep that it demanded to be heard.

"There is one question that has always haunted me... What will happen to my father and mother? What will happen to me, to my children, after we die? Where will we go? Will we ever meet again?"

Her words struck a chord.

There was a shift in the atmosphere—an unspoken sorrow, a universal fear, a truth so undeniable that it bound them all in a quiet moment of understanding.

The group fell into silence. No one rushed to answer. Vasudeva, Padma, Apeksha, and Akshaya simply nodded, their eyes reflecting the same unspoken emotions. They, too, had wrestled with these questions and had felt the same fear gnawing at the edges of their souls.

The wind blew gently, rustling the temple bells hanging at the archway. Somewhere in the distance, a monk's voice rose in prayer, his chant merging seamlessly with the breeze.

Just then, Kiran, standing near the threshold of the Buddha Hall, signalled to them. His face was calm, his gesture subtle—yet its meaning was clear.

"It's time for the next session."

The devotees slowly rose from their seats, some still lost in thought, others wiping away silent tears. They walked towards the hall, their hearts heavier yet somehow lighter—as though the weight of their questions had finally been acknowledged, even if not entirely answered.

And in that moment, they knew—they were exactly where they were meant to be.

# CHAPTER VIII

## The Interlife

*"The interlife is not a pause, but a sacred space of reflection and choice, where the soul reviews its past and consciously shapes its next journey, guided by the wisdom it has gained."*

*– Shree Shambav*

### Synopsis

*This chapter delves into the concept of the interlife, a metaphysical space between lifetimes where the soul reflects on its previous incarnation and prepares for its next. Drawing from various spiritual teachings, the chapter explores how this period of reflection serves as an opportunity for growth and understanding, allowing the soul to assess the lessons learned and the challenges faced during its most recent life. The idea of "soul contracts" is introduced—agreements made before birth that guide the soul's purpose and experiences in each lifetime. The chapter also explores how the soul, with the assistance of spiritual guides, makes important choices regarding its future path, including lessons to focus on, relationships to heal, and personal growth to achieve. Additionally, the chapter investigates how the interlife serves as a preparatory phase, where the soul actively participates in shaping its destiny, while still being influenced by larger universal laws. Finally, it addresses how experiences in the interlife may support or challenge the idea of free will, considering whether souls are free to choose their paths or are guided by predetermined plans. Through this exploration, the chapter provides insights into how the soul evolves and consciously steers its spiritual journey over multiple lifetimes.*

**The Interlife: A Realm of Reflection and Choice**

The hall was wrapped in a deep, contemplative silence. The devotees sat in anticipation, their minds brimming with questions that had long haunted them.

Guruji, seated with an air of eternal patience, looked at Vidyarthi, who had just asked, "Guruji, what happens after death? What is the soul's journey between lives?"

Guruji smiled, his eyes reflecting a wisdom that transcended lifetimes.

"Vidyarthi, imagine a river flowing toward the vast ocean. As it journeys, it nurtures life along its banks, carves through mountains, and reflects the changing sky. But what happens when it reaches the ocean? Does it disappear? No—it merges, only to rise again as mist, forming clouds before falling back as rain to begin another journey."

The devotees leaned in, hanging on to every word.

"Such is the cycle of the soul," Guruji continued. "It travels through lifetimes, gathering experiences, touching other souls, learning, unlearning, and evolving. But between these journeys, between one life and the next, there exists a sacred space—the interlife—a realm of reflection, choice, and divine preparation."

**A Realm Between Worlds**

A hush spread through the hall as Guruji's voice deepened with meaning.

"Many ancient texts and spiritual seekers describe the interlife as neither entirely material nor entirely ethereal—a vast, luminous realm where time, as we understand it, ceases to exist. It is here that the soul, having shed its earthly body, stands before the mirror of its own actions—not in judgment, but in deep understanding."

*Apeksha, her voice trembling, asked, "Guruji, does the soul feel pain in that space?"*

Guruji's gaze softened.

"Not in the way you think, my child. The soul does not experience pain as the body does. Instead, it watches its past life unfold like a grand cosmic play. Every word spoken, every action taken, every sorrow inflicted or received—it all returns, not as a punishment, but as a lesson. The soul feels the love it gave, and it feels the suffering it caused—not to be condemned, but to truly understand."

A tear slipped down Sujitha's cheek. "Then what happens next, Guruji?"

**Soul Contracts: The Blueprint of Life**

"Before taking birth again, the soul enters a sacred space where it chooses its next life," Guruji explained. "These are known as soul contracts—agreements made with other souls before descending to Earth. These contracts are not punishments or rewards but carefully chosen lessons. Just as a student selects subjects before entering a new grade, the soul chooses experiences before stepping into a new body."

Vidyarthi furrowed his brows in thought. "Guruji, does this mean that our suffering is something we chose?"

Guruji nodded gently.

"Suffering is not given; it is chosen for growth. A soul that wishes to understand patience may choose a life filled with trials. Another who seeks to learn compassion may decide to care for a loved one in great suffering. What appears as misfortune is often a deeply intentional lesson, agreed upon long before birth."

Sam, who had been listening in silence, finally spoke. "But Guruji, why would a soul choose pain? Why would it agree to loss and suffering?"

Guruji's expression was serene yet filled with immeasurable depth.

"A river does not weep when a leaf floats away from its surface. It carries the memory of that leaf in its currents. Souls come into our lives not to stay forever but to teach us something essential. When their lesson is complete, they move on. But the love, the connection—it never dies. It remains woven into the fabric of our being, forever."

*Sam looked down, his hands trembling. "Does this mean the people we lose were always meant to leave us?"*

Guruji nodded slowly.

*"Loss is an illusion of the physical world. In the interlife, souls reunite with those they have known before. Those who were our parents, our children, our beloved friends—many of them will return in new forms in our next journey. Sometimes, the mother we lost in this life returns as a daughter in the next. Sometimes, an enemy reappears as a sibling, offering a chance for reconciliation. These are the sacred cycles of the soul's journey."*

## The Role of Spiritual Guides

*Vasudeva, deep in thought, asked, "Guruji, are we alone in this process? Who helps us understand all this after we die?"*

Guruji's face radiated a knowing smile.

*"You are never alone, Vasudeva. In the interlife, the soul is met by* ***spiritual guides****—beings of light and wisdom who help it make sense of its journey. Some of these guides may be souls you have known before—an ancestor, a teacher, a dear friend who has crossed over. Others may be divine beings assigned to your spiritual evolution. They do not dictate your choices, but they illuminate the path, helping you understand which lessons still remain unfinished."*

*Astyn, who had remained quiet, finally spoke. "Guruji, if all this is true, why don't we remember it when we are born?"*

Guruji chuckled softly.

"If a student enters an exam already knowing the answers, what is the purpose of the test? Forgetting is part of the process, my child. It is the veil that makes the experience of life meaningful. But the soul carries whispers of its past—sometimes in dreams, sometimes in unexplainable feelings, and sometimes in a deep sense of knowing. If you sit in stillness, if you listen closely to your inner voice, you may remember fragments of the agreements you made before coming here."

The devotees sat in complete silence, absorbing the immensity of Guruji's words.

Finally, Guruji exhaled deeply, his voice dropping to a gentle whisper.

"The interlife is not just a space between death and rebirth. It exists in every moment of transition. When you lose someone, when you change paths, when you stand at the crossroads of transformation, you are—whether you realise it or not—in the interlife. It is the space of endings and new beginnings."

He looked at each devotee, his eyes filled with infinite love.

"Let this wisdom not be just knowledge, but an experience. Go within. Reflect. And when your time comes, may you walk into the interlife not with fear, but with understanding."

The flames flickered. The wind outside howled softly, as if nature itself had bowed in reverence to the truth spoken. The devotees sat unmoving, lost in the vast, sacred silence of realisation.

*Roopa, her voice filled with quiet curiosity, asked, "Guruji, what is the interlife, and how do spiritual teachings describe its purpose in the soul's journey?"*

**The River Between Two Shores**

Guruji said, "Roopa, imagine a great river flowing between two lands—one shore is the life you leave behind, and the other is the life you are yet to enter. The river itself, that space between, is the interlife—a sacred pause in the soul's eternal journey."

The devotees leaned in, drawn into the world his words painted.

"Many believe that when we leave the physical body, we are simply gone, but the soul never ceases to exist. In the interlife, the soul pauses, not to be judged, but to understand. It stands before a mirror—not one made of glass, but of truth. Every action, every word, every thought is reflected back. But there is no punishment, only learning."

*Roopa asked, "Guruji, does that mean we relive everything?"*

Guruji nodded.

"Yes, but not in the way you might think. You do not merely see your past life; you feel it. Every moment of kindness, every act of love—it washes over you like a warm embrace. But equally, every moment of pain you cause to others returns—not as punishment, but as an experience. You feel the sorrow you inflicted, not because a higher power demands it but because the soul itself seeks to understand. It wishes to grow."

A hush spread through the gathering. The night wind rustled the leaves as if even nature paused to listen.

## Choosing the Next Journey

*Apeksha, deep in thought, asked, "But what happens after that, Guruji? Do we just wait?"*

Guruji smiled.

"No, my child. Just as a traveller does not stay forever in a resting place, the soul does not remain in the interlife. It prepares. It chooses."

The devotees exchanged glances.

"Before taking birth again, the soul enters a sacred council, often guided by higher beings—spiritual guides who have walked this path before. Together, they review what was learned and what remains to be understood. The soul does not simply return to another life by accident—it chooses its next experiences with great care."

Bhavya furrowed her brows. "But Guruji, why would a soul choose to suffer?"

Guruji exhaled softly, his voice carrying both compassion and deep knowing.

"Imagine a sculptor standing before a block of marble. He does not weep at the stone's roughness. He does not curse the chisel that strikes it. Instead, he knows that every cut, every chip, is shaping something beautiful. The soul, too, chooses experiences—not to suffer for suffering's sake, but to refine itself, to understand, to awaken."

"A soul that wishes to understand patience may choose a life filled with waiting. A soul that seeks to master compassion may be born into hardship, so it may learn to embrace others in their pain. Every challenge is a lesson written in the ink of divine wisdom."

*Dev, who had been silent, whispered, "So… every difficulty we face was chosen?"*

Guruji nodded.

"Not all struggles are preordained, but many of them are. Have you ever met someone for the first time and felt as though you've known them forever? Have you ever walked into a place and felt an unexplainable connection? These are echoes of soul contracts—agreements made before birth. Some souls promise to meet again, to guide, to love, and even to challenge one another. Sometimes, the one who breaks your heart in this life is the same soul who, in a past life, once saved you."

*Sam exhaled sharply. "But what of those who hurt us deeply? Are they part of our soul contract, too?"*

Guruji's gaze softened.

"Yes. Even those who bring us pain are sometimes the ones who, at another time, loved us most. A soul may agree to play the role of a betrayer, not out of cruelty, but to teach a lesson only they could give. Sometimes, the greatest teachers arrive disguised as suffering."

**The Ultimate Realisation**

Guruji looked at them all, "Vidyarthi, the interlife is not simply a waiting room between lives—it is the sacred space where the soul rediscovers itself. It is the realm where the veil is lifted, where all illusions fall away, and only truth remains. It is there that you will see yourself—not as a body, not as a name, but as pure, radiant consciousness, eternal and ever-expanding."

"And when your time comes to cross that river, may you do so not with fear but with the knowing that nothing is ever truly lost? The ones you love, the ones who have left, the ones you are yet to meet—all are but travellers in this great cosmic journey, destined to find one another again."

*Vasudeva, his voice steady yet laced with curiosity, asked, "Guruji, how do theories of soul contracts and life purpose shape the decisions made in the interlife?"*

## The Weaver and the Threads

Guruji, after a pause, said, "Vasudeva, imagine a weaver sitting before an intricate loom. Each thread is a life, each knot a decision, and each pattern a destiny unfolding. The weaver does not simply throw the threads together randomly—every strand is placed with care, each colour chosen with intent. This is how the soul prepares for its next journey in the interlife."

The devotees leaned in, drawn into the world, his words painted.

"Before a soul returns to the physical world, it enters a sacred space—a realm of reflection, wisdom, and preparation. It does not return blindly; it chooses. It remembers every lifetime it has lived; every lesson learned, every bond formed. And then, guided by higher beings—some call them spiritual guides, others call them the Council of Elders—the soul begins the work of weaving its next life."

*Bhavya's brows furrowed. "Guruji, why would a soul choose to suffer? Why would it sign a contract that leads to pain?"*

## The Sculptor and the Stone

Guruji exhaled softly, his voice carrying both compassion and deep knowing.

"Bhavya, if you were a sculptor, would you cry every time your chisel struck the marble? Would you curse the hammer for shaping the stone? No, because you would know that each strike is a step toward something beautiful. The soul, too, is an artist—shaping itself through experience. It does not see pain as punishment but as a tool for transformation."

"A soul that wishes to understand patience may choose a life of waiting. A soul that seeks to master love may be born into circumstances that test its ability to forgive. A soul longing for strength may place itself in the midst of great hardship, not as suffering, but as a lesson written in the ink of divine wisdom."

*Padma, her voice barely above a whisper, asked, "But what of those who hurt us deeply? What of betrayal, abandonment, and loss? Are they part of the soul contract, too?"*

Guruji's gaze softened, and he looked at each of them with infinite tenderness.

"Padma, have you ever watched a great dancer perform? Notice how they do not move in only one direction, nor do they stay in the light alone. They weave between shadow and illumination, creating beauty in the contrast. Life, too, is a dance between joy and sorrow, love and loss, union and separation."

"Yes, sometimes the very people who hurt us are souls we once loved in another lifetime. A dear friend may take on the role of an enemy, not out of malice but because the lesson must be learned. A child lost too soon, a lover who walks away, a betrayal that cuts deep—these, too, are part of the design."

*Alice wiped a tear from her cheek. "Guruji…, then why don't we remember? Why don't we recall our soul contracts?"*

## A Test of True Learning

Guruji smiled gently.

"Imagine you are given the answers to every exam before you sit for the test. Would you still learn? Would the knowledge be real, or would it simply be memorised? The soul chooses to forget so that the experience is genuine. Yet, it leaves behind clues—déjà vu, a sudden connection with a stranger, an unexplainable pull toward a place or a person. These are whispers from the interlife, reminding us of the contracts we once made."

"The forgetting is not a punishment—it is an opportunity. Because if you choose love without remembering why, if you choose kindness without knowing the reason, then that choice is pure. It is untainted by obligation. And that, my children, is the true test of the soul."

## The Web of Souls: Eternal Connections

*Vasudeva, still deep in thought, asked, "So Guruji, are we destined to meet the same souls again and again?"*

Guruji nodded.

"Yes, Vasudeva. Just as a river returns to the ocean, souls return to one another. Some souls agree to walk together through many lifetimes—sometimes as lovers, sometimes as family, sometimes even as adversaries. These are the ones who shape us the most. Do not be surprised if a stranger feels at home or if an enemy feels oddly familiar. The threads of destiny are woven tightly, and nothing is by chance."

Guruji said, "Vidyarthi, the interlife is not a place of judgment, but of understanding. It is there that the soul sees the full picture, the grand design. It is there that it chooses its next chapter, not with fear but with wisdom. And when your time comes to return to that space between lives, may you not go with regret but with the knowing that everything—every joy, every sorrow, every meeting, and every farewell—is part of something far greater than you can yet comprehend."

**The Luminous Path:**

A gentle breeze carried the scent of jasmine and sacred basil through the ashram, weaving through the silent gathering of devotees.

*Padma, her voice filled with curiosity and reverence, asked, "Guruji, what role do spiritual guides play in helping souls reflect and prepare for future incarnations?"*

Guruji, seated on an asana, closed his eyes for a moment as if listening to something beyond the reach of ordinary hearing.

**The Lantern Bearers of the Soul**

"Padma, imagine you are walking through a vast, ancient forest. The path before you is covered in mist, and the road behind is barely visible. You carry a lantern, but its glow is faint. Just when the darkness feels overwhelming, you see a figure ahead, holding a brighter light, waiting to guide you. This, my dear, is the role of a spiritual guide."

He paused, watching the flickering expressions on the devotees' faces.

"Spiritual guides are souls of immense wisdom who have transcended their own cycles of birth and death. They exist not to dictate but to illuminate—to hold the lantern so that the soul may see its own path. In the interlife, when a soul steps beyond the veil of the physical world and into the realm of reflection, these guides are there, waiting with patience and love."

*Bhavya leaned forward, her eyes searching Guruji's face. "Guruji, do we know these guides? Have we met them before?"*

Guruji smiled.

"Yes, Bhavya. Often, they are souls we have walked with across many lifetimes. Some were once our teachers, our friends, and even family. Others may never have incarnated at all, existing only in realms beyond this one, serving as guardians of wisdom. But no matter where they come from, their purpose remains the same—to help us remember who we truly are."

**The Sacred Mirror:**

"When a soul leaves its body, it does not dissolve into nothingness. It enters a realm where the illusion of time softens, where the boundaries between past, present, and future fade. Here, the spiritual guides meet the soul, not with judgment but with deep compassion. The soul is shown the tapestry of its past life—not as a list of achievements and failures, but as an intricate story woven with love, suffering, joy, and lessons."

"It is like standing before a sacred mirror," he continued, his voice calm yet powerful, "a mirror that does not distort, that does not flatter or condemn. The soul sees itself as it truly is—not just the actions taken, but the intentions behind them, the ripple effects of every word spoken, every kindness offered, and every moment of pain inflicted."

*Vasudeva spoke softly, "But Guruji, wouldn't this be painful? To see all of one's mistakes so clearly?"*

Guruji nodded gently.

"Yes, Vasudeva, it can be. But remember, pain is not punishment—it is a teacher. And the spiritual guides stand beside the soul, not to shame it, but to help it understand. To ask, 'What have you learned? How have you grown? What do you wish to experience next?' They help the soul see that every challenge was a stepping stone, every sorrow a sculptor shaping its wisdom."

**The Soul's Choice: Preparing for the Next Life**

"After reflection comes the great moment of decision. With the guidance of these luminous beings, the soul begins to weave its next journey. It chooses its family, its circumstances, its challenges—not as a victim, but as an architect designing the temple of its next life."

"Imagine an artist standing before a vast canvas," Guruji said, his voice filled with depth. "The artist does not paint blindly. They choose their colours with care.

A bold stroke of red for passion, a soft touch of blue for peace, a dark shade for lessons in resilience. The soul does the same. It does not ask, 'How can I have an easy life?' but rather, 'How can I grow? How can I serve? How can I love more deeply?'"

*Apeksha, her eyes shimmering with tears, whispered, "Guruji, does this mean we agreed to everything that happens to us?"*

## The Music of Free Will

Guruji's expression softened.

"Yes and no, Apeksha. Life is not a rigid script but a melody—one with a structure but also space for improvisation. Before birth, the soul chooses its primary lessons, its core relationships, and its destined meetings. But within that, free will is always alive. How we respond, how we grow—that is up to us. The spiritual guides do not interfere with this freedom, but they whisper, they nudge, they send signs—sometimes as intuition, sometimes as a dream, sometimes as a stranger speaking the exact words we need to hear."

He looked around at his devotees, their faces reflecting the firelight, their souls absorbing the ancient truth.

"When you feel lost, when life feels unfair when suffering weighs heavy on your heart—remember, you are never truly alone. The lantern bearers walk with you. And when your time comes to return to the interlife, to reflect and begin again, they will be there, waiting with love, ready to guide you home."

### The Eternal Symphony:

*Akshaya, his voice steady yet filled with the weight of curiosity, asked, "Guruji, how do experiences of the interlife support or challenge the idea of free will in the soul's journey?"*

### The Weaver and the Loom: Destiny and Choice

Guruji, seated in his usual stillness, let the question linger in the air, allowing its depth to settle within each heart present. Finally, with a gentle nod, he spoke, "Akshaya, imagine a weaver sitting at a loom, her hands skilfully threading together the intricate patterns of a vast and endless tapestry. The threads she uses are not random—they are chosen carefully, each colour holding meaning, each weave carrying the weight of past choices. But within this pattern, she has freedom. She can change the design, add new colours, and adjust the flow. This is how free will and destiny exist together, not as opposites, but as partners in the soul's unfolding journey."

He looked at the fire, watching the flames dance as if weaving their own unseen design in the air.

"The interlife is like the weaver's pause—where the soul steps back from the loom and observes the tapestry it has woven. Every choice, every experience, every joy and sorrow is visible, not as separate events but as a grand, interconnected design. The soul sees where the patterns are harmonious and where the threads become tangled. And in this space of deep reflection, it chooses how to weave its next story."

## The River's Path: Destiny as a Current, Free Will as the Oar

Guruji turned to the devotees, his gaze steady yet filled with warmth.

"Many ask—do we truly have free will if we are bound by karma, by past choices, by lessons we must learn? The answer, my dear ones, lies in how we understand fate. Imagine a river flowing from the mountains to the sea. The soul, before birth, chooses the river—the challenges, the lessons, the significant moments. But how we navigate the waters, how we respond to the rapids or the still pools, that is always within our hands."

*Vasudeva, deep in thought, murmured, "So the soul chooses the circumstances, but our reactions shape the journey?"*

Guruji smiled.

*"Exactly, Vasudeva. Free will is not about escaping the river but about learning to steer the boat. Some choose to surrender to the current, letting life take them where it may. Others fight against it, resisting the lessons. But the wisest souls learn to work*

*with the flow, understanding that even the roughest waters can lead to new shores of wisdom."*

## The Theater of Souls: Choosing the Roles We Play

*Padma, her voice barely above a whisper, asked, "Guruji, does that mean we agreed to all the pain we experience in life?"*

Guruji's expression softened, and he nodded gently.

"Yes, Padma, but not as punishment, not as suffering forced upon us. Think of life as a great play and the interlife as the moment when the actors step off the stage and gather behind the curtains. Here, the soul meets with other souls—those who were its family, its friends, even its enemies. Together, they decide what roles they will play in the next act."

*Bhavya's eyes filled with tears. "Even those who hurt us?"*

"Yes, Bhavya," Guruji said with deep compassion. "Sometimes, the greatest lessons are learned through pain. A soul that loves you deeply may choose to play the role of your adversary, not out of malice, but to help you grow. Imagine a master swordsman—if he only faces weak opponents, he will never sharpen his skill. So, too, the soul must face challenges to grow in wisdom and love."

## The Unwritten Pages: The Power of Choice

The devotees sat in silence, absorbing the weight of Guruji's words. Finally, Akshaya spoke again, "But Guruji, if so much is planned in the interlife, does that mean our choices here do not matter?"

Guruji's eyes sparkled with knowing.

"Ah, Akshaya, think of a book. Before it is written, the author may outline the plot, sketch the characters, and set the themes. But the details—the words themselves—are unwritten until the moment of creation. The soul may choose the lessons before birth, but how we live those lessons, how we embrace or reject them, is entirely up to us."

Guruji said, "At every moment, we are both the author and the protagonist of our own story. The interlife offers guidance, but the pen is always in our hands. That, dear ones, is the divine balance of free will and destiny."

A deep silence filled the air, not of emptiness but of understanding.

## A Pause Between Journeys

The afternoon sun hung high, casting golden light upon the ashram, filtering through the ancient trees. The scent of sandalwood and jasmine lingered in the air as Guruji, after a long, contemplative pause, gently instructed the devotees to take a break for their midday meal. A soft murmur of gratitude filled the space as the devotees slowly dispersed, making their way toward the food canteen, their minds still immersed in the depth of the morning's discourse.

The meal was simple yet nourishing, prepared with devotion, and served with humility. Some devotees, after their meal, sought refuge under the cool shade of towering trees, reclining against their sturdy trunks, allowing the silence to seep into their being. Others wandered into the Brindavan Garden, where the fragrance of fresh blooms intertwined with the soft hum of bees, creating an atmosphere of serenity. A few chose to take long solitary walks, their footsteps merging with the rhythm of their thoughts, reflecting on the wisdom imparted by Guruji.

Beneath the vast embrace of the ancient banyan tree, Padma and others gathered at their usual meeting place. The thick roots cascaded down like sacred threads from the heavens, a witness to countless discussions, contemplations, and revelations shared over time. The gentle rustling of leaves formed a soothing melody as they settled into quiet conversation.

"Tomorrow morning, we will be returning to our daily routines," Padma sighed, looking at the faces of those who had, over the days, become more than companions in learning—kindred spirits on the same sacred journey. "But I heard from Akshaya that the remaining course of our session will be discussed in the next retreat."

Vasudeva, ever perceptive, turned his gaze toward the distance and said with a soft smile, "Look, Akshaya is here."

As if summoned by the thought itself, Akshaya approached, his presence radiating a quiet strength as though he carried within him the very essence of Guruji's teachings.

Nita, unable to contain her curiosity, asked, "Akshaya, is it true that this session will continue in our next retreat?"

Akshaya nodded, a knowing glimmer in her eyes. "Yes. Guruji intends for us to continue the journey in the next retreat. There is still much to be explored, many layers yet to unfold."

A spark of anticipation flickered in Alice and Sofia's eyes. "Then we will be meeting soon again," they chimed in unison, their voices filled with excitement.

Aarna, Dev, and John exchanged smiles, their unspoken bond reaffirmed at that moment. There was comfort in knowing that their path, though temporarily diverging, would soon converge again under the guidance of Guruji.

Rohith, with curiosity lacing his words, asked, "Will the retreat be held in Kanchipuram or Kodaikanal?"

Akshaya, with a reassuring nod, answered, "It will be in Kanchipuram."

For a moment, there was silence, not of emptiness but of contentment—of souls finding solace in shared purpose, of knowing that this journey, though scattered in time and space, was one they would walk together.

Kiran, who had been quietly observing, finally signalled, gently reminding them that it was time to return to the Buddha Hall. One by one, the devotees rose, brushing the dust off their robes, their hearts a little lighter, their minds a little clearer. As they walked back, the banyan tree stood still, a silent witness to another moment woven into the tapestry of their spiritual journey.

And so, with each step, they carried forward not just words and lessons but the quiet promise of reunion, of deeper understanding, of the unfolding path that awaited them in the next retreat.

# CHAPTER IX

## Consciousness in Creating Reality

*"Consciousness is not a passive observer of reality, but the very fabric through which the universe is woven, shaping our experiences, perceptions, and the reality we live within."*

*– Shree Shambav*

### Synopsis

*The chapter delves into the profound role of consciousness in shaping our reality, not just during life but also after death and in realms beyond the physical. Consciousness is explored as the underlying force that organises, filters and gives meaning to our experiences, perceptions, and even our understanding of existence itself. By examining how consciousness influences our thoughts, emotions, and actions, the chapter sheds light on its power to manifest and shape the world we experience. It also explores the interconnectedness between thought, energy, and existence—how our inner world influences the external and how consciousness may transcend the physical boundaries of the body, continuing to shape realities in realms beyond death. The chapter also addresses the intersection of spiritual and scientific perspectives on this concept, comparing how different fields approach the idea of consciousness as a creative force. In doing so, it invites reflection on how understanding the true power of consciousness can transform the way we approach life, death, and the mysteries beyond.*

## The Infinite Weave of Consciousness

The air was thick with the fragrance of jasmine, and the distant sound of temple bells echoed through the ashram. The Buddha Hall held an atmosphere of reverence. Devotees sat in deep stillness, their eyes fixed on Guruji.

After a long moment of silence, Guruji spoke, his voice carrying the weight of ancient wisdom.

"Abhirami," he said, his gaze meeting hers with the warmth of the eternal, "The Role of Consciousness in Creating Reality is a truth deeper than the ocean and vaster than the sky. It is the unseen current shaping the world around us, the unseen brush painting the canvas of existence."

Abhirami leaned forward, her heart yearning for understanding. The others, too, listened with bated breath, sensing that what was about to be revealed was more than just knowledge—it was the essence of being itself.

## The Ocean and the Wave

Guruji continued, "Imagine consciousness as an infinite ocean, boundless and without end. Each individual life is like a wave rising from its depths. The wave believes it is separate, individual, and unique—just as we believe we are separate beings. But what happens when the wave dissolves back into the ocean? Does it cease to exist, or does it return to its true nature? Life is no different. Consciousness does not begin with birth nor end with death—it simply shifts form, like the wave merging back into the sea."

The devotees sat in silence, absorbing the profound analogy.

"During life," Guruji explained, "our consciousness shapes every experience we encounter. Every thought we nurture, every emotion we embrace, becomes the architect of our reality. The world we see is not separate from us—it is a reflection of the energy we project."

## The Mirror of Existence

*Padma whispered, "Guruji, does that mean our thoughts create our reality?"*

Guruji nodded, a soft smile playing on his lips. "Reality is not something we passively experience—it is something we actively create. Think of existence as a great mirror. If you stand before it with anger, it reflects anger. If you stand before it with love, it reflects love. The world is not happening to you, Abhirami—it is happening through you."

A hushed realisation passed through the devotees, as though a veil had been lifted.

**Beyond the Veil of Death**

"And what happens after death?" Abhirami asked, her voice barely above a whisper.

Guruji's eyes held the wisdom of lifetimes. "Just as dreams feel real while you are in them, so too does life. But what happens when you awaken? Death is but a transition, not an end. The moment consciousness sheds the body, it enters the realm beyond—the space where thoughts are no longer bound by time, where reality is shaped instantaneously by the mind. If one leaves the body in fear, they experience fear. If one leaves in peace, they enter peace."

*A shiver ran down Abhirami's spine. "So, even after death, our consciousness creates our experience?"*

Guruji nodded. "Indeed. That is why sages across ages have taught us to cultivate a peaceful mind, to purify our thoughts, and to nurture love—because the journey does not end when the body is left behind. It continues."

The Interwoven Fabric of Thought, Energy, and Existence

*Vasudeva, who had been listening intently, asked, "Guruji, how does consciousness connect with the physical world? If it is so powerful, why do we feel limited?"*

Guruji smiled, his voice carrying the softness of moonlight. "Consciousness is like the wind—it moves unseen but shapes all that it touches. The thoughts we hold become the energy we emit. That energy interacts with existence, weaving the fabric of our lives. If a person constantly dwells in sorrow, they unknowingly attract more sorrow. If they cultivate gratitude, life brings them more reasons to be grateful. Every thought is a seed planted in the soil of the universe. What you water with attention grows."

A deep stillness settled over the hall. The devotees were no longer just listeners; they were seekers on the threshold of a great revelation.

**The Dreamer and the Dream**

Guruji's voice softened as if he were speaking from the very heart of the cosmos. "In the great dance of existence, you are both the dreamer and the dream.

Life is not happening outside of you—it is unfolding within you, shaped by the consciousness you carry."

A gentle breeze rustled the curtains as if the universe itself had paused to listen.

"So, I ask you, Abhirami, and all of you—what reality will you create? What world will you shape? Will you choose fear or love, suffering or joy? The choice has always been yours."

Guruji smiled softly and began to recite a poem titled, **"The Dreamer's Awakening."**

Eyes closed, and in the hush of sacred stillness,
it was felt—not as a thought, fleeting and weightless,
but as truth, woven into the marrow of being.

*"What reality will be created?"*

No longer a wanderer adrift in the vast unknown,
not apart from the universe—
but the rhythm of its breath,
the quiet pulse between silence and song.

The ocean—
depths unfathomed, tides unbroken,
cradling both storm and stillness
in the arms of eternity.

The wave—
rising, falling, surrendering to motion,
never lost, only becoming,
always returning home.

The dream—
woven from whispers of stardust and longing,
a vision shaped by light unseen,
soft as dawn, infinite as dusk.

And the dreamer—
eyes closed, yet seeing everything,
not waiting for destiny,
but daring to create it.

A deep hush enveloped the devotees. For in that moment, they were not merely hearing words—they were witnessing the truth of their own being, the power of their own consciousness.

Abhirami closed her eyes, and for the first time, she felt it—not just in her mind, but in her soul.

She was not separate from the universe.
She was the ocean.
She was the wave.
She was the dream.
And she was the dreamer.

*Kieron asked, "Guruji, how does consciousness shape our perception of reality during life and after death?"*

Guruji closed his eyes for a brief moment, as if gazing beyond the fabric of the visible world. With a serene smile, Guruji opened his eyes and began, "Kieron, consciousness is not just an observer of reality; it is the very thread that weaves reality itself. It is like the sun that shines upon the ocean—when the waters are still, it reflects the light perfectly, but when disturbed, it distorts the reflection. The nature of your consciousness determines how you perceive existence."

He paused, letting the thought settle before continuing, "During life, your consciousness acts like a lens through which you interpret the world. Every joy, every sorrow, every experience is coloured by the state of your awareness. When the mind is clouded with fear, the world seems harsh and unforgiving. When the heart is filled with love, the same world appears beautiful and compassionate. Reality is not something separate from you; it is something shaped by the depths of your being."

Guruji's voice softened as he spoke of the afterlife, "After death, the body dissolves, but consciousness does not. It continues its journey, carrying the imprints of thoughts, desires, and emotions. Just as a dream does not vanish the moment you wake up but lingers as a memory, the soul carries forward its experiences into the interlife. The state of one's consciousness at the time of death shapes what one experiences next. If the mind is at peace, the transition is smooth, like a river flowing gently into the ocean. If there is attachment, fear, or regret, it may feel like a storm that pulls one into turbulence."

He then gave an analogy, "Imagine a sculptor working on a statue. Every stroke of his chisel, every detail he carves, shapes the final form. Life is that sculpting process, and consciousness is both the sculptor and the stone. If the sculptor is unaware, the statue remains rough and incomplete. If he is mindful, it turns into a masterpiece. Just as the sculptor does not cease to exist when he puts down his chisel, so too does consciousness not end when the body is no more—it continues its journey, carrying the impressions of its creation."

The devotees sat in silence, absorbing the profound words. The wind rustled through the trees, carrying the scent of sandalwood and jasmine as if nature itself bowed in reverence to the eternal truth.

Guruji looked at Kieron, his voice now a gentle whisper, "So, the key is awareness. To shape reality with clarity during life and to enter the realms beyond with grace, nurture your consciousness. Feed it with wisdom, with love, with the understanding that you are not merely experiencing reality—you are creating it."

*Martina asked, "Guruji, what is the relationship between thought, energy, and existence in realms beyond the physical?"*

Guruji closed his eyes for a brief moment, as if listening to a song that only the soul could hear. Then, with a serene smile, he opened his eyes and looked at Martina.

He began, his voice soft yet carrying the depth of an ocean, "Thought, energy, and existence are not separate threads but strands of the same divine weave. Just as a river is inseparable from the water that flows through it, existence itself is shaped and moulded by the movement of thought and energy."

He gestured toward the sky. "Imagine the cosmos as an endless ocean of energy. Every thought you have is like a stone dropped into that ocean, creating ripples that extend far beyond what the eye can see. In the physical world, the effects of thought are subtle, like ripples on the surface. But in the realms beyond—the realms of pure consciousness—thought is not a whisper; it is a force. It has the power to shape entire realities."

Martina and the devotees listened in awe as Guruji continued. "In the physical world, we often believe that existence is fixed, solid, something that happens to us. But in the higher realms, where the body is shed, and only the essence remains, existence is more fluid.

Thought is not just a passive reflection of the mind—it is an architect, a creator. Just as an artist brings a vision to life with colours and strokes, the soul, in its purest state, sculpts its own experience with thought and energy."

## The Traveller of Light

Long ago, in a time beyond time, there was a seeker—a soul that had wandered across many lifetimes, gathering wisdom like a river collects stones on its bed. This traveller, unburdened by the weight of the physical world, stepped beyond the veil of form into a realm of pure light.

At first, he was bewildered. There was no ground beneath his feet, no sky above his head, no horizon to guide him. Instead, he found himself in an endless expanse of shimmering energy, flowing like golden currents in an ocean without shores. He reached out, but his hands found nothing to grasp—no walls, no trees, no landmarks of any kind. It was a world without boundaries, where existence itself was fluid, shifting like the ripples of a dream.

As he stood there, unsure of where to go, a thought arose within him: *What is this place?* And in an instant, the space around him began to respond. The energy stirred like silk caught in an invisible breeze. Fascinated, he let his mind wander. He thought of a garden, lush and serene, a place where the soul could rest.

Before his very eyes, the golden currents of energy began to condense, taking form. Emerald green leaves unfolded, their surfaces glistening as though kissed by morning dew. Flowers of impossible hues bloomed—colours that had no name, glowing softly like tiny stars. The air filled with a fragrance so delicate, so profound, that it was as if the very essence of peace had taken scent. Birds of light, their wings translucent, appeared out of nowhere, singing melodies that resonated not in the ears but in the heart.

A sudden thrill rushed through the traveller. *Is this my creation?* He wondered. If a mere thought could bring forth such beauty, what else could be shaped by the mind? His excitement grew, and with it, so did the world around him. He imagined towering mountains rising into the heavens, their peaks touching the very fabric of eternity. At once, magnificent peaks surged from the golden mist, standing tall with an ethereal glow. He envisioned a river, and before him, waters of liquid silver began to flow, reflecting the infinite sky.

But then, a shadow of doubt crept into his mind. *What if I am lost? What if I never find my way back?*

The moment the thought surfaced, the entire realm trembled. The sky, once a boundless expanse of radiant light, darkened into an ominous storm. Thunder roared like the anger of forgotten gods, and lightning split the sky into jagged veins of fire. The tranquil river swelled into a furious flood; its silver waters now blackened with unrest. The air grew heavy, thick with the weight of fear, and the mountains that had once stood in silent grandeur now seemed to loom over him, their peaks sharp and menacing.

Panic gripped the traveller. He tried to run, but there was nowhere to go. The world was shifting around him, not by external forces, but by the storm within his own mind.

And then—deep within—he heard a voice. A whisper, gentle yet powerful.

*"You are not lost. You are not powerless. You are both the traveller and the creator of the path."*

The words resonated through him like a forgotten truth suddenly remembered. He closed his eyes, steadied his breath, and quieted his thoughts. He let go of fear, releasing it like a bird set free from a cage. He focused on peace, on love, on the stillness that lay beneath all things.

And just like that, the storm began to fade. The sky softened into gold once more. The river calmed, its surface returning to its silver serenity. The towering mountains stood once again as symbols of majesty, not of menace. The garden, though momentarily shaken, was still there, its flowers blooming with quiet grace.

The traveller understood. This realm was not governed by the fixed laws of the physical world. It was shaped by the movements of his own consciousness. Thought was not a passive thing here—it was the very fabric of creation. Fear could summon darkness, but love could summon light. Doubt could birth storms, but clarity could restore peace.

A deep stillness filled him, not just in this realm but in his very essence. He had not merely stepped into another world—he had stepped into the realisation of his own power.

And with that knowledge, he continued his journey, not as a wanderer lost in an unknown land, but as a creator walking the path of his own making.

Guruji looked at the devotees, his eyes gleaming with ancient wisdom. "This is the power of thought and energy in realms beyond. The soul does not simply wander—it manifests. This is why great sages teach us to cultivate purity of thought, to nurture love and wisdom, for what we carry within will shape what we see beyond."

A hush fell over the gathering. The wind whispered through the trees, as if nature itself bowed in agreement.

Guruji's voice softened, filled with deep compassion. "So, understand this truth: your thoughts are not mere shadows in the mind—they are seeds cast into the infinite field of existence. Nurture them well, and they will bloom into worlds of beauty, within and beyond."

**The Dance of Consciousness and Reality**

*Sujitha's voice carried the weight of curiosity, a question that had echoed through the minds of seekers and scholars alike for centuries. "Guruji, how do spiritual and scientific perspectives align or differ on the idea of consciousness creating reality?"*

Guruji smiled, his gaze distant as if peering into realms unseen yet ever-present. "Ah, Sujitha," he said gently, "this question is like a river that flows through two great lands—one of science, where knowledge is measured, observed, and dissected, and one of spirituality, where truth is felt, intuited, and experienced. Both rivers originate from the same source, and though they take different paths, they inevitably merge into the vast ocean of understanding."

He paused, letting the thought settle among the gathered devotees before continuing.

"Let me tell you a story."

**The Weaver of Light**

Long ago, in an ancient kingdom cradled between towering mountains and an endless sky, there lived a young artist named Arin. But Arin was no ordinary painter—his brush did not merely capture the world as it was; it revealed the world as it *could* be. His art was more than pigment on canvas; it was a whisper from the unseen, a bridge between thought and reality.

The villagers spoke in hushed tones of his miraculous gift. When he painted golden fields of wheat, the land would yield an abundant harvest, even in times of drought. When his brush touched the canvas with images of rivers teeming with fish, the fishermen's nets would overflow. His strokes carried energy beyond human understanding, as if the very gods had bestowed upon him the power to shape destiny itself.

But in the royal court, whispers turned to scepticism. The king, a man of reason and logic, dismissed these tales as mere coincidence. Yet curiosity gnawed at him. Was it chance? Was it an illusion? Or was there something beyond his understanding?

One day, he summoned Arin.

"They say you do not just paint," the king said, studying the young artist with sharp, searching eyes. "They say your brush bends reality to its will. But is it not simply the nature of things unfolding as they must?"

Arin met the king's gaze, his expression calm, knowing. "Your Majesty," he said, "may I paint something for you?"

The king hesitated for a moment, then nodded.

Arin unrolled a vast canvas and dipped his brush into a well of deep, luminous colour. But instead of painting the familiar wheat fields or rivers, he envisioned something never before seen—a grand palace. His hand moved with effortless precision as if guided by something greater than himself.

Slowly, a magnificent structure took form. Towers reached for the heavens, crowned with golden domes that gleamed like the morning sun. A bridge of shimmering glass extended over a tranquil lake, its waters reflecting the sky's endless expanse. Gardens unfurled in wild, celestial colours, bearing blossoms unseen in the known world. Every detail pulsed with almost divine energy as if the palace had always existed somewhere beyond the veil of time, waiting to be called into being.

When Arin finally stepped back, the court fell silent. The king, a man rarely moved by beauty, found himself unable to look away.

Something stirred deep within him—an inexplicable knowing, a certainty that had not been there before. This palace, which had never existed, could exist. The vision had taken root in his mind, solid and undeniable.

With newfound conviction, the king summoned his finest architects, engineers, and craftsmen. He handed them the painting—not as mere art, but as a blueprint, a map to something greater. Brick by brick, stone by stone, Arin's vision took shape in the waking world.

Years passed. And when the final golden dome was set into place, the king stood before the palace, seeing not just a structure of stone and glass but the undeniable truth of what had unfolded.

He turned to Arin, wonder in his eyes. "So, you do not shape reality with magic," he said, his voice hushed. "You shape it with vision."

Arin bowed, a knowing smile playing on his lips. "Your Majesty, is that not magic enough?"

The wind carried his words across the palace grounds, where they settled like seeds in the minds of those who listened.

For the first time, the king understood—creation begins not in the hands but in the mind. Reality does not merely unfold; it is *woven* by the dreamers, the visionaries, the ones who dare to see beyond what is, into what *could be.*

### Science and Spirituality—Two Paths, One Truth

Guruji's voice carried the weight of centuries of wisdom as he turned back to the devotees. "Just like Arin, we all paint our realities—not with brushes, but with thoughts, intentions, and beliefs. Science and spirituality approach this truth from different angles, yet they speak of the same mystery."

"In science," he continued, "quantum physics tells us that particles exist in multiple possibilities until observed—until consciousness interacts with them. This is not unlike the blank canvas of Arin's world, where reality takes form only when envisioned. Experiments in the quantum realm suggest that observation affects the behaviour of matter, hinting at a connection between consciousness and physical existence."

"In spirituality, we have long known this. The sages and mystics have taught that the world is but a projection of the mind. The Upanishads speak of *Maya*, the illusion shaped by perception. The Buddha spoke of reality as a mirror of the inner world. Great yogis have demonstrated how focused consciousness can alter bodily states, bend the laws of nature, and even manifest the seemingly impossible."

"But where science demands proof," Guruji said, "spirituality asks for experience. Where science seeks to measure, spirituality seeks to feel. One observes from the outside, the other from within. And yet, they are dancing partners in the same cosmic rhythm."

The devotees sat in silent awe. Sujitha's eyes gleamed with the light of realisation. "So, Guruji, reality is both discovered and created?"

Guruji nodded. "Yes, Like Arin's palace, reality is first imagined before it is built. What you focus on, you shape. What you believe, you become. The question is not whether consciousness creates reality—the question is, *what reality are you creating?*"

The air around them seemed to hum with unseen energy, as if the universe itself had leaned in to whisper its ancient secrets.

*Nita asked, "Guruji, in what ways can understanding the power of consciousness transform our approach to life and death?"*

Guruji closed his eyes for a moment, allowing silence to settle over the gathering like a warm embrace. "Nita," he said, his voice as gentle as the evening breeze, "understanding the power of consciousness is like a river realising it is not merely flowing toward the ocean but that it is the ocean in motion. It transforms the way we live, and in doing so, it transforms the way we embrace death."

The devotees leaned in as Guruji continued. "Let me tell you a story... Long ago, in a distant land, there was a man named Pushkara who feared death more than anything. From childhood, he had seen loved ones leave this world, their absence, carving hollow spaces in his heart. The finality of it haunted him. He became obsessed with escaping death, seeking out sages, healers, and even alchemists who promised immortality. But none could offer him freedom from his fear."

One day, a wandering mystic came to his village. The man radiated peace, his presence like still waters undisturbed by any storm. Pushkara, desperate for answers, fell at his feet and pleaded, "Tell me, O Wise One, how do I escape death?"

The mystic smiled. "Come with me."

He led Pushkara to the edge of a vast lake, its surface reflecting the sky so perfectly that it was impossible to tell where the water ended and the heavens began.

"Look into the lake," the mystic instructed.

Pushkara peered in and saw his own reflection staring back. 'What do you see?' asked the mystic.

"Myself," Pushkara answered.

The mystic picked up a small stone and dropped it into the water. Ripples spread, distorting the reflection.

"Now, what do you see?"

"The image is broken," Pushkara admitted.

The mystic smiled and waited. Slowly, the ripples faded, and the reflection of Pushkara's face returned unchanged.

"You believe you are this reflection, Pushkara. You believe you are this body, this fleeting form. But tell me, when the water is disturbed, does the sky itself break? Or does only the reflection waver while the sky remains untouched?"

Pushkara's breath caught in his throat. "The sky remains untouched," he whispered.

The mystic placed a hand on Pushkara's shoulder. "Then understand this: You are not merely the reflection in the water. You are the vast sky above it. This body will one day dissolve, just as the reflection may waver and disappear. But what you truly *are*—consciousness itself—remains eternal, untouched by time, birth, or death."

For the first time in his life, Pushkara did not feel fear. He felt the embrace of something greater than his limited self. He walked away from the lake that day, not as a man seeking to escape death, but as one who had begun to understand life.

Guruji paused, allowing the story to settle in the hearts of his listeners like seeds waiting to bloom. Then, with a knowing gaze, he spoke once more. “Nita, when we recognise that we are more than this temporary body, more than our fleeting identities and experiences, our approach to life transforms. We stop clinging. We stop fearing. We begin to live fully, embracing every moment as sacred. And when the time comes for this body to return to the earth, we do not meet death as an end but as a doorway—one we have walked through many times before.

Consciousness is the great river, flowing from one life to another, carrying with it the wisdom of all it has seen. When we awaken to this truth, we do not fear drowning, for we realise—we *are* the river itself.”

Silence hung in the air, thick with the weight of realisation. Nita’s eyes shimmered, not with sadness, but with something deeper—understanding. She bowed her head in reverence, whispering, “Thank you, Guruji.”

The others remained still, their minds dancing between the world they had known and the vastness they had just glimpsed.

# WRAP UP

## A Journey Through Life After Death

### The Eternal Dance of Devotion and the Interplay of Consciousness

Guruji exhaled softly and began, his voice weaving the story like a sacred thread binding the seen and unseen.

“Long ago, in the eternal realm of Goloka, where the fragrance of divine love fills the air, where the melody of Krishna’s flute keeps the cosmos in rhythm, there was a devotee—Sridhama. His devotion to Krishna was unmatched, unwavering, and absolute. But in his unwavering faith, there was also a blindness, a single-mindedness that saw Krishna as the sole object of love, dismissing all else. Even Radha.”

Guruji's voice softened, the weight of his words pressing upon the listeners.

"Sridhama could not bear to hear Radha's name chanted with such reverence. 'Why do you sing Radhe, Radhe?' he asked, his voice carrying the sharpness of disbelief. 'Only Krishna is worthy of devotion! Why do you place a mere woman on the same pedestal as the Divine?'"

Yet, the devotees of Radha continued, their voices rising in ecstatic chorus, 'Radhe, Radhe!' Their love for Her was unwavering, for they knew—without Radha, there is no Krishna; without Krishna, there is no Radha. They are not two but one, intertwined beyond mortal understanding.

But Sridhama, in his unyielding devotion, challenged Radha Herself. He sought to prove that Her name was but an illusion, a veil of Maya. And so, in his arrogance, he tested the power of Her Name.

A butterfly fluttered past, its iridescent wings shimmering like liquid light. "Say, *Radhe, Radhe*," Sridhama commanded.

The devotees, hesitant but obedient, chanted, 'Radhe, Radhe!' And in an instant, the butterfly was reduced to ashes. A gasp spread through the gathering.

Then came a bird, its song a whisper of the heavens. Sridhama's voice rang again, filled with certainty, "Say Radhe, Radhe once more."

Again, the devotees chanted. Again, the bird burned to nothingness.

A murmur of doubt slithered through the devotees. Was Sridhama right? Was Radha's name a force of destruction rather than liberation? Had they placed faith in illusion?

And then, from among them, a little girl stepped forward. Eyes filled with innocence, she looked up at Radha and spoke softly, "Say, Radhe, Radhe."

Fear gripped the devotees. Would this child meet the same fate?

But Radha, ever compassionate, gazed at the girl with infinite tenderness. She knew what none of them understood yet. That creation and dissolution are but two sides of the same breath of existence.

Meanwhile, Krishna, watching in silence, found Himself at an impasse. He was both the Supreme and the Beloved; He could not choose between the purity of Sridhama's devotion and the eternal truth of Radha's love.

And so, He withdrew, seeking solitude to reflect. "Give Me time," He said, "to understand who among you is the highest in devotion."

Krishna left, but not without setting a test. He instructed Sridhama, "Guard this door. Let no one enter."

And Sridhama, ever loyal, stood at his post.

Yet, within His heart, Krishna called for Radha, not with words, but with longing—an invisible pull that transcended speech, that existed beyond sound, beyond form.

And Radha felt it. Love, in its truest form, cannot be restrained. It is not a choice; it is an irresistible force, a magnet drawing soul to soul, self to Self.

She ran to Krishna, her very being aflame with divine yearning. But at the threshold, she found Sridhama blocking her path.

"Move aside," she implored. "He calls me."

"I hear nothing," Sridhama retorted. "Prove to me that He has called you."

"His voice is not heard with ears, but felt with the soul."

But Sridhama would not yield. Blinded by his own perception of truth, he mistook love for illusion. And in that blindness, he committed the greatest of acts—the act of separation.

He cursed Radha. "For a hundred years, You shall forget who You are. You shall wander the Earth, unaware of Your own divinity."

A silence followed. A silence so deep it felt as though the cosmos itself had paused.

And Radha, with a smile both sorrowful and knowing, accepted the curse. Because love does not resist—it surrenders. Because even separation, in the grand design, is a part of a union.

At that moment, realisation dawned upon the devotees. They had misunderstood.

For when they had chanted Radha's name, the butterfly had not perished—it had transformed. It had become the bird. And when the bird was called, it had leapt lifetimes and become the girl.

And the girl—oh, the girl—was now free.

With shining eyes, she turned to Sridhama and whispered, "You cursed Radha, but you do not know what you have done. I was that butterfly. I was that bird. And now, because of Her Name, I have transcended millions of lifetimes. I have been liberated."

At last, Sridhama saw. The illusion was not Radha but his own mind's limitations. And he fell to his knees, begging for forgiveness.

Krishna emerged then, His smile a mixture of mischief and divine purpose, for it had all been His Leela. The curse was not a punishment but a necessity—a veil is drawn so that love could be rediscovered, so that the eternal dance could continue, over lifetimes, across realms.

And so, the devotees resumed their chant, 'Radhe, Radhe!' But this time, the name was not mere sound—it was a bridge between the finite and the infinite, a name that held within it the secret of creation, dissolution, and liberation.

Guruji's voice trailed off, his eyes reflecting galaxies unknown.

He looked at his devotees, their hearts swollen with emotion, and spoke, his words soft yet thunderous:

"And so, consciousness is not bound by physicality. It is not confined to life or death. It moves, it shifts, it transforms, creating and dissolving realities as we call them forth. To awaken is to recognise that we are both the dream and the dreamer, both the butterfly and the boundless sky."

A silence fell upon the gathering, not empty, but full—full of understanding, of awe, of something unspoken yet deeply felt.

Nita, her voice barely above a whisper, asked, "Guruji… was this just a story?"

Guruji smiled, a knowing glimmer in his eye. "Is this life not a story too?"

And in that moment, they understood.

**The Night of Reflection: A Journey Continues**

Guruji, after a long pause, rose gracefully from his asana and began to walk slowly, signalling the close of the day's session. A profound stillness settled over the ashram, broken only by the rustling of leaves in the cool night breeze and the faint murmur of a distant prayer. Above them, the sky stretched vast and infinite, a celestial canvas where stars shimmered like silent witnesses to the mysteries unfolding in the hearts of each seeker.

Though Guruji had left the Buddha Hall, his words lingered in the air, reverberating through the minds of the devotees. They wove through their thoughts like an unbroken thread, binding them to a truth that felt just beyond their grasp—close enough to stir the soul, yet distant enough to beckon them forward. The retreat had ended for now, but the journey was far from over. In a few weeks, they would gather again in Kanchipuram, where the deeper mysteries of life, death, and the realms beyond would be unveiled.

As Guruji's figure disappeared into the night, the devotees stood in quiet reverence. Some walked away in silent contemplation, as if absorbing the day's revelations like parched earth welcoming the first drops of rain. Others lingered, seeking solace in whispered conversations, their voices hushed as though afraid to disturb the delicate fabric of understanding that had begun to weave itself within them.

Near the fireplace, a small group gathered—Akshaya, Vasudeva, Akanksha, and Apeksha—drawn together by an invisible bond, a connection forged through shared awakening. The glow of the fire flickered in their eyes, mirroring the quiet flame that had been kindled within them. The night stretched on, heavy with reflection yet light with the quiet promise of a truth that was still unfolding.

Nita sighed, her voice tinged with wonder, "The days have just flown away like the wind—like moments slipping through our fingers."

Espen and Astyn nodded, their eyes reflecting the unspoken transformation within.

"A new dimension has opened in my life," Espen murmured, almost to himself. "A thought I never imagined could exist… yet now, I can't unsee it."

John, who had been listening in quiet contemplation, turned toward Bhavya. There was a weight in his gaze, not of burden but of longing—for deeper understanding. "Bhavya, what happened next?" he asked.

Bhavya looked into the fire, as if searching for the memory within its dancing flames. The warmth on her face reminded her of the warmth she had once lost—the warmth of those who had left her, those she had mourned with grief so consuming that it had seemed impossible to emerge from it.

She exhaled, her voice steady but heavy with the echoes of past sorrow.

"As days went on, the pain only deepened. No matter how much my friends tried, the wound was too vast, too raw. The weight of loss clung to me like an unshakable shadow. I could not revive myself."

She paused, the night air filling the space between her words.

"One day, a neighbour who had seen my suffering said to me, 'Come with me to Kanchipuram. You will find solace.'

"My first question was, 'Will I find my loved ones?'

"She only smiled and said, 'You will find your answers.'"

The fire crackled, filling the moment of silence that followed. The devotees listened with rapt attention, feeling as if Bhavya's journey was their own, as if her questions mirrored those buried deep within them.

"With no other path left, I travelled to Kanchipuram. And as soon as I entered the ashram, something shifted. The air felt lighter, and the people smiled with a radiance I could not understand. There was a serenity there—an unspoken assurance that all was as it should be."

Bhavya's voice softened as if she were reliving the moment.

"After a long wait, Akshaya led me to meet Guruji in the Brindavan Garden. I expected a sage sitting in deep meditation, surrounded by scriptures and incense. But instead… I saw a simple man, immersed in life itself—feeding the birds, tending to the plants, whispering to the flowers as if they were dear friends."

She smiled faintly, shaking her head at the memory.

"And then, without even turning, he said, 'Bhavya… One day, we all have to go. This plant, these birds, myself, and you.'"

A hush fell over the group. The inevitability of that truth settled upon them like a gentle but undeniable weight.

"He looked at me and continued, 'This is the ultimate truth. Why do you cry about losing them? They have continued their journey. Their time with you was never meant to be forever. If they stayed, who would complete their path? Be happy for them, for they have moved forward. Death is an illusion—the soul does not end, and it only sheds its vessel to continue forward. And this applies not just to them, but to all beings.'"

Bhavya swallowed, her voice trembling with remembered emotion.

"Like a child, I wept. I wept for all the pain I had held onto. I wept for the truth I had refused to see. I wept because, in that moment, I understood."

Guruji placed his hand on my head and said, 'Soon, you will realise.'

"The moment his hand touched me, I felt it. A surge of energy, a current of something beyond words, rushed through me. Every doubt, every grief, every fear I had carried—dissolved like a mist before the morning sun.

"And now, I wonder… what would my life have been if I had never met Guruji?"

A heavy silence settled over the devotees, but it was not an emptiness—it was full. Full of emotion, of realisation, of something unspoken yet deeply understood. Some had tears in their eyes. Others simply closed their eyes, feeling the truth settle within them.

Above them, the vast night sky stretched endlessly, the stars twinkling like luminous beings bearing silent witness to their awakening.

No one spoke for a long time.

And then, softly, someone began to chant:

*"Radhe… Radhe…"*

The chant spread as if carried by an unseen wind. The fire crackled, the leaves rustled, and the stars shone on.

For the journey had only just begun.

# Life Coach and Philanthropist

Shree Shambav is the visionary founder of the Shree Shambav Ayur Rakshita Foundation (www.shambav-ayurrakshita.org). He founded this institution with a lofty goal: to recognise human identity across gender, ethnicity, and nationality. Through this organisation, he wants to assist all communities in realising their full potential and the intrinsic beauty of life.

Shree Shambav, a Life Coach, is dedicated to supporting people on their journeys of self-discovery and empowerment. He assists people in discovering who they are, determining what inspires and drives them, and overcoming limiting ideas. His approach clarifies what one wants in life, assisting people through goal-setting and a step-by-step process for achieving them. He empowers people to make deliberate and responsible decisions, allowing them to identify their blind spots and evolve as individuals via the use of numerous strategies and tools.

The foundation's bold, uncompromising, and compassionate ventures are always aimed at initiating the "Inner Transformation" process. They focus on spiritual growth, personal growth, and self-healing while emphasising that true progress lies in "Inclusive Growth and Co-existence." This philosophy drives all their initiatives, encouraging a holistic approach to development and well-being.

Under Shree Shambav's leadership, the foundation has launched several impactful movements:

Shree Shambav Green Movement: This mission is to create a healthy, green, and clean earth through responsible water conservation and greening initiatives. The movement strives to make the world a green paradise by encouraging sustainable living and environmental responsibility.

Shree Shambav Vidya Vedhika (Vizhuthugal): This project aims to help students and children by offering training, books, stationery, and uniforms. It aims to provide the next generation with the tools and resources they need to excel both academically and personally.

Shree Shambav and his foundation exemplify the spirit of compassion, transformation, and inclusive growth via their work, which has a profound impact on individuals and communities around the world. His work exemplifies the power of acknowledging and nourishing the human spirit, creating a world in which everyone can reach their full potential and appreciate the beauty of life.

# TESTIMONIALS

**Journey of Soul - Karma** - "We die in our twenties and are buried at eighty." Remember that nothing can stop someone who refuses to be stopped. "Most people do not fail; they simply give up." Shree Shambav deserves full credit. It allowed me to sit and consider what I might miss out on in life. The author has delved into every aspect of our daily lives. How can a seemingly insignificant change in these seemingly insignificant details bring us such joy? The Soul of Journey teaches you the "art of living" as well as the "art of dying."

**Twenty + One Series** - The rich cultural heritage offered a host in twenty + one short stories with incredible imagination, morals and values prevalent at a given time, influencing how people respond to a crisis or any situation. The author has recreated images with universal values and morals. The plentiful of fascinating from faraway lands would leave the modern play and story writers a cringe. The book supports trust and immeasurable values, instilling hope for the new generations.

**Death** - "Shree Shambav's 'Death - Light of Life and the Shadow of Death' is an extraordinary masterpiece that delves deep into the profound questions surrounding our existence and mortality. The book's opening statement, 'Nothing ever truly dies; it simply ceases to exist in one form before resuming it in another,' sets the stage for a thought-provoking exploration of death's multifaceted nature. Shambav's remarkable ability to navigate the philosophical complexities of death and our universal fear of it is both enlightening and comforting. This book is a testament to the power of understanding and acceptance."

**Whispers of Eternity** - "Reading 'Whispers of Eternity' by Shree Shambav was a transformative experience that left me captivated from beginning to end. Each section of this exquisite collection delves into the myriad facets of existence, offering poignant reflections on life, death, and everything in between. Shree Shambav's verses are a testament to the beauty of language and the power of expression, inviting readers to embark on a journey of self-discovery and spiritual awakening. Whether celebrating life's simple joys or grappling with the complexities of human emotion, this book is a timeless companion that speaks to the heart and soul of every reader."

**Life Changing Journey Series** - "Life Changing Journey Series II Inspirational Quotes" is a remarkable collection that illuminates the path to self-discovery and personal growth. With its inspiring quotes and insightful reflections, this book serves as a beacon of light in a world often shrouded in darkness. Each quote offers wisdom, guidance, and encouragement, reminding readers of their inner strength and resilience. A must-read for anyone seeking inspiration and enlightenment.

**Learn To Love Yourself -** "A Heartfelt Guide to Authentic Self-Love." "Learn to Love Yourself" invites readers on a transformative journey to embrace their true essence in a world often focused on external validation. Through ten insightful chapters, it gently reveals principles of genuine self-love, guiding readers to deepen their connection with themselves. Beyond surface positivity, it encourages the cultivation of resilient self-acceptance, from embracing one's unique qualities to setting empowering boundaries. With inspiring stories and practical wisdom, this book is a trusted companion on the path to inner peace, fulfilment, and joy, helping readers build lives that reflect their authentic selves.

**The Power of Letting Go** - This book has been a gift to my spiritual journey. Shree Shambav's insights into attachment, personal growth cycles, and forgiveness are enlightening. The concept of seven-year cycles resonated with me, helping me understand the natural phases of life. I feel more empowered to let go of what no longer serves me and step into a life of freedom and fulfilment. A truly beautiful read!

**A Journey of Lasting Peace** - "A Journey of Lasting Peace" feels like a trusted friend guiding you through the maze of self-discovery. The 18 transformative principles are both practical and deeply resonant, addressing everything from gratitude practices to the art of letting go. Each chapter is infused with warmth and wisdom, making it easy to apply the concepts to my life. I particularly appreciated the emphasis on physical health's connection to mental well-being; it served as a wake-up call for me to prioritise my health. This book is an invaluable resource for anyone serious about personal growth!

**Astrology Unveiled Series** - "Profound, Logical, and Inspiring". What stands out in Astrology Unveiled is the author's dedication to making Vedic astrology logical and approachable. Each concept flows naturally into the next, backed by examples and exercises. The insights into karma and life cycles add a philosophical depth rarely seen in astrology books. Perfect for anyone seeking spiritual growth alongside astrological knowledge!

**The Entitlement Trap -** "Thought-Provoking and Challenging" The book challenges readers to confront their own sense of entitlement, and that's not easy—but it's essential. The Entitlement Trap doesn't offer a one-size-fits-all approach. Instead, it's a thoughtful, layered examination of how entitlement can limit our growth. The chapter on "Defining Your Own Hill" was particularly impactful, as it pushed me to reconsider which challenges are truly worth pursuing. A thought-provoking read for those willing to do the inner work to create a life they can be proud of.

**Whispers of a Dying Soul** - "A Soul-Stirring Reflection on Life's Unspoken Truths" **-** *Whispers of a Dying Soul: Unspoken Regrets and Unlived Dreams"* is a deeply moving exploration of the unexpressed emotions and unfulfilled aspirations that shape our lives in ways we often don't realise. This book invites readers to confront the powerful, often hidden impact of regret while guiding them through a journey of introspection and healing. Each page opens a space to reflect on the choices that define us—from moments of unspoken love to neglected passions—offering a gentle reminder to live authentically and courageously.

**Whispers of the Soul - A Journey Through Haiku** - is a mesmerising collection that speaks directly to the heart. Each haiku is a delicate brushstroke capturing life's fleeting beauty and timeless wisdom, inviting readers into moments of deep reflection and peace. This book is a balm for the soul, guiding us to find meaning in stillness and connection in simplicity. The themes of nature, love, and mindfulness echo universal truths, resonating with quiet, powerful grace. It's a book to be savoured slowly, cherished deeply, and returned to often. Truly, it is a gift for anyone seeking calm and clarity in life's chaos.

**Whispers of Silence** - Unlocking Inner Power through Stillness by Shree Shambav is a rare gem that beckons readers to pause, reflect, and reconnect with their inner selves. In a world that never stops talking, this book offers a profound exploration of silence—not as a void but as a rich and transformative space.

From the first page, Shree Shambav's writing resonates deeply, blending scientific insights with spiritual wisdom in a way that feels both universal and deeply personal. The author's ability to bridge the tangible and the transcendent makes this book an invaluable guide for anyone navigating the chaos of modern life.

**The Power of Words - Transforming Speech, Transforming Lives -** "The Power of Words is a profound and enlightening guide that has transformed the way I approach communication. Shree Shambav masterfully uncovers the hidden influence of our words on relationships, self-perception, and overall well-being. This book doesn't just teach you how to speak; it inspires mindful communication that fosters connection and trust. The insights on replacing negative patterns like gossip and judgment with kindness and authenticity are truly life-changing. The practical strategies and engaging narratives make it an invaluable resource for personal and professional growth. A must-read for anyone striving to communicate with intention, clarity, and compassion. Highly recommended!"

**The Art of Intentional Living - Minimalism for a Life of Purpose -** "The Art of Intentional Living is a refreshing guide to finding clarity in a cluttered world. With practical wisdom and profound insights, it inspires you to simplify, prioritise, and live with purpose. A must-read for anyone seeking balance and fulfilment."

**Awakening the Infinite - The Power of Consciousness in Transforming Life -** "Awakening the Infinite is a transformative guide that expands the mind and nourishes the soul. With profound insights and practical wisdom, this book beautifully explores the power of consciousness, helping readers connect with their true purpose and inner potential. It is a journey of self-discovery, healing, and spiritual awakening, offering clarity and inspiration at every turn. A must-read for anyone looking to live with greater awareness, meaning, and authenticity."

# ACKNOWLEDGEMENTS

To my grandfathers, grandmothers, mothers, fathers, aunts, uncles, neighbours, sisters, brothers, friends, and teachers, they poured in endless moral stories, retellings of Ramayana, Mahabharata, Puranas, Upanishads, and so on.

My teachers, neighbours, and kindred souls. Who provided us with a stage to perform wonderful Puranic stories and were gracious enough to acknowledge our efforts.

The artists and translators of epics have served as a source of inspiration, invigorating our spirits, making these works accessible, and enabling us to grasp the profound depths and deeper dimensions they contain.

I also cherish the stimulating conversations I had with my wonderful mothers, Punitha Muniswamy and Uma Devi.

Our family's youngest member, Aadhya, who always overwhelmed me with questions, inspired this book.

I would likewise prefer to express gratitude to Mr Sivakumar, Mrs Roopa Sivakumar, Mr Akshaya Rajesh, Ms Akshatha Rajesh, Ms Apeksha Prabhu, Mr

Akanksh Prabhu, Mr Nikash Sarasambi, Mrs Spoorthi Nikash for their valuable inputs.

I must thank Mr Rajesh, Mr Savan Prabhu, Mrs Revathi Rajesh, Mrs Rajani Sarasambi, and Mrs Manju Reshma, who encouraged me and often suggested writing a book. Their unwavering belief that I had something valuable to offer kept me going during my writing sessions.

Love you all,

**Shree Shambav**

www.shambav.org

shreeshambav@gmail.com

# BOOKS BY - AUTHOR

## Journey of Soul - KARMA

"Journey of Soul – Karma" is a heartfelt exploration of life's profound truths in our increasingly complex world. Addressing challenges, inequalities, and the quest for meaning, this book brings the timeless concept of Karma into focus. It emphasises Karma not merely as philosophy but as a guiding principle for our daily lives, inspiring us to walk a path of integrity and purpose. Through this journey, readers gain insights into how actions shape destinies, encouraging a life aligned with truth and compassion. It's a beacon for those seeking a deeper, more fulfilled existence.

# Death - Light of Life and the Shadow of Death

In *Light of Life and the Shadow of Death*, the enigma of mortality is approached with clarity and compassion. Death is an inevitable certainty, yet it casts a lingering shadow of fear over our lives, stirring grief and despair as we strive to prolong our time on earth. This profound work examines the fate of departed souls and the heavy emotions we attach to loss. Yet, it offers a path toward accepting death and finding peace amid life's uncertainties. Exploring our origins, ethical values, and purpose unveils the sustaining truth of existence. The shadow of death, though daunting, is reframed as a shared, universal experience—one that calls us to confront our deepest fears with wisdom and grace.

## Whispers of Eternity 150 Plus - A Symphony of Soulful Verses

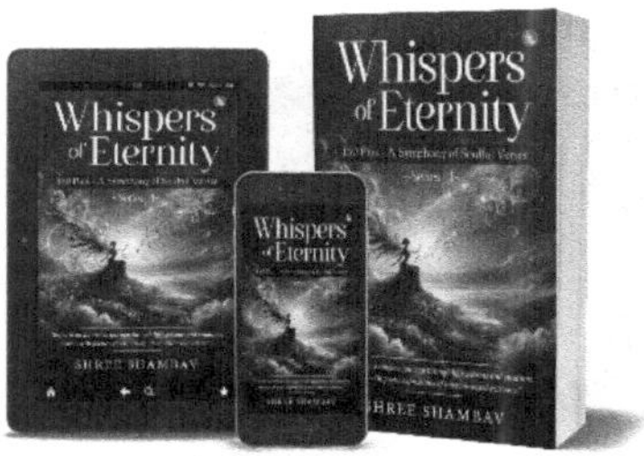


Step into the soul-stirring world of *Whispers of Eternity* by Shree Shambav, a collection of over 150 poems that capture the essence of the human experience. Divided into sections like "Through the Seasons," "Whispers of Hope," and "Threads of Unity," the book journeys through life's phases, emotions, and the universal connections that bind us all. Shree Shambav's verses touch upon nature, love, and spirituality, inspiring readers to find beauty in the everyday. Each poem is a finely crafted reflection, rich with insight and depth. *Whispers of Eternity* invites readers to pause, reflect, and embark on a timeless journey through the landscapes of the heart and soul.

## Life Changing Journey Series I and II

In Life Changing Journey - 365 Inspirational Quotes Series I, Shree Shambav curates a powerful collection of 365 original quotes across fourteen chapters, each crafted to touch the heart of our daily lives. More than a simple compilation, this series speaks directly to personal experiences with wisdom and depth. Quotes like, "The most beautiful things are unseen but can be felt," echo the quiet beauty of life's intangible moments. Another, "Giving up is easier; holding oneself up is wiser," provides a guiding light in challenging times. Life Changing Journey reveals the transformative power of carefully chosen words, inspiring readers to find strength and new perspectives on their paths. Through Shree Shambav's work, readers are reminded of the wisdom and resilience hidden within each day.

## Twenty + One - 21 Short Stories Series I and II

In *Twenty + One - Short Stories*, Shree Shambav brings to life the often-overlooked characters of nature—trees, animals, and mountains—revealing their intrinsic worth beyond mere utility. With poetic personification, he gives voice to these silent beings, some of whom are lucky enough to have names, titles, and rare human protection. Mountains, usually seen as mere landmarks, are depicted with reverence, emphasising their enduring presence. The stories build a bridge between humans and the natural world, showing that pain, grief, and resilience are shared across all forms of life. Shambav invites readers to empathise with the silent struggles of trees and animals, inspiring a fresh perspective on ecology and our responsibility towards the environment. This collection is a call to honour our connection to nature, encouraging readers to foster compassion and respect for all life.

## Learn To Love Yourself

*Learn to Love Yourself* is a powerful invitation to turn inward in a world focused on external validation and superficial measures. Through ten transformative chapters, each offering a key rule for self-love, readers are guided to uncover their inner beauty, cultivate personal strength, and develop a solid foundation of self-acceptance. This journey goes beyond momentary happiness; it's about building an authentic relationship with yourself that fosters resilience, joy, and fulfilment. From embracing your unique qualities and practising compassion to setting boundaries and pursuing what makes you come alive, this book provides essential insights and practical guidance. Let *Learn to Love Yourself* be your trusted companion on this path, inspiring you to unlock the limitless potential within and find true inner peace.

## The Power of Letting Go

*The Power of Letting Go* invites you to release attachments, fears, and expectations, guiding you toward true inner freedom and joy. With deep insights, practical exercises, and timeless wisdom, this book equips you to face life's challenges with resilience and grace. It explores the essence of attachment, embraces the power of seven-year growth cycles, and teaches the art of forgiveness as a key to a fulfilled life. Each chapter brings concepts to life through relatable analogies and real stories, making profound ideas both accessible and engaging. Let this book serve as your beacon for self-discovery and spiritual awakening, helping you navigate uncertainties and unlock your potential for a joyful, meaningful existence.

## A Journey of Lasting Peace

A Journey of Lasting Peace is a transformative guide to self-love, inner peace, and personal strength, where Shree Shambav leads readers through 18 powerful principles for discovering their true selves. Each chapter explores vital themes, from the quest for inner peace and the importance of self-awareness to the healing practices of mindfulness and yoga. Through practical strategies, reflective exercises, and heartfelt stories, this book offers a clear roadmap to a more authentic and fulfilling life.

Whether you seek to embrace imperfection, establish healthy boundaries, or reconnect with nature, A Journey of Lasting Peace provides the wisdom to navigate life's challenges and find enduring tranquillity. Perfect for anyone on a journey of self-discovery, this inspiring work gently reminds us that lasting peace starts within.

## Astrology Unveiled: Series I and V

Astrology Unveiled: Foundations of Ancient Wisdom invites you to unlock the mysteries of astrology, offering timeless knowledge rooted in the teachings of ancient sages. This comprehensive guide explores fundamental principles like Rashi, Graha, Bhava, and Divisional charts, making it an essential resource for beginners and intermediate students alike.

With logical explanations and practical applications, Shree Shambav skilfully blends ancient insights with modern understanding. Rich in examples, detailed explanations, and engaging exercises, this book serves as an illuminating path to mastering Vedic astrology.

Embark on a transformative cosmic journey, discovering how astrology can unveil your destiny, guide life's choices, and support your spiritual growth.

## The Entitlement Trap: Get Over It, Get On It

Are you feeling stuck in a cycle of blame and dissatisfaction? The Entitlement Trap: Get Over It, Get On It offers a transformative path to reclaiming your personal power. This insightful guide helps you break free from the mindset of victimhood and empowers you to take control of your life. Inside, you'll discover how to redefine success, prioritise your true values, and live with purpose. Through practical strategies, you'll learn to embrace simplicity, connect with nature, and leave a lasting legacy. Get ready to shift from powerless to empowered and create a life you love!

## Whispers of a Dying Soul: Unspoken Regrets and Unlived Dreams

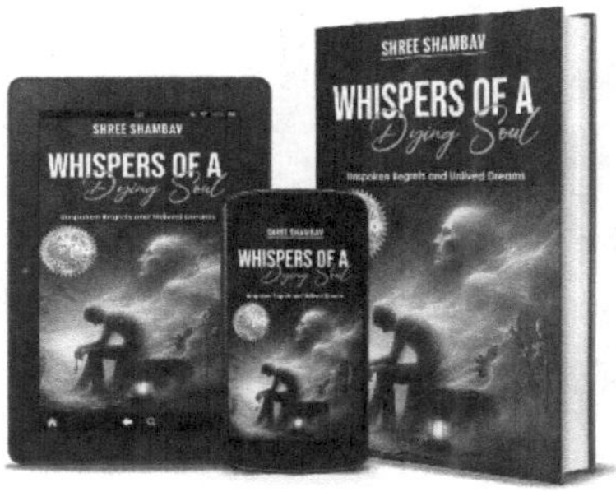


"Whispers of a Dying Soul" embarks on a profound journey that delves into the silent longings we often carry but seldom express. This powerful exploration uncovers the unspoken emotions that shape our lives—missed opportunities, unfulfilled dreams, and the quest for authenticity. Through heartfelt reflections and transformative insights, this book invites you to confront your regrets and turn them into powerful catalysts for growth and healing.

## Whispers of the Soul: A Journey Through Haiku Series I to IV

"Whispers of the Soul: A Journey Through Haiku" is a poetic invitation to pause and rediscover life's hidden beauty. This transformative collection of haikus explores themes of nature, mindfulness, love, and the human journey, offering profound reflections on universal experiences. Divided into five series, the book delves into nature's elegance, the depths of inner stillness, the tenderness of human connection, the passage of life's seasons, and the mysteries beyond the self. Each haiku captures fleeting moments with timeless grace, guiding readers toward peace, self-discovery, and a renewed appreciation for life's simplest wonders. This is more than poetry—it's a soulful journey.

## The Power of Words: Transforming Speech, Transforming Lives

*The Power of Words: Transforming Speech, Transforming Lives* illuminates the profound influence of our everyday language. This book explores how words can heal or harm, connect or divide, urging readers to embrace mindful communication. It delves into the "Sins of Speaking," such as gossip and judgment, while celebrating virtues like honesty, kindness, and authenticity. With practical strategies for transformation and a focus on the art of listening, Shree Shambav offers a roadmap to elevate our conversations. Perfect for both personal growth and professional development, this guide inspires readers to use their words to create peace, foster deeper connections, and lead a life of integrity and purpose.

## The Art of Intentional Living: Minimalism for a Life of Purpose

In a world that celebrates more, The Art of Intentional Living invites you to embrace less. This powerful guide explores how minimalism can transform every aspect of your life—your space, your time, and your mind—by removing distractions and focusing on what truly matters.

Through simple yet profound principles, you'll learn to:

- Declutter your physical and digital space
- Prioritise what aligns with your values
- Create time for meaningful connections and experiences
- Cultivate a life of purpose, peace, and clarity

## Awakening the Infinite: The Power of Consciousness in Transforming Life

In a fragmented world, Awakening the Infinite explores the power of consciousness to heal, transform, and unite. This book takes you on an experiential journey, revealing how awareness shapes reality and connects us to universal wisdom. Through spiritual teachings, introspection, and practical insights, it helps you uncover your soul's true purpose. With transformative practices, it guide you toward emotional healing, clarity, and personal growth. As you deepen your awareness, you'll forge a profound connection with yourself and the world around you. Embracing this journey leads to a life of mindfulness, authenticity, and purpose. Ultimately, it is an invitation to awaken the infinite potential within.

9 789334 249095

Printed at Repro India Ltd.